This innovative study examines emotional responses to socio-economic pressures as they are revealed in early modern English plays, historical narratives and biographical accounts. These texts yield fascinating insights into the various, often unpredictable, ways in which people coped with the exigencies of credit, debt, mortgaging and capital ventures. Plays discussed include Shakespeare's *The Merchant of Venice* and *Timon of Athens*, Jonson's *The Alchemist* and Massinger's *A New Way to Pay Old Debts*. They are paired with writings by and about the finances of the corrupt Earl of Suffolk, the privateer Walter Ralegh, the royal agent Thomas Gresham, theatre entrepreneur James Burbage, and the Lord Treasurer Lionel Cranfield. Leinwand's new readings of these texts discover a blend of affect and cognition concerning finance that includes nostalgia, anger, contempt, embarrassment, tenacity, bravado and humility.

Theodore B. Leinwand is Professor in the Department of English at the University of Maryland, and author of *The City Staged: Jacobean Comedy, 1603–1613* (1986). He is editor of *Michaelmas Term* in the forthcoming *Collected Works of Thomas Middleton*, and has published essays in *PMLA*, *ELH*, *Shakespeare Quarterly*, *Shakespeare Studies* and *Women's Studies*.

Cambridge Studies in Renaissance Literature and Culture 31

Theatre, finance and society in early modern England

Cambridge Studies in Renaissance Literature and Culture

General editor
STEPHEN ORGEL
Jackson Eli Reynolds Professor of Humanities, Stanford University

Editorial board
Anne Barton, *University of Cambridge*
Jonathan Dollimore, *University of York*
Marjorie Garber, *Harvard University*
Jonathan Goldberg, *Duke University*
Nancy Vickers, *Bryn Mawr College*

Since the 1970s there has been a broad and vital reinterpretation of the nature of literary texts, a move away from formalism to a sense of literature as an aspect of social, economic, political and cultural history. While the earliest New Historicist work was criticized for a narrow and anecdotal view of history, it also served as an important stimulus for post-structuralist, feminist, Marxist and psychoanalytical work, which in turn has increasingly informed and redirected it. Recent writing on the nature of representation, the historical construction of gender and of the concept of identity itself, on theatre as a political and economic phenomenon and on the ideologies of art generally, reveals the breadth of the field. Cambridge Studies in Renaissance Literature and Culture is designed to offer historically oriented studies of Renaissance literature and theatre which make use of the insights afforded by theoretical perspectives. The view of history envisioned is above all a view of our own history, a reading of the Renaissance for and from our own time.

Recent titles include

A complete list of books in the series is given at the end of the volume

Theatre, finance and society in early modern England

Theodore B. Leinwand

CAMBRIDGE
UNIVERSITY PRESS

PUBLISHED BY THE PRESS SYNDICATE OF THE UNIVERSITY OF CAMBRIDGE
The Pitt Building, Trumpington Street, Cambridge CB2 1RP, United Kingdom

CAMBRIDGE UNIVERSITY PRESS
The Edinburgh Building, Cambridge, CB2 2RU, United Kingdom
http://www.cup.cam.ac.uk
40 West 20th Street, New York, NY 10011–4211, USA   http://www.cup.org
10 Stamford Road, Oakleigh, Melbourne 3166, Australia

First published 1999

Printed in the United Kingdom at the University Press, Cambridge

Typeset in Times 10/12 pt   [CE]

A catalogue record for this book is available from the British Library

ISBN 0 521 64031 8 hardback

For Joan

Contents

Acknowledgments

Finding my way into this book has entailed some felicitous false starts. Several essays in which I explored ways people high and low on the early modern English social ladder negotiated the distances that separated them were meant to grow into a book. They appeared in print but never coalesced because I seemed to have said as much as I had to say, and because my own thesis – my allegiance to the concept of negotiation – had begun rather predictably, and so tediously, to drive my argument. There followed an introduction to a book on Jacobean London's middling sort, those who were climbing on the intermediate rungs of the ladder. I began with Shakespeare and I had planned to move on to Jonson, Middleton, Heywood and so on – precisely the playwrights who figure in *Theatre, finance and society*. But once again, a project founded upon what distinguishes diverse socio-economic sorts failed to sustain my interest. Perhaps increasing age, perhaps a small but unmistakable move to the right, were abetting a turn in my attention from distinction to affiliation. In any case, I found myself more and more attracted to the notion that constraints and opportunities, pressures and pleasures, pertain at every rung on the ladder. Consequently I have found it more interesting to discover the precise, not the opposed, ways a peddler and a royal agent cope with the need for credit.

Finding my way into this book has been, then, not really a climb but a walk along an unforeseen path. Most of the progress I made took place at the Folger Shakespeare Library. It is difficult for me to imagine a better place to go about one's business. When I did take to the road, I profited from responses I got at the City University of New York Graduate Center, at the Strode Center at the University of Alabama, at several Shakespeare Association of America meetings, and at the Sixteenth Century Studies Conference. The University of Maryland has supported me with a General Research Board fellowship and my colleagues in the English department invited me to present a first draft of the first chapter at one of our Renaissance Reckonings.

In the past, I have tried to repay some of the personal debts I have

incurred while wrestling with notions like the middling sort and negotiation. Here, I want to thank those who have either helped me to see my
final topic more clearly or encouraged me to believe that it is a subject
worth pursuing. For help with a quick question, for talk over lunch, or
for reading through one or more chapters, I am grateful to Jonathan
Auerbach, Kent Cartwright, Neil Fraistat, Mary Fuller, Marshall
Grossman, Lindsay Kaplan, Bob Levine, Beth Loizeaux, Bill Loizeaux,
Nancy Maguire, David Miller, Gail Paster, David Sacks, James Siemon,
and Julie Solomon. Dorothy Stephens waded through numerous pages
when she had more pressing things to do. In those places where I have
met her standards of argument, this book is the better for it. I came upon
Elizabeth Hanson working at the Folger Library on material related to
my own after I had already covered quite a bit of ground. She was and
continues to be a generous and shrewd reader. While I have learned to
welcome the hard questions she asks, I take comfort in the knowledge
that, as often as not, she does not expect that anyone can answer them.
Finally, I must acknowledge Frank Whigham, who has seen me through
from start to finish. His company – his friendship and his counsel –
makes for one of the chief satisfactions of doing this work.

　　Sarah and Jesse belong here too. Joan stands apart.

Introduction: affective economies

Theatre, finance and society is an interpretive inventory of responses to socio-economically induced stress. Not so much what early modern English people thought of their circumstances, nor solely what those exigencies felt like, my subject is the amalgam of cognition and affect that enables coping mechanisms and coping strategies – from routines that were mostly passive to those in which men and women seized the initiative. Then as now people made something of their debts, their risks, and their losses. Then as now people responded to and acted upon their economic encumbrances and opportunities in various and often unpredictable ways

There is no way exhaustively to canvass an entire historical moment's repertoire of socio-economically aroused affect. One may, however, look at particular dramatic texts, at biographical records, and at historical episodes for evidence of varieties of emotional engagement. While drama and historical narratives lend themselves to the recovery of affect, unlike an essay, a treatise, or a pamphlet, they do not and they need not self-consciously set out to know what they feel or think, although the feelings represented in them are bound up subtly with the knowledge they depend upon. Early modern English drama, biography, and history everywhere enact the likes of embarrassment and contempt and rage, but they have not often been mined for their affects. They have not often been read as indices of the emotional life of the past, despite the fact that in different forms, terms, and circumstances, that part of experience must have been as meaningful then as now.[1]

What *has* been written about, and for some time now, is the way the early modern English period complexly elaborates an historical transition, at once epistemological, ideological, and material, from what has been variously rendered as status to contract, from sacred to secular, ascription to achievement, finite to open, fixed to contingent, use to exchange, bounty to profit, feudal to (nascent) capitalist.[2] Such forward-looking if retrospectively construed trajectories have much to commend them, and I evoke them not as straw men, but in earnest. These *longue*

1

durée, diachronic markers organize the past and so afford it a structure that empowers argument. Still I think we ought not merely to re-mark these enabling structures; rather, we want to follow the cultural historians' lead when they ramify and complicate large-scale structures in terms of their more fine-grained operations. We may make sense of epistemic transitions by analyzing qualities of "social experience and relationship" as well as the "affective elements of [historical] consciousness."[3] We should be able to take any critical element – say, credit or venturing – within a full-blown structural reconfiguration and reveal its variety and vitality. And we may begin to investigate "objective causes for their subjective effects" and affects, just as Marx correlated alienation with estranged labor and Weber, deferred gratification with the rise of capitalism.[4]

I do not imagine that in the chapters that follow I have identified the full panoply of affects that can be teased out of the dramatic and non-dramatic material that I consider. Held up to the light by someone else, these scenarios would undoubtedly reveal different affective features. Material looked at in different contexts necessarily reveals different facets. I try to demonstrate this very necessity by turning twice to *The Merchant of Venice*, offering two complementary though not wholly consistent readings of the play. Looked at in terms of credit relations, Antonio's sadness appears to be a form of dismay that generates nostalgia. Looked at in the context of adventuring, his sadness is equipment for living, something that serves him in the world of high finance. Gilles Deleuze and Félix Guattari have written that affect can take the form of an "active discharge of emotion . . . projectiles just like weapons."[5] Such affects are neither mere sensations nor responses; they have the capacity to do work. In the first instance, Antonio's sadness leads to thoughts of death, in the second, sadness affords socially useful *gravitas*. Other readings are of course possible, and other feelings, like self-pity, may be attributed to Antonio. The coherence of this book depends upon its sustained attention to socio-economic pressures brought to bear on the lives of dramatic characters and historical personages, but the catalogue of affects that I work with could be enlarged. Neither guilt, remorse, envy, disgust, fear, nor grief is prominent here, but most of these emotions will be seen to merge with those I do dwell on. Each no doubt was felt in its own right and its experience must in many cases have been inflected by socio-economic determinants.[6] If I attend instead to embarrassment or contempt or outrage, it is because these are among the affects that seem to be in play across the particular economic modalities I discuss. This is not, however, a zero-sum game; a financial relationship like indebtedness may stimulate multiple affects and often one more readily than another.

While my terminology throughout this volume – from credit crunch to nostalgia to venture capital – is often anachronistic, the economic categories and attendant affective responses that I describe are, I think, not. As will become clear if it is not already, credit, debt, mortgages, and venturing were fully within the realm of experience of early modern English people. Of course, so was affect. Wittgenstein argues that a complex emotion like grief is less an irrecoverable, private, inner state than it is a response deeply implicated in the social world, "a pattern which recurs, with different variations, in the weave of our life."[7] Affect-laden qualities like tenacity and humility that I discern on and off the early modern English stage are no less bound up with the mundane negotiations of *homo economicus* as he was imagined and as he lived, be this Timon of Athens or James Burbage, Subtle and Face or Walter Ralegh. Neither the plays nor the historical events that I take up require a vocabulary, even an awareness of their own, of affect for something like what we may identify as bravado or anger to be present. Affect necessarily erupts from within the interstices of relations and it abides in conjunction with "appraisals and judgements."[8] Part and parcel of epistemology, what has been termed emotionality can be understood only in terms of social (and here, economic) conventions.[9] But the relation of affect both to cognition and to external factors is neither uniform nor especially easy to delineate. Silvan Tomkins, a formidable if idiosyncratic student of affect, tries to encompass every possibility: "[a]ffect can determine cognition at one time, be determined by cognition at another time, and be interdependent under other circumstances."[10] "Reason without affect would be impotent," Tomkins writes, "affect without reason would be blind."[11] Our knowledge is never perfect and our affects are rarely dormant. At one moment affect signals a knowledge deficit (filling in where confusion reigns), at another, a knowledge overload (expressing a conviction that lacks clear social sanction).[12] When he approaches the subject of affect as response and, as Wittgenstein would have it, as avowal, Tomkins is no less equivocal. "The recalcitrance of affects to social and cultural control is no more nor less real than their shaping by powerful cultural, historical, and social forces."[13] The space of recalcitrance that Tomkins carves out for affect I will on occasion make the grounds for agency.

Tomkins also explores the degree of freedom that inheres in affect. While we are generally clumsy when we attempt to control our affects, we do seem to have the wherewithal to vary their intensity and direction. Affects do not merely respond to economic circumstances, they themselves stimulate response, expand and contract, vary in relation to one another, answer now to the scarcity of stimulus, now to its surfeit.[14] In chapter 2 I describe ratios of humility to bravado expressed by characters and playwrights alike. Such sentiments are both voluntary and indicative of command economies. Affective economies are also implied when Tomkins argues that without "the capacity to turn affect both on and off for varying periods of time, the freedom to invest affect in one or another object, to shift affect investment, to overinvest affect, to liquidate such investment, or to find substitute investments would not be possible." Nevertheless Tomkins seems to me to be at his aphoristic best when he quips that affects "are the primitive gods within the individual."[15] We are theirs and yet they are ours too. They and we lack fine motor skills; moreover affects, compared with drives and sensations, operate within a realm of greater internal freedom and wider external scope.[16] They participate in the social world and they can be roughly gauged according to the innumerable evaluations and conceptualizations that we form as we first approach a scene and then upon our arrival. When Robert Cecil appraises the beleaguered Ralegh's capacity for exhausting expenditure of energy, writing that Ralegh "can toil terribly," we get an ambiguous account of freedom and control. Ralegh is actively, even violently, trying to assert order amidst the chaos I describe in chapter 4. But Cecil, who precedes Ralegh in time and place (he has arrived on the scene first and he, not Sir Walter, is in the Queen's good graces), can make terrible toil seem by turns awesome, pathetic, and comical. Ralegh's fervid labors are at once a sign of his own calculated investment of affect and evidence of the possibility that his affect has gotten the better of, or diminished, him.

Cecil's commentary on Ralegh reads like a character reference, or a critique of a part played after a particular fashion. I too am prone to blur the distinction between what we might call lived affect and its representation. This seems to me inevitable when, as is the case with the cast of characters and historical subjects I discuss, what is felt is more often than not enacted. While plays, biographical material, and fragments of historical narratives may require that we pay attention to, say, social class (the affects that I take up in chapters 2 and 3 are largely the consequence of status infringements), they can tolerate a good measure of theoretical indifference to genre and formal mediations where affect is concerned. Affect is not so much oblivious to, as it is variable within, the very conventions and plots which render it accessible. It has both a degree of transparency within, and maneuverability across, discursive boundaries. History is therefore neither mainstay nor warrant for the readings that follow, rather it is another repository. Insofar as affect is concerned, history and theatre are, surprisingly, equally capable of confirming or confuting one another. Letters, depositions, statutes, petitions, pamphlets, and play scripts all have their own generic and sub-generic rules and expectations; but rather similar sorts of affect are recognizable across different kinds of writing, just as manifestly distinct affective responses arise within common circumstances. To add the dimension of mutable socio-economic interpellations is to exacerbate still further the volatility of affect across genres. Credit, whether it puts pressure on reputation, solvency, or both, seems equally (here in comedy, there in tragedy, elsewhere in the life of the Jacobean court) capable of generating feelings of longing, of deracination, and of invincibility. Venturing may correlate with painful endeavor whether one's investment is on the high seas or in shares in a theatrical enterprise like the Blackfriars. The non-dramatic material that I consider in tandem with successive plays owes its place in each chapter sometimes to the suggestive range of a particular affect, more often to the heterogeneity of a particular economic contingency. Multiple, even contradictory, styles of knowing and behaving are the inevitable concomitant to socio-economic obligations.[17] Consequently, my readings of plays and historical records are taxonomic not paradigmatic, local not totalizing.

To found one's argument on *grand récit*, or to depend upon an overarching category like the early modern "market" or "marketplace," is to accomplish, as I have noted at the outset, a good deal of important conceptual work.[18] Often, however, words like "exchange," "commodity," "circulation" – especially "market" – function largely as metaphors in such arguments.[19] They serve as tacit markers of structures and practices that we acknowledge but that we can neither feel nor locate with much precision. We still live in a market society, if one that has drastically transformed the nascent capitalist techniques typical of the late sixteenth and early seventeenth centuries. But neither now nor then do I think it rings true to think in terms of what *the market* felt like. The fungibility and placelessness that are Agnew's subject, like the contingency of value that underwrites Engle's work, derive from market-induced exigencies that require a more local habitation and a name.[20] Or names, since a gesture complementary to the totalizing embrace of the market is to level at some one, synecdochic practice – say usury – and to allow it to stand for an enormous range of socio-economic factors. Thus, after the fashion of one variety of Shakespeare criticism, a focus on Shylock *qua* moneylender (although his intentions place him more within the realm of folklore than capital) obscures the diversity of fiscal relations prevalent in Venice/London. Of course, from dozens of STC entries to the work of R. H. Tawney, it is clear that biting usury was a hot-button topic in early modern London.[21] But usury by no means exhausts either the discursive or the affective range of indebtedness. Usury suggests predation; credit enables borrowers in a specie-scarce economy.[22] Usury has an ominous ethical tenor; credit customarily entails honor, trust, and reputation.[23] A usurer victimizes; a creditor invests in a borrower and inaugurates an at least partially reciprocal relationship.[24] A paradigmatic deployment of usury – as bogeyman or touchstone, as a typifying practice or the butt of early modern moral economists – or of any other single economic practice, distracts attention from the ethical, epistemological, and affective freight carried by a host of other socio-economic determinants that were experienced both on and off the early modern English stage.

Recourse to master tropes like "the market" and "commodification" also obscures the extent to which the early modern English economy (at the level of custom or practice) and the law were still emerging from medieval antecedents. Generalized talk about "exchange" fails to register just how far from modern were early modern procedures.[25] Commercial law, for instance, begins to take shape only late in the seventeenth century. The law-merchant and mercantile customs were in no way held to have the force of common law. Contracts were difficult to enforce in Stuart England and one court regularly undermined the standing of another in the course of protracted disputes.

The common law . . . was slow to recognize that customs between merchants could originate a legal duty and had difficulty apportioning responsibility between principals and agents. Partnership and factorage disputes had to be settled by invoking the law of debt or relations between masters and servants. To sue a multiple partnership, it was necessary to sue in the name of each partner. *Common law followed words rather than intentions*; fictitious pleadings had to be employed to consider contracts made overseas.[26]

Liquidity and fungibility still lay well into the future.[27] The assignability and more generally the negotiability of most sorts of bills of exchange and of promissory notes was extremely limited at the Shakespearean moment.[28] So too were remedies for debtors and for creditors. Age-old customs like sanctuary saved debtors from creditors; unrestricted terms of imprisonment incapacitated debtors willing to work out repayment schedules. "It was not until 1705–6 that a statute addressed the difference between fraud, negligence and misfortune or between short-term cash-flow problems in an otherwise sound business and long-term insolvency."[29] Merchants relied on custom and often turned to arbitration, but lawyers picked apart the former and the courts were slow to enforce the latter. Of course, the Elizabethan and Jacobean drama with which this book is concerned predates by nearly a century the Bank of England, paper money, and the National Debt.[30] Land still took precedence over trade, real property over exchange values. Shakespeare purchased acreage in and around Stratford and a Blackfriars tenement. Antonio, Timon, Touchstone, Quomodo, and Overreach – to mention but a few of the characters I discuss in the chapters that follow – often if not always speak to the backward-looking character of socio-economic history. Much the same might be said even of men on the make like James Burbage and Thomas Gresham, Lionel Cranfield and Walter Ralegh. Inductive procedures which try to make sense of Burbage's credit relations or Ralegh's venturing reveal much about the mixed early modern English economy that deductions about the consequences of "the market" overlook. Affect is but one such unremarked category.

Each of the following chapters is triangulated according to one or another economic modality, affect, and text. Insofar as the early modern English economy is concerned, I have made my approach from very close to the ground. That is to say, while I acknowledge the resonance of terms like credit and interest, I primarily aim to explore their mundane, often pedestrian fiscal sense. For the most part, I begin with a practice within the economy. The next step is to make sense of the way it ramifies in the social, psychological, and affective realms. Venturing, for example, is for my purposes first and foremost to be associated with potential profit. To the extent that it entails risk, it comprehends solvency – individuals' assets, their capacity to withstand loss – as well as some things less numerable, like tolerance, comfort level, or exposure. When venturing shades into seemingly effortless plunder, it has the potential to awaken both compensatory effects and affects. Subtle, Doll, and Face set out to make something out of nothing, but their venture tripartite turns out to be extraordinarily labor-intensive. Robert Cecil invested in privateering voyages but did what he could to conceal his investments and proclaim his innocence. *The Merchant of Venice*'s Antonio balances the exhilaration and exoticism of far-flung foreign ventures with carefully displayed sadness. Because venturing correlates with status, it is significant that Antonio is a merchant and Bassanio a gentleman, a scholar, and a soldier; that Subtle and Face threaten to expose one another's past; that Cecil is nervous about notoriety. Economic practices were pervasively, if differentially, marked by social entitlements. There was no one, consistent, *homo economicus*.

Each chapter that follows also assesses the affective dimension of an economic practice as it is represented in a variety of dramatic and non-dramatic narratives. Such affect is not necessarily predictable. Nor, as I have suggested, is it sensible to restrict one's conception of feelings to what might be called a language of primary emotions. While happiness

or fear might well pertain, a host of affect-laden sentiments, psychological processes, and activities are also evident. An understanding of affect
responsive to epistemology, to culture, to class, and to intention enables
a more nuanced and wide-ranging account of actors caught up in the
early modern economy. I write not only about sadness and rage, which
register unremarkably within the horizons of affect, but about hybrid
sentiments like embarrassment, nostalgia, and humility, and about still
more taxonomically indeterminate capacities like tenacity.[31] While tenacity may be more recognizable as a character trait than an emotion, it
nonetheless answers to what one feels (and makes others feel) as well as
to what one is or thinks. Indicative of intensity, anathema to an
aristocratic bearing like *sprezzatura*, adjunct to choler but opposed to
phlegm, tenacity denotes an obduracy that is at once felt and understood,
emoted and meant. In a particular economic environment, it can (like
most of the affects I discuss) take the form of a response, as evidence of
interpellation, and of a tactic, as evidence of agency. Tenacity is what is
wrought up in us in view of economic exigencies and opportunities; in
Tomkins's terms, it is susceptible to the force of emotion and to the
clarity of reason, it confirms the interdependence of affect and cognition.
A similar case might be made for the affective import of nostalgia, akin
to melancholy, something we feel as much as we think, a kind of
yearning, loss, or denial. In chapters 2 and 3, I describe responses to
economic distress that are cognizant of affect and yet affect-poor. These
are cases in which cognition overtakes, or struggles to overtake, affect.
Timon revels and then rages, but most of his energy goes into decoupling
affect from the economy. His utopian endeavor is to render both what he
is and what he feels indifferent to economic circumstance. Such an
exemption from fiscally induced affect is precisely what Richard Easy, in
Michaelmas Term, has already been endowed with. Where Timon
struggles tragically to win for himself a reprieve from economic entail-
ments, Easy's obliviousness comically sets him free.

   Texts make the remnants or intimations of past affects and economic
relations accessible. The plays and the historical and biographical
material that I discuss are in the first instance determined by the
economic modality that gives each chapter its title. Antonio and Shylock
are creditors. In *Eastward Ho* and *Michaelmas Term* debtors abound.
Much of *A New Way to Pay Old Debts* turns on a mortgage, and *The
Alchemist* is propelled forward by a venture tripartite. The non-dramatic
narratives that I have constructed are also about credit, debt, mortgages,
and venturing. Each one further unfolds the affect identified in the play
with which it is paired, forging a substantive chain linking plays to
economic phenomena, then complementary historical narratives to

affects. *The Merchant of Venice* has to do with credit, Antonio's nostalgia is bound up with his accreditation, and in the non-dramatic fragment I pair with the play, Queen Elizabeth deploys her credit rating as a form of what I call tactical nostalgia. To take another instance: indebtedness inspires characters in *Eastward Ho* to calibrate a serviceable ratio of humility to bravado, and these same affective postures are recalibrated by Jonson and Chapman when they find themselves imprisoned for their play. Each play is paired with an economically apposite non-dramatic scenario in order to suggest the multiplicity of affective experiences and to test the reliability as well as the cogency of distinct sorts of evidence. I try not to privilege either on-stage or off-stage expression; similarity and difference provide more appropriate terms for discrimination.

The characters and historical personages that I discuss in chapter 1 are caught within a net of credit relations. In relation to Shylock and Bassanio, Antonio stands as surety and creditor. He is also a debtor whose own creditors extend beyond the characters whom we meet in the play. His saddening acknowledgment that his scope in Venice is comprehended largely in terms of his solvency occasions in him a neurotic form of nostalgia, an affect-intensive longing for a self-image untrammeled by exchange values, or for death. In her role as creditor and debtor, I discover in Queen Elizabeth considerably more tolerance for the inevitability that one's credit answers to a blend of solvency and reputation. In contrast to Antonio's passive dismay, Elizabeth reveals a shrewd and an aggressive penchant for accommodating herself to the exigencies of credit. The Queen's nostalgia does not so much immobilize her (like Antonio) as it equips her with a velvet glove of benevolence that covers a hard fist of self-serving fiscal policy. Credit and affect in the middle section of the first chapter turn on embarrassment. The Gresham of Heywood's *2 If You Know Not Me* like the Gresham who served successive Tudor sovereigns adopts two discordant bodily postures: he always seems to be both looking over his shoulder and flexing his muscle. Either way, he betrays his vulnerability and his suspicion that he is about to be discovered and so embarrassed. While the preemptive moves that he carries out – like the building of the Exchange – are meant to safeguard his credit, a nagging sense of incipient humiliation never entirely disappears from either Heywood's Gresham or from the historical factor's epistolary apologies.[32] An edgy hyper-elation describes the affect expressive of Gresham's acute self-consciousness, as well as the defensiveness which I take to be the more strictly cognitive aspect of his *habitus*. Always worrying aloud his singularity, Gresham remains first and last indebted to his playwright or his sovereign. The unavoidable liaisons of accreditation also hold sway in *Timon of Athens*. Timon's singularity does not derive from a prodigious, Gresham-like financial capacity within the realm of the economy; rather it corresponds to his impossible desire to deliver himself from economic exigency *tout court*. Set alongside the typical Jacobean strategy for exemption, epitomized at the end of this chapter by Thomas Howard, the Earl of Suffolk's staggering financial corruption, Timon's irrational repudiation of the bonds of credit becomes deeply moving. A tragic solipsism like Timon's, which has the virtue of probity, appeals forcefully to audiences caught up in the quotidian dependencies and compromises (in Suffolk's case, scandals) of credit relations.

Distinct affective responses to indebtedness underwrite the three plays and paired non-dramatic materials I discuss in chapter 2. Jonson and Chapman, imprisoned for *Eastward Ho*, and the play's apprentice, Quicksilver, suggest what we might call achieved affect. Miming humility and staging bravado at varying intensities for the benefit of diverse creditors, playwrights and character alike mitigate their obligations by manipulating the range of acceptable responses to debt. They produce or perform affect suitable to a normative ethics of credit and debt from the moment their workaday craft – play-writing and apprenticing to a goldsmith – fails them. Insufficient deference to their creditors lands them in prison. Credible affect bails thems out. Correspondingly unpremeditated affect is my subject in the middle sections of this chapter. *Michaelmas Term*'s Easy's insouciance and James Burbage's tenacity, in comparison with Quicksilver's or Jonson's studied affect, seem innate. Easy's easiness – something of a shock and a respite in the hectic financial capital – is precisely what we come to realize his nemesis, Quomodo, longs for. Moreover, Quomodo's shenanigans look differently when measured against Burbage's stubborn fabrication of a theatrical enterprise out of next to no capital and barely manageable debt. The observable repertoire of affect associated with written bonds thus expands as a consequence of Middleton's plotting, while insofar as *Theatre, Finance and Society* is concerned, the middle portion of chapter 2 looks back to sealed bonds in *The Merchant of Venice* and forward to those in *A New Way to Pay Old Debts*. My final consideration of debt has a distinctly socio-economic valence in keeping with the debtors in *Greene's Tu Quoque* and those lodged in early modern English debtors' prisons who imagined themselves to be victims of status infringements. Not surprisingly, their humiliation and deprivation gave rise to feelings of outrage and a desire for revenge. A debtor's degradation (the mostly material aspect of a debtor's indignation) was at once known and felt; and yet for all of its genuine wretchedness, such abjection proved amenable to comic recuperation on the stage and to unexpected reassignments of social disinction in the Hole itself.

In chapter 3 I turn to mortgages and so to the affect consequent upon the inveterate, *un*easy alliance between land and capital.[33] Feelings of bitterness, betrayal, and anger pervade Massinger's *A New Way to Pay Old Debts* even as they punctuate the mortgagor–mortgagee relationships that occupied so much of the time of Jacobean financiers like Lionel Cranfield and Arthur Ingram. Here again, it is difficult to distinguish status infringement from economic hardship. Lord Lovell is disgusted by the potential adulteration of his pure blood; Prince Charles was contemptuous of the notion that a businessman could make discriminations about points of honor.[34] But the intensity of affect aroused by mortgaging seems especially to follow from the inevitability of the reciprocal bond between landed and monied gentlemen. Their anger rose with their deepening recognition that neither could do without the other, that theirs was a relation not of opposition but of mutual dependence, even collusion. Together they participated in the vigorous early-seventeenth-century "land market," a conjunction of terms that since the nineteenth century, at least, indicates the extent to which landed interests and monied interests worked through one another – were often one and the same. It is then reasonable to wonder whether the truly remarkable figure in *A New Way* is Sir Giles or Lord Lovell. The former has caught our attention, though surely he would have come off as a familiar brutish creditor in his day. The latter, however, was a genuine anomaly: a wholly unencumbered courtier and landowner. Such freedom from fiscal obligation would have been truly extraordinary; and yet even so endowed, Lovell affects the very same rage and contempt as those less well positioned than he. When land changes hands, in plays like *Michaelmas Term* and *A New Way*, and in the swaps or purchases carried out by Ingram and Cranfield with country landowners and with each other, it does so to the predictable accompaniment of resentment, humiliation, and intimidation. These affective terms, I point out at the end of chapter 3, are also apposite to Sonnet 134, Shakespeare's mortgage sonnet.

In chapter 4 I return to *The Merchant of Venice* and pair it with *The Alchemist*. I read Shakespeare's play in tandem with an evaluation of the part Ralegh played in the capture of a Portuguese carrack, the *Madre de Dios*, and I read Jonson's play alongside an account of holding shares in companies like the Children of the Queen's Revels and the King's Men. In all four cases, I try to recover the affective dimension of venturing. Risk – what Shakespeare would have called hazard – induces a measure of sadness in Antonio, and perhaps in Ralegh too. While this does not hold true for the likes of Subtle and Face, they do join with almost every other significant character in my last chapter (the important exception is Lovewit) in shouldering an affect-laden burden of laboriousness. The

prospect of quick and easy profit stimulates the offsetting, even anticipatory, affect that we recognize in the pain of toil. So Antonio exerts
himself to the point of bating; Ralegh toils terribly; Jonson sweats to
write a line; Subtle protests the pains he has taken; and Blackfriars'
backers like Samuel Daniel, as well as the players who insisted on their
right to become shareholders in the King's Men, demanded compensation for their labor and pain. Any risky investment that might pay off
handsomely required affective ballast (an implicitly ethical security
deposit) in the form of effort; better still, patently exhausting work.
Before early modern English people could rationalize profit, they had a
lively sense of what it felt like, or at least of what they thought it ought to
feel like. As profit-taking increasingly came to be normalized, legiti-
mating affect might fall by the wayside or be sublimed into cleverness.
Those like Cecil and Lovewit and perhaps Shakespeare (dyer's hands
notwithstanding), who seem to have been averse to high risk and
therefore exempt from painful toil, could bank instead on their office or
their wit. Is it then entirely fortuitous that, rightly or wrongly, we tend to
associate pronounced affect and strain with the bricklayer's son but not
the bailiff's, with Ralegh but not King James's beagle?[35]

1 Credit crunch

There was among men and women in the latter part of the sixteenth century a dawning, sometimes consuming, awareness that both rural and urban life, agriculture, industry and trade depended on credit. In England, where there was a chronic shortage of coin, "the use of credit was almost ubiquitous."[1] From laborers to the Duke of Norfolk, from widows to Queen Elizabeth, English people were lending and borrowing. They were engaging in the sorts of verbal, personal, usually reciprocal and non-institutional monetary transactions upon which depended the livelihood of communities of tradesmen and gentlemen, farmers and citizens alike. But they were also beginning to participate in, and to take notice of, more "rational, impersonal and pragmatic money-lending practices" that took the form of penal bonds and written contracts, and were characterized by profit and self-interest.[2] We may gauge the social and psychological force of this awareness if we keep in mind the interplay of two related meanings of "credit": trustworthiness (one's worth in the realm of belief) and solvency (one's worth in the realm of finance). The sometime congruence, sometime friction, registered in these distinct senses of credit is readily felt in dramatic texts sensitive to linguistic slippage.[3] I take as my examples Shakespeare's *The Merchant of Venice* and (with Thomas Middleton) *Timon of Athens*, and Thomas Heywood's *2 If You Know Not Me, You Know Nobody*. The credit crunch staged in these plays may also be seen to have taken its toll on the likes of Queen Elizabeth, Thomas Howard, Earl of Suffolk, and apropos the Heywood play, Thomas Gresham. That these plays signal different structures of feeling answerable to the same historical pressures suggests that the early modern English experience of the operations of credit was both elastic and profound.

I

In *The Merchant of Venice*, a very nuanced elaboration of credit relations proceeds from Shakespeare's only sustained imagining of a merchant.

13

Antonio, the eponymous merchant, acts in a manner that is at once historically recursive and psychologically neurotic. By recursion, I do not mean an historical necessity of return, whereby that which is superseded in the course of a transition must be repeated in order to identify or consolidate its supersession. I mean something more along the lines of what I will call neurotic nostalgia: the human potential not so much for denial of, but resistance to change which is already overtaking one, change to which one knows oneself to have contributed.[4] Such resistance takes the form of a return or recursion to prior, if still consequential, formations: for example, recourse to gift-giving as if in an economy of abundance on the part of a merchant increasingly enmeshed in an economy of scarcity; or recourse to the spirit of the law from within a culture tending toward its letter.[5] Of course, what makes return or recursion viable is the fact that orientations that are progressively being overtaken can continue to seem ever so *au courant*. Furthermore, by recursion I intend not quite what Freud meant by the compulsion to repeat, the urge "to restore an earlier state of things" that we have been "obliged to abandon under the pressure of external disturbing forces," but repetition that devolves from the disturbing forces the one who repeats has him or herself awakened.[6]

Recursion traces those steps between now and then that are not necessarily traversed in a straightforward fashion. It corresponds less to a rearguard effort to stymie or retard than to a knowing return to that which is being superseded by those who themselves are abetting this supersession. Recursive subjects act out their alienation from their cultural moment. Needless to say, there are other ways of responding to the awareness that one is caught up in, or is even an exemplar of, an historical moment's version of the socially or economically dominant. One might, for example, play the part to the hilt or give up altogether. Or one might suffer embarrassment or seek exemption (partially recursive adaptations which I explore below). When we do find recursion, however, and after it fails, as it almost inevitably does, we find death. More precisely, we find a death-wish and a desire to secure after death a reputation (credit) that is commensurate with the resumptive self that has been overtaken. Death, then, signifies integrity or wholeness, an end to the disquieting recognition of the gap between desire and the desire to be without desires, to be interest free.[7] In the Freudian account, repetition is bound up with a death *drive*. Recursion, however, operates at the level of consciousness, where the death drive knows itself as a death *wish*, and for the purposes of say, drama, can be thematized as such. For what alternative do we have when we find ourselves sick with what we have become and at least temporarily incapable of imagining what else we might be?

Sick with what we have become. Or, as Antonio puts it in *The Merchant of Venice*, surely one of the most famous of all texts on credit in western history, "In sooth I know not why I am so sad" (1.1.1).[8] Almost at once, the merchant of Venice will give over the mercantile exchange values with which his merchandising aligns him in order to recur to an idealized version of values no longer in the ascendant. This recursion transpires, however, in front of an audience that would have taken the merchant to be, in Georg Simmel's words, "the personified function of exchange."[9] From Salerio's stylized account we learn that Antonio's

> argosies with portly sail
> Like signiors and rich burghers on the flood,
> Or as it were the pageants of the sea,
> Do overpeer the petty traffickers
> That cur'sy to them . . .   (1.1.9–13)

Like London's Lord Mayors, whose investiture entailed costly shows both on the Thames and through the city streets, Antonio's ships are the pageant-worthy "ventures" (1.1.21) of a rich burgher. However, their aristocratic bearing, their overpeering, corresponds to Antonio's unrealizeable commitment to extricating himself from the *burgerlich* exchange funotion. That there is no escape is evident when Salerio's aggrandizing verse is recontextualized "upon the Rialto" in Shylock's prosaic market analyst's account: Antonio "is a good man . . . he is sufficient . . . he hath an argosy bound to Tripolis, another to the Indies . . . a third at Mexico, a fourth for England" (1.3.13–18). Shylock stipulates that Antonio "is sufficient," not merely well-off, but a credible risk: "sufficient" is the technical word for Antonio being qualified by his means to enter into a bond.[10] "I may take his bond," Shylock asserts. "Be assur'd you may," responds Bassanio (1.3.24–25). Here, too, the technical language of finance is in play; to be assured is to be made certain (in the sense of surety) or to be made secure (in the sense of posting some sort of security) or perhaps, to be insured: "I will be assur'd," Shylock asserts, and "that I may be assured . . . may I speak with Antonio?" (1.3.26–27).[11]

Two scenes earlier, when we first hear Bassanio speak with Antonio, we learn that Antonio's sufficiency – his exemplary status in the world of financial and commodity exchange – is by no means confined merely to the world of commerce.[12] Bassanio's description of his relationship with Antonio, his merchant friend and creditor, has embedded in it all of the hallmarks of English city merchants' moneylending to improvident aristocrats. Bassanio seeks to prolong his debt to Antonio; he would have his creditor advance him new funds and roll over old debt into new. Thus Bassanio speaks of his own "faint means" failing to "grant continuance" (1.1.125), that is, to support his style of living. It is of course from Antonio that he now seeks "continuance" or debt prolongation. And while Bassanio says he does not mind foregoing his customary high style, finding himself, as he says, "abridg'd / From such a noble rate" (1.1.126–27) – indeed, even though we are about to learn that Antonio "lends out money gratis" (1.3.29) – all of Bassanio's talk of "great debts" and "debts I owe" and "rest[ing] debtor" cannot help but make a phrase like Bassanio's "Nor do I now make moan to be abridg'd / From such a noble rate" sound like a barely veiled request that Antonio adjust the interest rate he charges on loans to gentle, "noble" men like Bassanio.

Whether in his antagonistic relationship with Shylock or in his friendship with Bassanio, Antonio is locked into thoroughly early modern credit relations. To Shylock he stands as the guarantor of Bassanio's debt, as a security who has assured the moneylender of his sufficiency.[13] To Bassanio he stands as creditor, having permitted Bassanio to "[t]ry what my credit can in Venice do" (1.1.180), even as he, the lender and not the borrower, has felt it necessary to "assure" Bassanio of his "purse . . . person . . . [and] extremest means" (1.1.137–38). Enmeshed in a seemingly wall-to-wall Venetian credit economy, Antonio, who knows not why he is so sad, is poised on the cusp of recursion. Sick that he is taken to be the paradigmatic sign of capital in the form of credit not only by Shylock and Bassanio, but by himself, Antonio knowingly recurs to an economy even more primitive than one within which he can boast that he takes no interest ("excess" – 1.3.57), to an economy in which three thousand ducats of liquid capital is backed by one pound of solid flesh, in which credit relations signify not solvency but friendship (1.3.56–59), and in which a sealed and notarized (1.3.140) financial bond can take the form of an archaic, potentially lethal bond.[14] Antonio can commit himself only to a (self-)interest-free economy beyond the pleasure principle, or to death. Thus while Walter Cohen shrewdly points out that "the penalty for default on the bond is closer to folklore than to capitalism: stipulation of a pound of flesh . . . is hardly what one would expect from *homo economicus*," he twice gets things backward when he writes that "[a]s a traditional and conservative figure, he [Antonio] nearly becomes a tragic victim of economic change; as the embodiment of progressive forces, he points toward the comic resolution."[15] Rather, as the play's representative of "bourgeois mercantilism" (Cohen, 202), Antonio models economic change. Beating a retreat from this role to his sad "part" (1.1.78–79), he at once faces backward in history and toward death, not comic contrivance.

But before the turn toward death comes the failure of recursion. Antonio's nostalgic fantasy that his arrangement with Shylock is but a "merry bond" uncontaminated by interest-taking, operating outside of profit and loss (Shylock tells him that "A pound of man's flesh . . . / Is not so estimable, profitable neither" – 1.3.161–62), inevitably runs up against the reminder that Antonio is fully caught up in the circulation of Italian capital. Suddenly, in Act 3, we learn that just as Antonio has extended his credit to many others beside Bassanio ("I oft deliver'd from his [Shylock's] forfeitures / Many that have at times made moan to me," explains Antonio – 3.3.22–23), so Antonio is himself in debt to many creditors beside Shylock. As Tubal announces: "There came divers of Antonio's creditors in my company to Venice, that swear, he cannot choose but break" (3.1.103–05). In his letter to Bassanio in Belmont, Antonio writes that his "bond to the Jew is forfeit" and that his "creditor*s* grow cruel" (3.2.315–16, my emphasis). Antonio would have it that, as one who lends gratis, he can sidestep the sorts of interestedness that motivate a credit economy. But Shylock keeps reminding us that precisely when Antonio steps back from profit-driven credit financing – when he lends gratis – he becomes the greatest source of competition in the financial marketplace. "[F]or were he out of Venice," Shylock asserts, "I can make what merchandise I will" (3.1.117–18).[16]

But it is not only in his dealings with Shylock that Antonio tries vainly to distance himself from financial operations. It does not escape our recognition, nor Antonio's, I think, that his dealings with Bassanio express not the bonds of gift-giving and bounty to which he would recur, but the bonds of a fully monetarized economy.[17] For all that Antonio would found his creditor relationship with Bassanio on friendship and on love (1.1.154; 3.3.319; 4.1.270–73; 4.1.446), he can never quite ignore the fact of indebtedness. If Bassanio's love persuades him to witness Antonio's death at Shylock's hands, then, Antonio writes to Bassanio, "all debts are clear'd between you and I" (3.2.317–19). If Bassanio will but repent that he loses a friend, then, declares Antonio at the trial, Antonio himself "repents not that he pays your debt" (4.1.274–75). By Act 3, Scene 3, Antonio acknowledges that "the trade and profit" (3.3.30) of Venice, that which has enabled his own livelihood, can and will insert itself into his neurotic economy of merry bonding and non-obligating bounty. And for Antonio, this acknowledgment presages death: the only relief from the credit crunch, the only freedom from desire (interest-taking), and the only locus of integrity that he can imagine. Sick with what he is and sick with what he cannot escape, he commences wasting away – even though at the start of the play he is confident that Bassanio would never be the cause of such depletion. In the play's first scene, he

says that Bassanio would never make "waste of all I have" (1.1.157).[18]
Now Antonio is so "bated" that he "shall hardly spare a pound of flesh"
(3.3.32–33) when Shylock raises his knife. After all is said and done, we
might well wonder whether entering into the bond is evidence of a death
wish on the part of sad Antonio. To have recurred to this folkloric mode
was to have stepped toward the impossible integrity of interestlessness,
toward death. Any sense we might have that his is a suicidal response to
Portia's interruption of his affective bond with Bassanio would be
complicated by our knowledge that Antonio is caught in an economy
founded upon interest.[19] The Antonio who appears in the famous court-
room scene proclaims himself "Meetest for death, – the weakest kind of
fruit / Drops earliest to the ground, and so let me" (4.1.115–16). The
only credit he finds it tolerable to concern himself with is his reputation
after death: "You cannot better be employ'd," he tells Bassanio, "Than
to live still and write mine epitaph" (4.1.117–18).[20] Needless to say,
Antonio intends his obituary to commemorate the imaginary, prior self
that his very concern with his epitaph indicates that he knows he has
superseded. Nothing ought to hint at the "waste of all" he has.

As Karen Newman has noted, Portia circulates in a structure of
exchange comparable to that which governs Antonio.[21] In debt to
Bassanio, in whose "account" she would stand "high" (3.2.144), Portia is
also his creditor, backing him to the tune of six thousand ducats to
"deface the bond: / Double six thousand, and then treble that"
(3.2.298–99). But Portia's response to the credit crunch is noticeably
different from Antonio's. In the trial scene she may recur to mercy, but
she insists on bonds, or contract (which is to say something different
from Karen Newman's assertion that "Portia short-circuits the system of
exchange" – 26). Moreover, though willed by her father into the marriage
market, she works both the symbolic/gift *and* the exchange/loan value of
the ring she offers Bassanio.[22] In Portia's dealings with Venetian men
and money, we detect tactical nostalgia. Her appeal for mercy is at once
sincere and calculated. So it is not surprising that in the end, when
Antonio – his ships restored and his "purse" filled with half of Shylock's
wealth – is sent packing for Venice and the mercantile identity he just
cannot seem to escape, Portia and Bassanio are ready to establish
themselves amidst a canny mixture of old-fashioned good housekeeping
and modern estate management.

Rather than succumb to neurotic nostalgia in the form of socio-
economic recursion, Portia – though as caught up within the play's credit
relations as is Antonio – does her best to work that which is residual as
well as that which is emergent in Venice. One might say that where he
bates, that is, becomes dejected, she negotiates. In her pursuit of a non-

neurotic accommodation to the credit crunch, we see signs of the advantages that may in some circumstances accrue to those who are not forced to operate under the bright lights of exemplarity. Neither a merchant nor a man nor threateningly "new," Portia has in her favor a degree of flexibility. In fact, her deft and energetic, often witty, maneuvering has a distinctly Elizabethan feel to it. It is not just that Portia and Elizabeth are interpellated by the wills of their dead fathers. Indeed, when *Merchant* was written in the mid-1590s, Elizabeth was done with her strenuous negotiations in a marriage market into which she too was rather "willed." But she (like the espoused Portia) was by no means done coping with credit.[23] Like all of Europe's early modern sovereigns, Elizabeth was from the very beginning to the end of her reign both a creditor and a debtor; she was constrained by and worked hard to control her credit rating.

Richelieu may well have been the first to declare that "les finances sont les nerfs de l'état" – not merely "dc la guerre".[24] In 1588, Philip II confided to his secretary that "the thought of obtaining money had become his sole occupation."[25] Of course by then Philip had already twice sent European money markets into disarray by declaring Spain bankrupt. He would do so again in eight years. Like Bassanio, who turns to Antonio for a second loan to give him the wherewithal to repay the first ("if you please / To shoot another arrow that self way / Which you did shoot the first" – 1.1.147–49), Philip would weather a period of embarrassment with his creditors, then work with them to consolidate his short-term liabilities into fixed-interest bonds. Layer upon layer of consolidated debt would form beneath each new stratum of liabilities.[26] Also in 1588, the Venetian Ambassador in Spain writes to the Doge in Venice that Philip is "running short of money"; the Duke of Parma has "sent bills of exchange for a million two hundred thousand crowns, on which the King will have to pay twenty-two per cent, in less than three months. His Majesty has raised other loans here, but with great difficulty, and at a high interest, for private individuals are unwilling to advance money in fear of a suspension of payment." On 9 May 1590: "Here they think of nothing else except raising money" (*CSP Venetian*).

Contemporaneously, in France Henri III was pawning royal rubies, diamonds, and pearls, and coming to terms with the fact that he "lacked sufficient credit to attract . . . substantial loans." When Henri of Navarre assumed the throne as Henri IV in 1589, he was forced to sell off his patrimonial lands or mortgage them to creditors. In December 1589, he commented to the Duke of Wurttemberg that "rien ne me combat tant aujourd'hui que le défault d'argent."[27] In 1592 he tried to keep the Swiss mercenaries on his side, explaining to them that "les grandes affaires que nous avons eues a supporter sont la seule cause du retardement qui a esté au payement des debtes dont nous vous sommes redevables." He knows that Spain is trying to win over the Swiss by saying that the French "payer mal . . . [leur] debtes," but he insists that the Spanish are "plus coupable que nous, comme tant de banqueroutes qu'il [Philip] a faictes . . . sont assez de tesmoignages."[28] By 1593, Henri was auctioning his abjuration of Protestantism to the highest bidder. And when around 1599 Sully began to take over the King's finances, he found, according to an account Sir George Carew claimed to have gotten direct from Sully, "all things out of order . . . full of confusion, no treasure, no munition, no furniture for the king's houses and the crown indebted three hundred million." Sully in turn basically took the Crown through bankruptcy, ignoring its creditors to the greatest extent possible.[29]

Late in 1588, Queen Elizabeth's own "financial position was beginning to provide cause for serious anxiety. She was still a long way from bankruptcy, but one of the three sources from which hitherto she had financed the Spanish war – the accumulated savings of a decade of peacetime economy – was within sight of exhaustion. The other two sources – the ordinary revenues of the crown and its extraordinary income from parlimentary grants – could not be expanded sufficiently to make good this loss . . . Accordingly the government had now to turn to the moneylenders to bridge the gap."[30] To look closely at, for example, the brief period from 1588 to 1590, is to discover the degree to which the likes of Walsingham, Burghley, and the Queen herself, like Philip himself and Henri himself, were preoccupied with credit and with debt. And though we may listen to Burghley fretting in the summer of 1588 about "how to get money here in specie, which is our lack, but by exchange . . . which will not be done but in a long time," I want to focus on Elizabeth's tactics for dealing with her credit crunch.[31]

Elizabeth began the war with Spain with some £300,000 in her treasury. By September/October 1588, she was down to £55,000.[32] But in November, Burghley listed among what he called "necessary debts": "Low Countries £75,000, naval supplies £10,000, the Household £10,000, the Ordnance £8000 . . . £50,000 to repay the city of London, and an unspecified sum for repairing ships and building new ones."[33] Unable to come up with money in specie, the Crown turned to the London companies for another loan of nearly £50,000. Here, Elizabeth was merely following in the footsteps of all the Tudor monarchs who turned to London merchants for short-term loans.[34] Then, in December, the counties were served with a forced loan for a comparable amount. R. B. Wernham notes that "London citizens went off into the country to avoid paying . . . and a considerable number of gentlemen . . . had to be interviewed by the privy council before they would yield what was required of them. Domestic loans were . . . paid unwillingly; they yielded inadequately; and they had to be repaid eventually."[35] There was recourse in 1589 to Parliament, which came through with a grant, and "rents on Crown lands were raised and 'stalled debts' were called in and recusancy fines stepped up."[36] This still was not enough. So in late February 1589, Elizabeth sent merchant adventurer William Milward to Germany to borrow £100,000. R. B. Wernham suggests some of the nuts and bolts of the Elizabethan credit crunch: on the Queen's behalf, Burghley instructed that Milward

was not to promise more than ten per cent. interest; and he was to carry himself at first as a private merchant coming for his own trade, not using the queen's name lest that should encourage lenders to raise their rates. For the same reason he was to take up the money in several portions and at several times; and he was to offer the queen's bonds under the great seal as security only in the last resort, if bonds on the merchant adventurers or on the city of London proved unacceptable.

(I interrupt Wernham here to note that when the Queen turned abroad to pay back domestic loans, she required the Corporation of London – its merchants – as a loan guarantor. As Elizabeth turned to Germany secured by the City, so Bassanio turns to Shylock secured by Antonio, the merchant of Venice.) Wernham continues, emphasizing that

this was one of the biggest foreign loans attempted during Elizabeth's reign. Only urgent financial necessity could have compelled a return upon such a scale to the long abandoned practice of foreign-borrowing.[37]

But this was not all. In June 1589, coincidental with Milward's report home that the Germans were not interested in advancing so large a sum, Henri III's envoy de Buhy arrived in England in search of 100,000 écus (which I believe would have been equal to 250,000 English crowns, or about £45,000). The King of France had finally allied himself with Henri of Navarre and together, they wanted Elizabeth to believe, they would finally rout the Catholics – if only, that is, she could come up with the cash they needed for a levy of 22,000 German soldiers. There is a long history behind such a request, one that always involved German mercenaries, appeals to the English for money, and sixteenth-century Dutch–French–Spanish religious and trade conflict but, suffice it to say, at this particularly austere fiscal moment all Elizabeth could offer was her credit, not cash. She would send someone to Germany, of all places, to second Henri's agents' attempt to borrow 150,000 crowns. De Buhy insisted that he required cash. Perhaps we should factor in here the comments on de Buhy's affairs of de Buzanval, Navarre's agent in

England. He says that he understands the Queen's "burdens, but it would destroy her reputation for inexhaustible resources to show the Germans that her treasure is exhausted." Furthermore, while he "knows that her Majesty offers her credit in Germany . . . some of his [Henri III's] counsellors tell him that a King of France should not lose his state for credit" (*CSP Foreign*, 26 June 1589). We might add here William Camden's claim that in the court of Narvarre, "*'les Anglois'* was a slang name for creditors whom it was intended to balk."[38]

So although Elizabeth really did want to get the Germans in motion and pursue her foreign policy on the Continent, and although in July she informed the Lord Mayor of London that she needed the City's bond for £60,000 which she intended to take up in Germany – a sum far larger than had been demanded but part of which would seemingly go toward satisfying what became de Buhy's modified demand for a grant of cash to go with the Queen's pledge of her credit – the Queen still felt it necessary to write in her own hand in French to Henri III to protest de Buhy's stubbornness. What follows is my translation of some of Elizabeth's idiosyncratic French: de Buhy, Elizabeth writes,

asked me for so large a sum that, having in my arms so many and diverse burdens, I couldn't presently content him with ready cash. But I offered voluntarily to engage myself for the entire sum with several Princes, merchants, or cities . . . Nevertheless, he took considerable, if not extraordinary liberty with me, saying that he would be carrying merely paper, and that he had need of the other kind of money. I cannot believe that you will commend him for such language, scorning as it does such contractual bonds as oblige and are honored by all Christian princes, among whom, when it comes to the credit of my word [le credit de ma parole], I do not put myself in a rank inferior to that of he who possesses the Indies.

In a postscript, the Queen adds,

I cannot hide from you, my dear brother, that notwithstanding the pertinacious de Buhy, I am presently sending a gentleman among the German princes to encourage them to aid you with men and money; in extending to them my credit [en leur donnant mon credit], I do not doubt that yours is already in Hamburg hands, and I hope it will bear fruit. (*CSP Foreign*, 26 June 1589)

Insofar as credit relations structure the marriage market, Portia and Queen Elizabeth discover that money is incarnate in them: women, as an incarnation of capital, mediate exchange. But Elizabeth finally opted out of the marriage market and Portia exerts considerable influence over it. Capable of making a crucial distinction between flesh and blood, Portia is not about to confuse her trust fund with her fund of trust. She secures the latter on the ring she gives Bassanio, her "vantage to exclaim on" him (3.2.174). In the letter from which I have quoted, Elizabeth tempers

any nostalgia when she acknowledges that trusting Christian princes –
the credit of her word – is distinct from but calibrated according to her
solvency (the credit she can and will extend in Germany). When Antonio
tells Bassanio that he may "try what my [Antonio's] credit can in Venice
do," he makes an offer identical to the one Elizabeth made to Henri III
when she wrote of the agent she was sending to Germany to raise funds
secured by her credit. The *OED* cites Antonio's line when it defines credit
as "solvency and probity" – as what I have been parsing as money and
trust, and what Elizabeth distinguishes in her two references to her credit
in her letter. But Antonio fixates on only probity and trust, as if what he
offers Bassanio were not money, as if he were offering something perhaps
not quite magical, but still founded like *kred in faith and belief.
Imagining that "there is much kindness in the Jew" (1.3.149), he hands
over to Bassanio his trust fund. He willfully ignores the extent to which
credit and banking permeate what Marx calls our "*moral . . .* [and] *social*
existence . . . under the appearance of mutual *trust*," though in fact
(Marx argues) they are predicated on "*distrust* and a total estrangement."
Shylock and Antonio's "merry bond" literalizes, or brings out, the folk
material latent in Marx. "In the credit system," he writes, "*man* replaces
metal or paper as the mediator of exchange. However, he does this not as
a man but as the *incarnation of capital and interest . . .* Money has not
been transcended in man within the credit system, but man is himself
transformed into *money*, or, in other words, money is *incarnate* in
him."[39] If Antonio's money is incarnate in him, and if Antonio is
"sufficient," then a pound of flesh makes sense. But if Marx is right, then
Antonio, and I suppose I, have misrecognized Antonio's extension of his
credit in the bond as simple recursion. That which seems old is after all
new, nostalgia is prophecy.[40] There has been a recursion, but into the
future. "[A]lthough it is true that the medium of exchange has migrated
from its material form [commodity or metal] and returned to man it has
done so only because man has been exiled from himself and transformed
into material form."[41]

II

Diverse sorts of credit relations constellate Antonio, Bassanio, Shylock,
and Portia according to varying ratios of trust to solvency, and interestlessness ("gratis") to self-interest. Unimpressed by and unsentimental
about Antonio's resistance to his self-alienating personification of exchange, *The Merchant of Venice* indicates how widely credit casts its net,
catching up among others an improvident gentleman and a folktale
heiress. That even the Duke of Venice is implicated in "the trade and

profit of the city" (3.3.30) suggests a motive for invoking Elizabeth I's affiliations with the City of London, the former as both creditor and debtor, the latter as loan guarantor and creditor's creditor. The financial and metaphoric bonds that linked sovereign and merchant citizenry also frame Thomas Heywood's *2 If You Know Not Me, You Know Nobody* (1605) though, as in *The Merchant of Venice*, intra-city credit relations predominate. In Heywood's play the merchants of London are Thomas Gresham, merchant-citizen extraordinaire, and the haberdasher Hobson. Both men are preoccupied with credit, with their financial standing and with their reputation; but then, it turns out, so is everyone else in this play, from the peddler Tawny-coat to Queen Elizabeth herself. Credit in the city is never simply a matter of one's own "parole"; it is always systemic and relational and therefore always puts one in a position of potential dependence, vulnerability, or humiliation.

Anything but sad, Heywood's Gresham is buoyant, even elated. And yet he is noticeably defensive. Unlike Antonio, who bates under the sign of nostalgia, Gresham glows so brightly that he almost effaces the shadow of embarrassment that stubbornly trails behind him.[42] He has every reason to exult in his credit-rating nonpareil, but so long as his reputation is predicated on his sufficiency, he is compelled to look over his shoulder with a "how'm I doing?", an aggressive sort of uncertainty. The play opens with Gresham on the verge of investing a staggering £60,000 in a patent for Barbary sugar. The Barbary king's merchant testifies to Gresham's good name: "to his credite be it spoke, / Hee is a man of heedfull providence" (8–9).[43] Confidence in Gresham's heedfulness and "courtesie" (10) does not, however, preempt a tactful inquiry into the status of his portfolio: "be it without offence, / How are his present fortunes reckoned?" (11–12). Gresham's factor's response is a model of cautiousness:

> Neither to flatter nor detract from him,
> He is a Marchant of good estimate,
> Care how to get, and fore-cast to encrease,
> (If so they be accounted) be his faults.   (13–16)

Gresham's canniness (his "care") and his consequent credit rating (his "good estimate") are his faults. His is the embarrassment of riches; his are "especial vertues, being cleare / From avarice and base extortion" (17–18). Though good, at fault; though clear, by assertion, not assumption. Everyone from the off-stage audience to additional on-stage factors is teased with the necessity of extenuating on Gresham's behalf only to learn that such indulgences are, for the most part, unnecessary.

As if embarrassed that he has no need of credit, Gresham worries aloud his self-sufficiency: "How thrives our Cash?" he asks his factor. "[I]s it wel increast? / I speake like one that must be forst to borrow" (62–63). Though not forced to borrow, he cannot resist a defensive boast: "Dost not thou think that three score thousand pounds, / Would make an honest Marchant try his friends?" (66–67). Of course, unlike Antonio, Gresham need not try what his credit can do. And yet for all that he is obviously loaded with cash, he cannot help wondering about "the common rumour / Touching my bargaine with the King of Barbarie" (70–71). Gresham flaunts his triple-A credit rating even as he seeks confirmation that he can attract venture capital. First his factor seemingly paradoxically asserts that "Tis held your credit" that Gresham needs no credit, being able on his own to "part with so much Cash"; then he assures his boss that "London will yeelde you partners ynow" (72, 76, 82).[44] Gresham responds not by acting to limit his liability but by stimulating his international operations in Venice and Portugal: "where much is spent, / Some must be got" (86–87). Though "but a Marchant of the Cittie, / And taken in a manner unprovided" (74–75), Gresham, like Cleopatra, can on his own replenish what he exhausts.

It has been suggested that Heywood's play aims to "show merchants and mercantilism in the best possible light . . . to legitimize and celebrate their activities and existence within the city"; that it focuses on middle-class "fantasies of prosperity and munificence," and celebrates "social and economic change" tempered by "medieval Christian values."[45] But this is to neglect the extent to which 2 If You Know Not Me explores the embarrassment with which its financiers encumber themselves. When Gresham's prodigal–trickster nephew John first appears on stage, he tries to shore up his reputation with an engaging, early modern attempt to jive his uncle. That this and later scenes bear out the surmise that young John has a way to go before he can outmaneuver his adroit uncle ought to redound to the elder Gresham's credit. No fool he (see 960–62). There is, however, something seemingly gratuitous about Heywood's revelation that the big-time merchant has cozened his nephew of his patrimony (170–71 and 922–25). Just as Dekker casts suspicion on the origins of Simon Eyre's wealth, so Heywood momentarily insinuates a moral lapse on Gresham's part. And just as some have zeroed in on aspersions Shakespeare casts on Antonio, it is reasonable to fasten onto this bit of cozening to suggest that Heywood has gone out of his way to embarrass Gresham.[46] But it is our sense of the pressure Heywood's Gresham (like Antonio) puts on himself that the play keeps returning to, and that suggests the more telling social and psychological, as opposed to the moral, costs of the credit crunch. We no more need Heywood's glances at theft than we need the critic's aggressive proof of Antonio's kinship with

Shylock to make out these merchants' uneasy efforts to secure their own credentials.

In *The Merchant of Venice*, Antonio cannot imagine a meaningful way to establish that he is "a good man" (1.3.11) in the context of the modern credit economy that underpins his ventures. He tries to locate himself within an extra- or pre-economic sphere of endeavor, only to have Portia reinscribe him in his business function and excuse him from Belmont. *2 If You Know Not Me*'s Gresham also finds it difficult to establish that he "is as good a man" (430) as another. Riches alone do not guarantee his credibility. Thus the insistence on Gresham's antagonist Ramsey's part "That *Ramsie* is as good a man as *Gresham*," when answered by Gresham's "And *Gresham* is as good a man as *Ramsie*" (420–30), results in a disturbing, if still comic, unconfirmability. Their stand-off resumes a few lines later:

RAM. Do not I know thy rising? GRESH. I, and I know thine.
RAM. Why mine was honestly. GRESH. And so was mine. (452–53)

The possibility that Gresham dealt dishonestly with the "Land-seller" with whom Ramsey thought he already had cut a deal is like the theft of Jack Gresham's patrimony. The facts in either case would facilitate our arrival at a reliable credit rating for Gresham. But Heywood does not take Ramsey v. Gresham to court and we never do get the sort of certainty about Gresham's off-stage probity that we would like.[47] Instead, we have simply the merchant's word, his assertions ("my right's my right" – 465). Confronted with mirroring wealth (Ramsey threatens that his "purse, / Shall make him [Gresham] spend" – 426–27), Gresham discovers that rich does not make right. And if the lawyers and the courts are written off by this play as inadequate to the task of confirming a merchant's probity, then Gresham must set about fashioning an alternative institution that will secure his good word, his name, his credit. What is striking about Gresham's construction of the Exchange is that, unlike Antonio, Gresham can imagine a way to accredit himself within an economic context. The Exchange, which Gresham pitches nostalgically as "a credite to the Land" (1,143), marries self-interest and magnanimity, good deal and gift.

It would be cynical to conclude that Gresham's benefaction of the Exchange and then his college is merely a compensatory response to having amassed great wealth, a counter-example against which to measure the rich citizens who Gresham himself says "live like beasts, spend time and die, / Leaving no good to be remembered by" (813–19). Thousands of merchant-citizens' endowments and the play's own "Gallerie . . . / Of many charitable Citizens" (760–61) suggest that wealth and piety were not deemed antithetical.[48] However, when Gresham builds on behalf of tradesmen and merchants, not the poor, he effectively trumps self-interest. He gives a place where others may get and thereby secures his reputation within what in 1623 Edward Misselden called the "circle of commerce." As the play's Dean of St Paul's puts it, Gresham's burse "Will be a Tombe for you [Gresham] after your death" (1,241). Like Antonio, Gresham looks to death. Where the former would escape his mercantile identity, would secure his credit on anything but mercantile exchange, the latter sets out to memorialize his exchange function as benefaction. The Exchange, to which "the Lombard Street merchants . . . carried thither their insurance business," represents part of the policy Gresham takes out on his reputation.[49] If there is any residue of embarrassment, the Queen can still be brought on to proclaim Gresham's burse the Royal Exchange and to knight the merchant (2,102–07).[50] If neither wealth nor the courts nor the Dean of St. Paul's can assure Gresham's reputation, then the Queen may serve as final arbiter. Elizabeth is not embarrassed, so Gresham need not be either.[51]

After all, as we have seen, Elizabeth too had to cope with the intersection of her reputation and her treasure. And it was none other than the historical Thomas Gresham whose job it was, as Royal Agent, to secure her "honor and credit."[52] Elizabeth's credit *qua* integrity governs *1 If You Know Not Me*, but Part II twice displaces Elizabeth's credit *qua* fiscal anxieties. In the first instance, we see Elizabeth borrowing money not via Gresham, as history would have suggested, but from the haberdasher Hobson. She sends to him for one hundred pounds. He responds that "she shall have two [hundred]" (1,117). Later, when Hobson and the Queen finally meet at Gresham's Exchange, Hobson tells her,

> When thou seest money with thy Grace is scant,
> For twice five hundred pound thou shalt not want.
> QUEEN. Upon my bond.
> HOB. No, no my Soveraigne,
>   Ile take thine owne word without skrip or scrowle.
> QUEEN. Thankes honest *Hobson*, as I am true mayde,
>   Ile see my selfe the money backe repayd . . . (2,088–94)

Magnanimity here resides with the comic merchant. While the Queen thinks in terms of bond and repayment, Hobson, as if embarrassed that Elizabeth might be embarrassed by the instruments of credit transaction, is satisfied with her word (precisely what Elizabeth's phrase, "la credit de ma parole," would have led one to expect). Consequently, the Queen need no longer offer as her guarantee her "bond" – over which she has limited control – but can instead swear on her virginity, rhyming maidenhood and repayment (mayde/repayde) according to her sovereign economy.

The second, more curious, displacement of the Queen's credit crunch takes place at the very margin of the text, at the point of the play's abrupt turn to what the Quarto title page calls "the famous Victorie of Queene *Elizabeth* in the Yeare 1588." Madeleine Doran has speculated that Heywood wrote "a sort of epilogue on the defeat of the Armada" for *Part 1*. Furthermore, when what Doran takes to have been two separate plays (*The Troubles of Queen Elizabeth* and *The Life and Death of Sir Thomas Gresham, with the Building of the Royal Exchange*) were amalgamated into *1 and 2 If You Know Not Me*, the Armada episode was "detached" from the end of the earlier play and appended to the later play. This is still more complicated, since there are short and long Armada scenes: Doran argues that when, c. 1632, "it was desired to revive the original *Queen Elizabeth* play," Heywood revised and expanded the epilogue.[53] Whether or not we accept all or parts of Doran's speculative narrative, we may make some non-bibliographic sense of an Armada coda to a play about a man who died nine years before the event (Gresham died in 1579, Hobson in 1581) if we think in terms of credit relations.[54] The loan from Hobson and the life of Gresham constitute jest-book style and high-finance preparations for the test administered to Elizabeth's "honor and credit" in 1588.[55] The Queen's famous victory is inescapably tethered to City capital. Her goodwill toward Gresham and Hobson reciprocates their willingness to accredit her.

As S. T. Bindoff notes, the Royal Agent's "principal task was to negotiate the loans of which the English government stood in constant and sometimes desperate need."[56] And this could be embarrassing when Gresham's employer forced him to arrange the prolongation of debts. Thus in 1552, Gresham writes to the Duke of Northumberland, "yt shall be no small grief unto me, that in my tyme, being his Majesty's [Edward VI's] agent, anny merchant strangers shulld be forssid to for bear their monny agaynst their willes . . . else in the end the disonnestye of this matter shall hereafter be wholly layde upon my necke." Gresham explains that he told the Fuggers that "there was no other remeddy" but that they must "forbere with the King's Majesty at this tyme; and that they would have them [their debts] prolongyd for another yere." This "matter dyd not a littil abash me," notes Gresham. After all, "I was fayne to give forth my owne [word] that this monny shuld be paid at the just daye, or else the King's Majesty could never have hadd yt." Rather than "resseve shame and discredit," Gresham would (so he says) rather be "dischargyd of this office of Agentshipe." Needless to say this is but "the smallest matter of all, so that the King's Majesty's [honour] and creditt be not spotted therebye."[57]

Just what was at stake in such dealings as the likes of Gresham were involved in is suggested by correspondence from the next reign. Prepared to make do without the experience of a Protestant factor, Mary fell prey to the inept agency of Christopher Dauntsey. By the time Gresham was called in to clean up Dauntsey's mess (more probably his corrupt dealings, which would cost Mary an extra two percentage points on loans in the neighborhood of 200,000 florins), the Queen was bound to follow through on a high-interest loan from one Lazarus Tucker, in Antwerp. "[F]or this Lazzerus Tucker is a very extreme man, and very open mouthed"; and "this matter toucheth the Queene's honnor and creditt." Having acknowledged Dauntsey as her servant, Mary ought not to be surprised that Tucker "doth now ground himself not a littill upon that worde." Gresham could manipulate the Queen's credit only so much – in this instance she "mayc not looke to have no monny under xiii or xiiii *per cento*: wychc, with pollitycke [read Gresham's] handeling, might as well [have] been had for at xi or xii upon the hundred, and the merchaunts right glad thereof."[58] Once they clear up this matter, and after a few months have passed, word of Mary's bad bargain will have died down and Gresham will pick up where he left off under Edward VI.

It has already been noted that throughout her reign Elizabeth was compelled to attend to her credit rating. Something of her fiscal reputation is evident in a later sample of Gresham's correspondence with his superiors. In 1562, the Royal Agent writes to Burghley from Antwerp: "[t]hese monny men be affraide to deall annye forther with the Queene's Majestie, by the reason they cast so manny doutes of this trobellsome world . . . here ys soche great dowtes caste upon our Estate, as the creadyte of the Queene's Majestie and all the whole nacyon ys at a stay; and glad ys that man that maye be quit of a Inglishman's bill!"[59] A year later, Gresham tells Cecil of necessary "prolongations for the making of the newe bandes [bonds]" and of his intent to leave England for Flanders, "for the better preserving of the Quene's Majestie's honor and creadit, and sattisfication of the creditors: for, dowghtless, my being there shall somewhat mollyfie and sattisfie them." While the Royal Agent has it within his power to preserve the Queen's credit ("whiche hath bin, and is, all my care"), Elizabeth in turn has the power to preserve Gresham's "poore name and creadit; which is the chefest substance that God hath sent [him]."[60] The appeal for mercy in *The Merchant of Venice* provides a glimpse of both the risks and the tactical deployment of nostalgia in the arena of credit; the mutual accreditations between Elizabeth and Gresham suggest that both tactical embarrassment (exposing the true credit of her word and of his) and its risks (royal wrath and default) were no less the Queen's than her agent's.

2 If You Know Not Me's exfoliation of plots might well come off as hodgepodge were it not that in almost every scene the anxieties that attend the "sattisfication of the creditors" are its subject. Hobson risks embarrassment and the ruin of his credit if Jack Gresham, "a very extreme man, and very open mouthed," lets it be known that Hobson has been with a French courtesan ("I hope these honest Gentlemen," Hobson begs, "Will save my credite" – 1,996–97). Timothy Thin-beard confesses to owing Thomas Gresham £500 that he has spent on whores. John the Upholster, in debt for £50, faces arrest by a sergeant who looks to be bought off: "if he wil stretch some 4. or 5. li being the sums so great he shal passe, weele make him sweare he shall not tell he was arrested, and weele sweare to the creditor we cannot meet with him" (678–81). The same trick has already worked with "Sent the Perfumer, Tallow the Currier, Quarrell the Glasier" (683–84). By the end of the play, having "neither money nor credite" (2,388–89), Jack Gresham is staving off nameless creditors who even appear on stage. To "somewhat mollyfie and sattisfie them," he impudently tries to marry the richly left widow, Lady Ramsey. But she, though seemingly charmed by his cheek, settles for discharging his debts rather than offering him her hand.

Finally, running through the play like one more thread, there is the peddler Tawny-coat. He first appears at Hobson's shop to pay for the wares he last took on credit and to refill his pack with new consumer specials ("Pay the old debt, and penne and incke for newe" – 226). He is soon back on stage, anxious to repay £10 he forgot to give Hobson. Once he establishes his credit (his good name) by insisting on his debt (Hobson cannot at first find the debt in his books and so will not accept the proffered £10), Tawny-coat stuffs his pack and is in for £20 more. But when he next appears, he enters "with a spade," having become one of the "wretched miserable" men who "dig living out of stones" (1,577–78). Between his last appearance and this, the peddler has himself extended credit to his "helpelesse neighbours in distresse" (1,651); but their "poverties" have prevented repayment. Consequently, Tawny-coat defaults on his debt to Hobson and the latter sues his bill (1,617). Tawny-coat fears that the haberdasher now will "seaze my houshold stuffe, imprison me / And turne my wife and children out of dores" (1,619–20).[61] But Hobson, who it turns out is on the verge of his own credit attack in France, forgives Tawny-coat's debt ("old *Hobson* nere will eate / Rather than surfet upon poore mens sweat" – 1,693–94), and several scenes later we learn that the former peddler has become "an able Citizen late chosen / A Maister of the Hospitall"

(2,130–31). Like Antonio at the end of *The Merchant of Venice*, his pack is once again full, his credit has been restored, and he is a "good sufficient man . . . God hath blest / His travaile with increase" (2,133–35).

From Heywood's insignificant John the Upholster to Timothy Thinbeard to Tawny-coat to Jack Gresham to Hobson to Thomas Gresham and Queen Elizabeth, the large and small humiliations ("travaile") attendant upon credit relations (indebtedness, mostly) constitute a master trope governing social, economic, and psychological bonds. Though sovereigns did not go hungry and diggers could hardly count on becoming masters, an all-pervasive money economy exacted its differential dues from the richer, middling, and poorer sorts. Burghley instructs Gresham on the Queen's behalf, informing the Royal Agent that "She, having great sums to be paid . . . (which cannot be paid of her own treasure, having lately acquitted large debts there . . .) has resolved that he [Gresham] shall renew those debts due in February for six months longer . . . She means to procure [read require] the loan of 30,000*l*. sterling from her merchant adventurers to acquit so much of her debt in February . . ." (*CSP Foreign*, 18 January 1561). The seventeenth-century London artisan William Wallington was enmeshed "in a continuous round of petty debt." The turner's "survival rested on a network of small creditors who sustained him" and "[t]here is no evidence that he was ever completely out of debt."[62] Even "the *Labouring-man* that hath neither house or home of his owne to hold his head in but liveth onely of his bare & bodily labour is to be accounted a poore man, whose necessitie is such sometime as he must need borrow."[63] All in all, as Richard Porder preached at Paul's Cross in 1570, "every man will give credit now," "not only money men, Merchant men, and Citizens . . . but also Noblemen, Courtiers, Gentlemen, Grasiers, Farmers, Plowmen, and Artificers, yea, I would the clergie were free."[64] But if "everyone" gives credit, then everyone must be borrowing. If the "Prince and his subjects, the Maister with his servants, one freend and acquaintaunce with another, the Captaine with his souldiers, the Husband with his wife, Women with, and among them selves, and in a woord, all the world choppeth and chaungeth," then anyone might be "at a stay and taketh daies for the payment of his debts."[65] Some will profit and some will break, or go bankrupt: between 1543 and 1624, Parliament issued four bankruptcy statutes, each of which aimed to protect creditors and "assumed the bankrupt's delinquency."[66] It was toward the end of this period that Shakespeare's and Middleton's *Timon of Athens* staged a default still more spectacular than Antonio's in *The Merchant of Venice*.

III

Perennially insolvent, Philip II exercised a sort of royal prerogative, a license to publish his bewilderment when confronted with financial matters. Toward the beginning of the Spanish debt crisis of the mid-1570s, he wrote: "I have been given these papers relating to Exchequer affairs. I understand that they are from a Genoese who is expert in these matters . . . I think that some of the things he says are good although he should comprehend them better than I since I am absolutely ignorant in these matters."[67] Early in 1580, Philip protested (or confessed or boasted) to the knowledgeable royal *contador* (auditor), Francisco de Garnica, that as for "exchange and interest, I can never get them into my head, I'll never understand them."[68] Although Philip surely appreciated the extent to which each and every move he made was predicated on "cambios y interesses," he seems to have been more interested in manipulating the consequences of his ignorance than mitigating it. Of course, he might well have worked to fortify his benightedness. For one who can imagine the nitty-gritty of credit and debt only as disabling, the motive for ignorance is powerful indeed. Why admit to paying attention to something which only wears you down? Why not try simply to exempt oneself by tacit fiat from the fiscal obligations entailed by the credit crunch?

Questions like these complicate attempts to distinguish ingenuousness from disingenuousness when Timon of Athens asks his steward:

> How goes the world, that I am thus encounter'd
> With clamorous demands of debt, broken bonds,
> And the detention of long since due debts
> Against my honour?   (2.2.41–44)[69]

"How goes the world" suggests one in, but perhaps not fully of, the economy – an exemplar *malgré lui*. But willfully or just unavoidably? Is Timon pretending ignorance of his credit rating or has he really been in the dark? One recent account of these lines would have it that "Timon acts flabbergasted . . . He professes amazement." Such a Timon would be at least somewhat disingenuous (he "acts" and "professes"). But this same account goes on to argue that it is "not so much that Timon is a fool as that his gift ideology lets him ignore money's commodity-form."[70] If truly blinkered by ideology, then would not Timon be genuinely amazed? In this critic's formulation, Timon stands in a not-quite-passive relationship to an ideology which "lets him" ignore things. But if his ideology licenses him to ignore the credit crunch, he could – if he would – pay attention. The same Timon who will momentarily register his astonishment ("you make me marvel") at his state of affairs nonetheless insists on his capacity, "I might so have rated my expense / As I had leave of means" (2.2.128–31). When Timon speaks of being "encounter'd / With clamorous demands," he sounds passive, beset by reality, if not by ideology. But Timon's "clamorous" indicates anger, disdain, even something like what may well have been Philip's pride at not understanding "these matters."

The Folio's "debt" and "debts" (which H. J. Oliver accepts) have exercised editors. Malone advanced "date-broken" for "debt, broken." Following Hanmer, Wells and Taylor remove "debt" and cite Wilson and Maxwell's argument that it represents an "undeleted false start. 'Debt' was probably abandoned as the next line was conceived."[71] The Folio's seeming redundancy may, however, represent a semantic distinction that springs from lexical indistinction. Just as Elizabeth wrote of her credit/monetary worth and her credit/reputation, Timon marks a difference between debts derived from financial bonds (what he owes because of what he has borrowed) and debts "against" his honor (something we may read cautiously against the grain – like Bassanio's "noble rate" – as pertaining more to his word than to bookkeeping). *Timon of Athens* makes it difficult for us to determine whether Timon has been unwilling or simply unable to figure out how to apply for his own benefit the distinction managed so adroitly by Elizabeth. Though he is first a bounteous host and then, apparently, a diametrically opposed type, a misanthrope, wealth (or gold) continues to attach itself to Timon and he continues to do what he can to give it up. Prone to neither nostalgia nor embarrassment, Timon (somewhat like the Folio Lear, who would "unburdened crawl toward death") would first nonchalantly, then aggressively, exempt himself from the debts incurred, not just from borrowing but from giving. In the end, Timon will turn from the encumbrances of credit to his enfranchising epitaph, to memorializing his credit-function not, as would Antonio, in terms of friendship and love (or as would Gresham, in terms of exchange), but in terms of exemption: *"Seek not my name . . . Pass by and curse thy fill, but pass and stay not here thy gait"* (5.4.71–73).

The encumbrances that will eventually cause Timon to break are displaced, during his first appearance in the play, onto Ventidius. He is in debt, "his creditors most strait" (1.1.99), and Timon will "free him" (1.1.106). The will to "ransom," "enfranchis[e]," "help," and "support" (1.1.108–11) a Ventidius beset by "clamorous demands" answers precisely to Timon's own desire for immunity. Having discharged Ventidius's debt, Timon next actualizes a dream in which a servant can win instant credit and so be made an "equal husband" (1.1.143). Timon imagines that with just a little "strain" (1.1.146) he can eliminate one of the oldest impediments to marriage, in effect do away with the need for credit rating by leveling all people's wealth. An old Athenian enters, attacking Timon's servant Lucilius's credentials. Timon instantly accredits his man by "build[ing] his fortune" (1.1.146). A story-book expenditure, something commensurate with Hobson's wish-fulfilling technique, mitigates desperate fact. Again and again, although he imagines he could rate his expense, and although he is a man of "large fortune" (1.1.56), one who has kept a lord's father's "Credit with his purse; / Supported his estate" (3.2.69–71), and drawn on his own "fortune" when "neighbour states . . . trod upon" Athens (4.3.95–96), Timon tries to float free of the net of credit in which he swims. Not just when he is flush and hospitable, but even when he is in the woods, Timon exercises the prerogatives of wealth to relieve himself of its pressures.

Nothing sets Timon more apart from his creditors – who pay uninterrupted attention to their cash flow – than his commitment to depletion, to spending himself out ("'tis not enough to give" – 1.2.218). "[E]xtremity" (4.3.301), the expenditure of "open bounty" (5.1.57) to which the play keeps referring, does not require knowledge ("Unwisely have I given" – 2.2.178). Neither does the wave-of-the-hand sort of problem-solving represented by Timon's "Let all my land be sold" (2.2.149). Timon is not merely "senseless of expense," he refuses "to *know* how to maintain it" (2.2.1–2; my emphasis). He just "pours it out" (1.1.275), leaving his steward to settle the "accompts" which he then throws off (2.2.137–38). Such giving ought not to be understood, however, in terms of the moral judgment attendant on prodigality or the social relations entailed by potlatch.[72] Before he breaks, at least, Timon may reasonably deny that he is prodigal. And he is borne out by the play's dozen or more references to "bounty" which complicate easy moral assessment. When Timon does accept the possibility that he is prodigal (4.3.280), it is yet another moment of confusing moral valence: he is handing out gold with which to cause destruction. It is also difficult to convince oneself that the essence of potlatch is at work here, that Timon has a proleptic desire to obligate others to him. Unlike Coppélia Kahn, a skeptical, psychoanalytically inflected reader of Timon's motives, I do not find it difficult to accept Timon's word when he says, "there's none / Can truly say he gives, if he receives" and that "I myself would have no power" (1.2.10–11 and 36).[73] What counts is that at the very center of the Athenian credit economy, Timon is trying to exempt himself via the "[m]agic of bounty" (1.1.6). Whatever the effect of Timon's gifts on those who benefit from him, the play focuses our attention on Timon's anti-economic gambit, his "raging waste" (2.1.4).

He gives/spends or wishes himself poorer (1.2.98) or imagines that his fortune is as much his "brother['s]" to command as his own (1.2.102). Neither the moral profit of generosity nor the social profit of largesse motivates Timon.

Timon accepts gifts for the same reason he turns to the lords for money: to keep spending. Give "two brace of greyhounds" to Timon and secure "fair reward" (1.2.186–88); give him "a beggar's dog" and receive gold; give him a horse and get twenty in return (2.1.5–10). These are not the circuits of exchange, of give and take. For Timon, economics corresponds to waste. When in 1605 and 1606 King James was farming the customs and turning to Parliament for subsidies (which were termed "supply" and, later, "support") that would permit him to satisfy his most pressing creditors, he could in good conscience assert that he was trying to do the country's business. For all that it might be said he was incapable of living within his means and that he was too bountiful, during the debate over the Great Contract in 1610 James could and did protest that he was willing to make retribution, to arrive at some sort of *quid pro quo*. It further could be asserted in his defense that "for a king not to be bountiful were a fault."[74] But when Timon's servant appears before Lucullus and explains, "in my lord's behalf, I come to entreat your honour to supply" (3.1.15–17; cf. "supply" at 2.1.27, 2.2.196, 3.2.34, and 4.2.47), and Lucullus responds by criticizing Timon's spending and bounty (3.1.25 and 39), something different is going on. Though mostly through representatives like Cecil, James was ready and able to deal, to negotiate, to work the economy, and to argue the prerogatives and necessities of sovereignty. But Timon, who stands for expenditure and nothing else, who has no fiduciary competence or no desire for it ("Thy lord's a bountiful gentleman: but thou [Flaminius] art wise" – 3.1.39–40), imagines himself released from economics altogether. He lives amidst the exacting credit economy that rules his creditors and racks his steward, but he acts as if he were not subject to its laws. His recursion from preeminent wealth to magic, to the pre-social or the imaginary, constitutes a fantastic repudiation of interpellation, an at once infantile and yet tragic exemption by fiat that renders Antonio's nostalgia comic (and pathetic) by comparison.

Timon's attempt to will his immunity from the ravages of this economy (his steward asks, "Who would not wish to be from wealth exempt"? – 4.2.31) has the effect of highlighting for us his immersion in it. Conversely, his exemplarity – his own creditors owe "their estates unto him" (3.3.6) – supports his conviction that his credentials permanently indemnify him. Whether we view his self-authorized exemption from the credit crunch as folly or arrogance or noble bearing, we understand his economic function to be determining. Like Antonio's nostalgia, and like Philip II's professed ignorance, Timon's desired exemption calls attention only to its impossibility. While we can imagine Bassanio or Heywood's Elizabeth beyond their economic functions, we cannot so imagine Antonio or Gresham, or Timon. In *Timon of Athens*, Alcibiades plays a role similar to Bassanio's in *The Merchant of Venice*. A. D. Nuttall argues that "Alcibiades' presence in the play has the effect of matching the structures of economic discourse, not with those of the higher morality, but with physical blood and death."[75] This suggests that we may conceive of alternative horizons of meaning – whatever they may be – for Alcibiades. This is not possible for Timon. Timon may be situated within an anti-economic discourse, but not one that is non-economic.

Even in the woods, he is first "dedicated beggar" (4.2.13) then burdened with gold. Just as his expenditure prior to his bankruptcy had no end beyond depletion, so his bounty in the woods, though motivated by rage, turns out to be mostly indifferent to effect. Timon says that he gives Alcibiades gold to pay his soldiers to "[m]ake large confusion" (4.3.129); but when Alcibiades refuses his "counsel" (4.3.132), Timon still gives him the gold. He hopes that the whores he showers with gold so that they may "defeat and quell" (4.3.165) Athens will themselves perish ("ditches grave you all" – 4.3.168). He would be satisfied if Apemantus hanged himself even if all of Timon's gold were "shut up" in him (4.3.281–82). He encourages the Banditti to pillage Athens, but expects that they will "[r]ob one another" and that his gold will "confound" them (4.3.448 and 452; later, he will give the Painter and the Poet gold to "rid . . . villains from your companies" though he clearly deems each of them an "arch-villain" – 5.1.99 and 107). And when his steward reappears, Timon gives him gold that he may "build [away] from men" (4.3.530). Just as Timon's desire for freedom from the demands of credit is projected onto the enfranchisement of imprisoned Ventidius at the start of the play, so, near the end, Timon imagines his steward living "rich and happy" but alone. Rather than a community of men exempt from lending and borrowing, an Athens without an economy, Athenians will now be swallowed by prisons and withered by debt (4.3.534–35). Somewhere on the periphery, beyond commerce and beyond community, the steward will paradoxically "thrive" (4.3.537).

Also on the periphery, in the woods, Timon wastes away, liquidating himself into solipsism ("he is set so only to himself" – 5.1.116). But even after he has used up his own resources and all of what he has borrowed, after he has spent the "bounteous housewife nature['s]" gold (4.3.423) on Alcibiades, Phrynia, and Timandra, on Apemantus, the Banditti, the

Poet, the Painter, and on his steward, he still has to find his way beyond those who would again entangle him in some form of indebtedness. Just when he is ready to achieve his final relief, the Senators arrive with "heaps and sums of love and wealth" (5.1.151). They would draw Timon back into the circle of commerce, start him up again in the economy he wishes to escape. Thus their "recanter," "render," "recompense," and "return" (5.1.145–58): a language of *re*interpellation and *re*accreditation within the realm of solvency and indebtedness, profit and loss. Heywood's Tawny-coat, himself a bankrupt digging (like Timon, 4.3.297) with a spade among stones, welcomes Hobson's offer to reinstall him in the local economy. Timon, however, now can tolerate only an economy of death: "Graves only be men's works and death their gain" (5.1.221). In his final imagining of Athens, production and profit sponsor neither bounty nor exchange but solitude and death. While his steward may live apart, Timon must die "bereft" (5.4.70). The injunctions of his textually suspect epitaph – "*Seek not my name . . . Pass by . . . pass and stay not here thy gait*" (5.4.71–73) – follow from his final exemption from credit. A "wretched corse, of wretched soul bereft" (5.4.70), Timon finally "cannot choose but break" (*The Merchant of Venice*, 3.1.104–05). In time, the "turbulent surge shall cover" (5.1.217) even his monument, turning his epitaph into an anti-epitaph, a last refusal of credit.

Like Coriolanus, who would be author of himself though he is Volumnia's and the patrician's warrior, Timon would be unencumbered though he is at the center of Athen's credit relations. Beseiged by his creditors' servants, Timon asks, "Have I been ever free . . .?" (3.4.79), grudgingly but only momentarily acknowledging the omnicompetence of debt.[76] *Timon of Athens* seems to have been written between 1605 and 1608, toward the end of a thirty-year period during which the English "nobility first became heavily dependent on credit" and "the dangers of borrowing – high interest rates and the potential danger of forfeiting mortgaged estates – were very real."[77] Although it is not a brief for bounty, for thrift, or for "the middle of humanity" that Timon never knew, the play takes it as a given that indebtedness is, as Lawrence Stone puts it, "an almost unavoidable necessity" (4.3.391; Stone, 539). It then follows Timon's efforts to make a clean break with the entire economics of indebtedness. If after all of his folly and invective, we still feel the resonance of Timon's efforts, it may be because Timon eschews corruption, the most notorious aristocratic accommodation to the Jacobean credit crunch.

Corruption, which in an economic context represents a tactical exemption from the exactions of desire and indebtedness, will serve as my last alternative in this partial inventory of credit relations. It is clearly the alternative favored by the Athenian Senate and Timon's creditors (in large measure, Middleton's creations, it appears), and it was the exemption of choice for countless aristocrats in Jacobean England. As Linda Levy Peck has argued, "corrupt practices actually functioned as the normal means by which the Crown and the aristocracy maintained their traditional political and economic control."[78] While James himself was responsible for creating and tolerating a "culture of political corruption" and while the King frequently exempted courtiers from the penalties designed to give teeth to reform efforts, there was a whole cadre of subjects eager to cash in on the expanding bureaucratic regulation of trade, monopolies, licenses, and offices.[79] But Peck's evidence must be crossed with Lawrence Stone's if we are to appreciate the extent to which corrupt economic practices were motivated by a desire to escape indebtedness and maintain expenditure.[80] Just as the Great Farm – with its attendant bribes paid to gain concessions and corrupt dealings among customs farmers – was organized in 1604–05 to provide for the financially constrained Crown a new source of credit and income, so powerbrokers like Thomas Howard, Earl of Suffolk, and Robert Cecil, Earl of Salisbury, protected these farmers because the former were so deeply in debt to the latter.

An exemplary courtier profoundly caught up in Jacobean credit operations, Suffolk was continuously in debt because of his remarkable extravagance: as he himself confessed, "The fault of the expense was my folly."[81] Looming large amidst such folly was Audley End, begun in 1603 and completed in 1616 at a cost of at least £80,000 (Stone notes the "well-authenticated" if not entirely reliable story that Suffolk told the King that his total expenditure on what was the largest private house in the land came to £200,000). But Suffolk was also set on providing for all ten of his children who survived childhood. Expensive tours of the Continent, substantial allowances, large property settlements, and major expenses at Court constituted an extraordinary drain on the income even of one "so lavishly rewarded by the Crown [Lord Chamberlain of the Household, Captain of the Gentlemen Pensioners, and finally Lord Treasurer], so fortunate in inheriting property from relatives [between 1614 and 1620, Suffolk and his eldest son had a total landed income of at least £8,000 a year], and so morally unrestricted in the pursuit of corrupt gains" as was Suffolk.[82] Always faced with new expenses and always in debt, Suffolk and his wife Katherine worked hard to exempt themselves from the credit crunch by means of a wide variety of corrupt dealings. Typical of these was Suffolk's manipulation of the farm of the customs and impositions on currants. Right from the start of the grant in 1604, Suffolk drew a handsome profit. But in 1609, after protests from the

Levant Company resulted in a lowering of the rate, Suffolk took advantage of his close ties to Cecil (now Lord Treasurer) and renegotiated the grant on terms which Stone calls "scandalous" (273). The new, twenty-one year lease to Suffolk's subcontractors entailed a pre-arranged bribe of £20,000. This phenomenal sum was eventually converted into an annuity to the Earl which in 1610 was paying him £3,000 a year, perhaps £5,000 a year in 1612.[83]

Deeply in debt to customs farmers who were themselves indebted to him for their piece of the action, Suffolk, like Timon, not only turned to them when he was pressed for cash but, corruptly (and unlike Timon) took advantage of the office of Lord Treasurer to see to it that they continued to advance him funds. In 1614, Suffolk borrowed £10,000 from the farmers. When, shortly thereafter, he became Lord Treasurer, he required £2,000 a year of the same men to save them from the obstructions Suffolk's new office would permit him to set in their way. After some manifest chicanery on the part of a Suffolk agent, the farmers agreed to pay the Earl £1,500 a year for seven years. This sum, writes Stone, "was to be used to pay the interest and to reduce the capital of Suffolk's private debts to them."[84] Meanwhile Suffolk's wife, the Countess Katherine, exacted bribes from the Spanish – the ambassador made over to the Howards some portion of £11,000 in 1609 – and from military commanders in Ireland. The latter agreed to pay the Earl and Countess £1,000 a year ("to be allowed and defalked out of the money assigned" for Ireland) in order to guarantee the transfer of the "residue" necessary for their support, though sums due them were still "converted to the Earle's occasions" by Suffolk's agent (Keep, 721–22).[85] Indeed, this same agent, the Teller of the Tallies in the Exchequer, Sir John Bingley, routinely dipped into the Treasury "without warrant or orders" (Keep, 724) on the Earl's behalf, sold official licenses in Suffolk's name, and did his best to help the Earl and his wife to profit from the awarding of royal grants.[86] At the Countess's bidding, Bingley at various times took "divers greate somes of money out of his Maty's Treasure and imployed the same about their own or other private uses & made divers payments for their own gain & left those payments & disbursements undone for wich the said moneys were particularly assigned" (Keep, 721).

Finally there was Arthur Ingram, financier and long-term Suffolk client, creditor, and operative, "a creature of the house of Suffolk" (Upton, 62). Suffolk was already deeply in debt to Ingram when he assumed the Lord Treasureship, but he was able to continue to pay off his man with preferment, if not money. Thus Suffolk's (and Robert Carr's) support temporarily got Ingram the post of Cofferer of the Royal

Household, a placement which occasioned concerted resistance on the part of all of the officers of the royal household and drew from Anthony Weldon the quip that this was to set a thief to catch a thief (Upton, 70). Together, Suffolk and Ingram used the former's control of the Exchequer and the latter's ready cash to force holders of royal promises to accept discounted returns on Exchequer tallies or letters of privy seal. Surely it was better to get something of what one was owed by the Crown than to get nothing (in the case of Sir David Murray, though owed £3,000, the knight had to settle for £2,000 and watch Suffolk pocket the rest – Keep, 726). Together, Suffolk and Ingram conspired to mislead the King (and cost his treasury well over £13,000) so that in 1617 Ingram could renew his contract for the alum farm, avoid penalties due on the 1615 contract, and kick back a profit to the Earl and his wife. And it was to Ingram (along with Lord William Howard) that Suffolk conveyed his estate to protect it from the Crown and unfriendly creditors when, in 1619, he was found guilty of "divers misemployments of his Maties treasure and other miscarriages and misdemeanours" as well as "divers extortions briberies and oppressions to the wrong and injurye of his Maties Subts" (Keep, 717).

Despite income from land, office, and what John Chamberlain called "extortion, concussion, and oppression, besides briberie and false dealing," Suffolk still found himself, in 1618, owing £40,000; the sum soon rose to £50,000 plus interest.[87] As if to punctuate his exemption from the sentence of credit, Suffolk did hardly anything "to reduce the burden of [his] debt before his death in 1626."[88] It may well be that there is nothing surprising about Suffolk. Thomas Ratcliffe, third Earl of Sussex, died owing £16,600; Robert Dudley, Earl of Leicester, died owing £68,500; Sir Christopher Hatton, £64,700; and Henry Hastings, third Earl of Huntington, £37,400. In the four years before his death Salisbury borrowed £61,000; he repaid only £36,000.[89] What stands out, however, is a Cecil's or a Howard's calculated, tactical exemption from the ravages of indebtedness by means of corruption when flourishing, then a final balk by means of death (that heirs were subsequently encumbered with debt seems hardly to impinge on these successful exemptions).[90] In its Jacobean context, Timon's fantastic repudiation of accreditation, his giving and dying, strikes one as neither narcissistic nor a gesture beyond the pleasure principle. Timon indulges in neither comic nostalgia nor chronicle embarrassment. There is instead an awful probity to his doomed effort to obliterate the inescapable credit relations endemic in Athens and London, to get himself free at last.[91]

IV

To the discursive markers which identify change in early modern
England with which I began, we may add commonwealth and political
economy. What had been conceived of as reciprocity (common wealth)
between one person and another, between sovereign and subject, is
increasingly understood in terms of *quid pro quo* (contract). The design of
the Great Contract is indebted to countless, if lesser, commercializations
of bonds in England. The discursive force of moral obligations was
mitigated by an increasing tolerance for instrumentality, or one sort of
instrumentality gave way to another, and to its remoralization.[92] What
we may learn from the dramatic and historical evidence examined here,
however, has less to do with an epistemic shift than with affective, lived,
tactical responses to change. Change that is remarked upon is also
change that is felt. Frustration, exhaustion, embarrassment, rage, nonchalance, bravado, these are some of the "affective elements of
consciousness" as it fitfully extends and accommodates itself to what I
have called the early modern English credit crunch. Or perhaps, given my
allegiance to the local, I can skirt the implicitly (and surprisingly)
Hegelian resonance of Williams's phrase by amending it to "elements of
consciousnesses." Not just princes but peddlers, merchants and nobles,
brothers and others were now differently, now comparably, devising,
improvising, or falling into one or another line as a result of the exactions
of credit.

2 Debt restructuring

To say that credit relations permeated most layers of early modern English society is but another way of saying that most contemporary production was founded upon debt. Given the chronic shortage of specie, what currency there was, was in seemingly constant circulation. While one certainly might have been victimized by a usurer, it is probably more likely that one would have been enabled by a creditor.[1] The ubiquity of credit relations meant that one and the same person was often at one and the same moment both a borrower and a lender.[2] "Credit was so common," writes Craig Muldrew, "that most people eventually accumulated numerous reciprocal debts over time."[3] It appears increasingly to occur to early modern English people that a theologically opprobrious nomenclature suited to others, to "not us," would no longer serve a population forced to recognize some version of themselves in these others. "He" is a prodigal, but "I" am a debtor. "He" is a usurer, but "I" am a creditor. Such confident and normative distinctions begin to break down in the early seventeenth century.[4] When we are *all* borrowers and lenders, what Kenneth Burke calls a religious psychology is converted by credit into a commercial psychology.[5] In such circumstances, any successful remoralization of accreditation and indebtedness would have to respond to historical change. Muldrew's revisionist account of seventeenth-century market relations entails an explicit rejection of Marx's conviction that credit relations are founded upon distrust and estrangement. Observing that as markets expanded "cultural stress on the ethics of credit actually increased," Muldrew concludes that "a new flexible law of contract which emphasized trust developed."[6] Of course, such an emphasis on trust is a tacit acknowledgment of the possibility of distrust. Comic reconciliations are often ethically charged adjustments made in the face of socio-economic disorientation.

Like the theatres in which they were played (about which more, later) and like the urban economy which they staged, the Jacobean comedies to which I turn in this chapter – *Eastward Ho*, *Michaelmas Term*, and *Greene's Tu Quoque* – are premised upon debt. Each, in its own way, manifestly capitalizes on, even as in a restrained manner it moralizes, debt. Each play discriminates among sorts of indebtedness while acknowledging its inevitability. Each is a study in debt management in which the fact of indebtedness is not a cause for embarrassment, but one's inability successfully to superintend one's debt is. Just as surely as default follows indebtedness in each comic scenario, imprisonment or its specter follows default. The sergeant's appearance on stage – more precisely, the clap of his hand upon a debtor's shoulder – signifies the end of bravado or an awakening from obliviousness. With the sergeant, the outraged debtor then proceeds to prison, to some sort of repentance and, finally, to reintegration, often with renewed bravado, into the community of adroitly managed debt. This thoroughly comic trajectory is a consequence of a generic imperative, a requisite if fantastic swerve away from the grimly familiar telos of mismanaged debt. On stage, the ratio of debtor's bravado to humility favors the former. In a theatrical context, even indifference to one's indebtedness can underwrite a comedy and stimulate pleasure. Off the stage, the imprudent ostentation of bravado could rarely have been so successful as even-tempered tenacity. A Londoner's fiscal recklessness or inattentiveness might lead to close and unending imprisonment, to unending litigation, or to Virginia. Still more darkly, any of these possiblities might be interrupted by death.[7]

The early modern English borrower's credit depended upon his or her trustworthiness, as it was rated not only by lenders but brokers, friends, associates, kin, and courts. Both debtor and creditor had to calculate intention, reputation (a mostly classical or secular set of external properties bound up with socio-economic status), and character (a theological, vaguely Protestant set of internal properties bound up with piety).[8] The comic borrower's self-confidence is a fantastic, if dramatically effective, response to a desire for mastery in a world of contentious, unpredictable, often inexplicable accreditation and discrediting.[9] Condensed within each play's moments of exhilaration and humiliation are Jacobean comedies' acknowledgments that what is at stake in a default is the loss of one's reputation and of one's patrimony. To ruin one's own credit is to incapacitate oneself socially and economically, and to vitiate the trust one has built up. "Credit lost is like a Venice glass broke." "He that has lost his Credit is dead to the world" (Tilley, C815 and C817).[10] In dramatic terms, to be discredited is to lose one's force as an operator, an improviser, a seemingly self-determining subject in the play of metropolitan capital. To be, as we now say, in the hole (out of money and deeply in debt), was to be consigned to the humiliations of the Hole, that portion of the Wood Street Counter "that stinks many men to death."[11] The gallant, apprentice, or trickster become broken debtor, "stript of his estate, his body Imprisoned, his liberty tyed up, his credit destroyed, and his friends banished," forfeits his maneuverability and so momentarily grinds to a halt his dramatic progress.[12] A comparable blockage afflicts his patrimony. Irredeemable indebtedness signals the dissipation of what was one's to inherit and one's to bequeath. Because bankruptcy undermines regimes fundamental to the transmission of property in early modern England, it is not surprising that such dislocation registers most particularly in the comic domain of marriage. Nor is it surprising that staged fantasies of indebtedness should proceed toward recovery. Successful financial reorganization engendered restored economic elasticity and the possibility that consanguinity or conjugality might either better position one in terms of debtor-creditor relations, or somehow limit their force.

I

Chapman, Jonson, and Marston's *Eastward Ho* (1605) begins with two sustained autobiographical statements responsive to conflicting sets of intentions but equally fixated on accreditation and indebtedness. The first vita is that of the cheeky apprentice, Francis Quicksilver:

Why, 'sblood, sir, my mother's a gentlewoman, and my father a justice of the peace and of quorum; and though I am a younger brother and a prentice, yet I hope I am my father's son; and by God's lid, 'tis for your worship and for your commodity that I keep company. I am entertained among gallants, true; they call me cousin Frank, right; I lend them moneys, good; they spend it, well. But when they are spent, must not they strive to get more? Must not their land fly? and to whom? Shall not your worship ha' the refusal? Well, I am a good member of the City if I were well considered. How would merchants thrive, if gentlemen would not be unthrifts? How could gentlemen be unthrifts if their humours were not fed? How should their humours be fed but by whitemeat and cunning secondings? Well, the City might consider us. I am going to an ordinary now: the gallants fall to play; I carry light gold with me; the gallants call, "Cousin Frank, some gold for silver"; I change, gain by it; the gallants lose the gold, and they call "Cousin Frank, lend me some silver." (1.1.26–47)[13]

Quicksilver's self-assertion has as its proximate cause his master Touchstone's objection to his being dressed inappropriately for an apprentice: he is decked out with "Sword, [and] pumps" (1.1.22) like a gallant. But the real trigger seems to be Touchstone's mention of Quicksilver's "indentures" (1.1.25). For this is to remind the would-be gallant not only of his actual social placement but of his economic entailment as well. The apprentice's response is multivocal. His initial lines are successively compensatory then explanatory. He is an apprentice but his origins are gentle; in other words, "[God]'sblood" as well as his mother's and his father's should guarantee that his temporary obligations as an apprentice do not discredit him. Nonetheless, the often expressed fear that apprenticeship resulted in a derogation of status was not easily assuaged, not even in the face of widespread acknowledgment, dating back at least half a century, that numerous sons of gentlemen were apprenticed in London's great companies.[14] A dozen or more years after *Eastward Ho*, Edmund Bolton was worrying "*Whether Apprentiship extinguisheth Gentry*" and vociferously refuting those who would lay "*the barbarous penaltie of losse of Gentry*" on younger sons in city trades.[15] Thus, just as soon as Quicksilver has palliated his current status by insisting on his pedigree, he proceeds to explain it, invoking primogeniture conjunctively ("I am a younger brother and an apprentice") but surely understanding its causal force. To the extent that we can distinguish social from economic determinants, it may be said that the economic origin (primogeniture, and the preservation of the family estate that it was meant to insure) of the apprentice Quicksilver's current social status is strategically insulated both fore (blood) and aft ("my father's son") by the social origins of his current economic status. And yet, in an age when patrimony was in critical relation to social and economic identity, even this buffer might prove unreliable: like Prospero, who must accept that Miranda is his daughter because his wife "said" she was, Quicksilver can only "hope I am my father's son."

Having begun with his credit rating, his avowal of his patrimonial credit and his acknowledgment of his chief debit, his indenture, Quicksilver goes on to advertise his expertise in the realm of urban socioeconomic exchange. That he can pass among gallants derives, we are tacitly to understand, from the pedigree he has just declared. Whereas the goldsmith Touchstone's presence in such company would automatically suggest self-interest, Quicksilver boasts that he can satisfy both himself and his master's "commodity" by insinuating himself among gallants. Passing as their "cousin Frank," he would have Touchstone believe that he is acting as the citizen's factor. This would normally be the role of a scrivener who made it his business to know which merchants had money to lend and which gentlemen were needy. But a scrivener would typically broker a loan between a goldsmith and a borrower. Here, Quicksilver suggests that he himself is a creditor for whom brokering is merely a secondary function. "Unthrifts" in debt to "cousin Frank" pawn their land to the goldsmith in order to pay off the disguised apprentice. Handsomely requited, Quicksilver then closes down the gallants' credit lines, leaving their estates firmly within the goldsmith's control. In fact, as Touchstone reminds Quicksilver, the cash he has been disbursing is not his own but his master's. Consequently, precisely who is

calling the shots here is difficult to determine. Both Quicksilver and, for
different reasons, Touchstone would have us believe that Quicksilver is
running the scam. Yet Touchstone knows exactly how much of his own
"cash" he is being "gallanted out of" (1.1.50–51) – "seven score pound"
– and when he refers to "the accounts" and to the money being "yet in
the rear" (1.1.68; 70), he can only be referring to his own books. The
goldsmith has all along been backing his apprentice, though he has
shifted the risk onto Quicksilver's, and, tellingly, Quicksilver's father's,
shoulders ("your father's bond [the indenture] lies for you" – 1.1.69). For
all his bravado (in moral terms, *because* of his bravado), Quicksilver
fares poorly at debt management.

Which brings us to the second autobiographical assertion, that of
William Touchstone:

as for my rising by other men's fall, God shield me. Did I gain my wealth by
ordinaries? no! By exchanging of gold? no! By keeping of gallants' company? no!
I hired me a little shop, bought low, took small gain, kept no debt book,
garnished my shop, for want of plate, with good wholesome thrifty sentences . . .
And when I was wived, having something to stick to, I had the horn of suretyship
ever before my eyes. [*To the audience*] You all know the device of the horn, where
the young fellow slips in at the butt end, and comes squeezed out at the buccal.
[*To Quicksilver*] And I grew up, and, I praise Providence, I bear my brows now as
high as the best of my neighbours . . . (1.1.51–68)

The goldsmith's *apologia pro sua vita* has all the hallmarks of bourgeois
thrift and risk-aversion. Touchstone describes a prudent, modest, and
steady ascent to the top of urban retailing. But if we are to make out the
source of his success, as opposed to the myth of his origins, then we must
look to his wiving and subsequent thriving. That Mistress Touchstone
had the "wherewithal" (1.2.118) to help set up William is confirmed
when we learn that it is seemingly *her* mother's land (this property will
motivate much of the plotting in *Eastward Ho*) worth £2,000
(4.2.269–70) and capable of yielding an annual income of £100 per
annum (1.2.102–03) that is to be passed on as a gift to their daughter
Gertrude. Touchstone's rise thus anticipates Sir Petronel Flash's hoped-
for climb on the back of a wife's dowry. The goldsmith has in his wife
"something to stick to," something to cling to for support as well as
something into which he may thrust. In his relationship with Mistress
Touchstone, as in his apparent arrangement with his ordinary-haunting
apprentice, unexceptionable cautiousness obscures calculated aggression.
Such policy, I take it, is what is represented by the "horn of suretyship"
that Touchstone refers to next.

Ostensibly, the horn is cautionary. Called to mind by the "something"
to which he is stuck, it is the cuckold's horn, the proverbial alarum to

domestic vigilance . . . and to fiscal policy too. He seems to be saying that, like the "thrifty sentences" which garnish his shop, the horn reminded him never to obligate himself to pay for the debts incurred by others (precisely the fate of *The Merchant of Venice*'s Antonio). The "device of the horn" may, however, have a more ominous import. Perhaps Touchstone betrays an earlier willingness to prostitute his own wife in order that he might rise in the world. Then too, C. G. Petter notes that "Touchstone alludes to the notorious method by which London merchants cheated young country gentlemen of their fortunes and land." In one sixteenth-century panel

an enormous horn hang[s] across a tree. At the far left stands a wealthy citizen, dressed to suit his affluence. He supervises a character, dressed like Quicksilver . . . who is thrusting a victim into the opening of the horn; his unhappy face and an arm emerging from the narrow end (buckle). The citizen holds a rope, loosely tied around the victim's legs. To the right stands another ragged, woebegone gallant (i.e., the gallant, fleeced).[16]

Once again, we have a suggestion that the goldsmith has been employing his apprentice in sharp dealing, "rising by other men's fall." But there is a still more nasty measure of Touchstone's potential for aggression here. For he may as well still be talking about his youthful wiving as about his buying and selling when, prior to a pun on "grew up" and subsequent to phallic wordplay about sticking, Touchstone refers to a "young fellow" slipping in at the butt end and squeezing out at the buccal (mouthpiece). When understood in sexual as well as economic terms, the "device" appears to be an amalgam of the latent contents of Touchstone's own nightmarish "horn" joke.[17] Wholesomeness and thrift (1.1.57) give way under a little pressure, revealing a predatory, sadistic, anal-retentive economy thoroughly at odds with Touchstone's pretensions.[18]

Debt, wiving, and patrimony. Touchstone keeps no "debt book" but neither does he say how it comes to pass that he "hired . . . a little shop." I am assuming that the place of "when I was wived" in his narrative sequence mutes the value of marriage to his career, just as his silence about his own parentage amplifies its importance. If Quicksilver is to be believed, Touchstone's "father was a maltman, and his mother sold gingerbread in Christ Church" (1.1.135–36). Quicksilver, as we have seen, is patently in debt and trumpets his "pedigree" (1.1.124). It is partly the work of the play to discipline him into marriage. In this regard, he is not so much the antithesis as he is a variant of sober, self-disciplining Golding, his "fellow-prentice, as good a gentleman born" (1.1.80–81). For Golding, no less than the prodigal Quicksilver, is on his way toward marriage in *Eastward Ho*, and his creditor is also Touchstone. The goldsmith indebts Golding to him by matching him with his younger daughter, Mildred: "I mean to give thee thy freedom; and with thy freedom my daughter; and with my daughter a father's love; and with all these such a portion as shall make Knight Petronel himself envy thee" (2.1.161–64). This transfer of daughter and dowry in its turn effectively reasserts the use value Touchstone found in his own wife. As a vehicle for a blatant transmission of property ("She's now mine . . . she's now thine" – 1.2.176–77), the Golding–Mildred marriage correlates the mystified commercial function of the good daughter with both the much-advertised economic value of the insufferable daughter, Gertrude, and the ostensibly commercial function of Quicksilver's punk, Sindefy. That marrying Sindefy is a variation on marrying Mildred is confirmed by the fact that the punk turns out to be the play's lone, truly conservative social critic. Mildred's-warmed over bromides (2.1.60–77) come off as both cheap and self-righteous when compared with Sindefy's acuity. But even this affinity does not exhaust Chapman, Jonson, and Marston's wittily counter-intuitive equation of industrious and dissolute apprentice-ships. For Quicksilver's sudden and incredible prison recovery is no less fantastic than Golding's overnight, miraculous rise to a deputy alder-manship, paying the debt he never promised. The comic exposure within the playhouse at the Blackfriars of Touchstone's and Golding's smugly politic behavior is in keeping with the mild sentence passed within the play on the reckless accounting practiced by Quicksilver and by Touch-stone's other son-in-law, Sir Petronel Flash.

When Touchstone dissolves Quicksilver's indenture and dismisses him from his house, the apprentice takes up residence with the play's other creditor, "the famous usurer" (2.2.11) Security. The *in loco parentis* role that overtaxed Touchstone has fallen to Security, whom Quicksilver regularly refers to as "dad" (2.2 *passim*). Quicksilver can now more easily pretend to serve Security in precisely the way he protested he was serving Touchstone: "I am now loose, to get more children of perdition into thy usurous bonds" (2.2.14–15). Helping Security to Sir Petronel's business and then helping the knight to the usurer's wife simply recapitulates Quicksilver's scouting out needy gallants for Touchstone even as he dips into the goldsmith's assets. Security, for his part, can provide Quicksilver with "his punks," his "wench," his wife-to-be Sindefy – the usurer's version of Mildred. One and the same stage thus variably figures surety and security, the goldsmith's shop, with its "horn of suretyship," and the "house . . . as 'twere the cave" (2.2.5) of Security. Touchstone's auto-biographical encomium to risk-aversion ("keep thy shop, and thy shop will keep thee"; "Light gains makes heavy purses"; etc. – 1.1.58–60) is succeeded by Security's equally ironic and self-serving lecture on "the safest course" how "honest men . . . live by lending money . . . with moderate profit, thirty or forty i' th' hundred" (2.2.118 and 111–13). And Golding's pedantic rebuke of Quicksilver (1.1.157–75) is supplemented by Sindefy's heartfelt cautions. With credit ratings on everyone's mind in *Eastward Ho*, the prodigal apprentice is as likely to be given a lesson in social deportment or debt management by a punk and a usurer as by an upright merchant and his virtuous heir.

Predictably, neither Quicksilver nor Sir Petronel heeds the abundance of advice on fiscal planning that the play has to offer. As a result, they are both ripe for exposure. But first Chapman, Jonson, and Marston cash in on the apprentice's bravura and on the knight's pyramid scheme (creditors eager to arrest Sir Petronel have backed the Virginia voyage that he aims to refinance with the proceeds of the sale of Gertrude's inheritance). Then they set the stage for the grand finale – Quicksilver's repentance – a performance so far over the top that renewed bravado vitiates whatever humility may momentarily have been felt. Because all Londoners depended upon one another as borrowers and lenders, each had to comply with an ethics of credit. We see the effects of this in *The Merchant of Venice*, where Antonio "cannot choose but break," having accepted prior claims made in the name of the "trade and profit of the city" (3.1.104–05 and 3.3.30). Quicksilver works aggressively (as Antonio conspicuously refuses to do) to sustain his maneuverability in the face of financial imperatives. When he trades on his "cracked credit" (cf. 3.2.349) or recites his "Repentance," however, he is not so much conforming to an ethics of credit as performing it, conforming to it *by* performing it.[19] Of course, there must be some punishment for the apprentice's "receipt" of his master's goods (4.2.267) and for his co-conspirator's secret sale of Gertrude's land to Security. But *Eastward Ho* rejects a punitive mode of socio-economic discipline and opts instead for a form of comic *self*-disciplining that still more closely aligns Quicksilver with Golding. There are minor humiliations meted out in Wapping, where Quicksilver washes ashore; on the Isle of Dogs, the debtor's refuge where Sir Petronel lands; and in the debtors' prison whose inmates eventually include Quicksilver, Sir Petronel, and Security. But the reconstitution, not the mortification, of a community of urban actor/agents (like Touchstone, Golding, and Quicksilver in Act 5) performing acts of mutual accreditation is the more deeply desired telos of the play.

In Wapping, Quicksilver despairs,

> O which way shall I bend my desperate steps,
> In which unsufferable shame and misery
> Will not attend them? (4.1.145–47)

Since even in his moment of desperation we hear something of Quicksilver's debts sperate (recoverable), or of his desperate debts (those irreclaimable), it comes as no surprise that he is soon up to his old "tricks" (4.1.225). Before we even come upon him in the Counter, the familiar terminus for Jacobean debtors in default, we know that Quicksilver has begun to "make shift" (4.1.268). His recovery begins with prison letters, supplications addressed to Touchstone and Golding. Golding hears "a great deal of humility i' these letters" (5.2.44) and decides to employ whatever credit he has with the gaoler on the prisoners' behalf. Touchstone reasonably equates "all suits, to all entreaties, to all letters, to all tricks" (5.2.82–83). He has not yet heard of Quicksilver's "'Repentance', or his 'Last Farewell'" (5.3.63), nor does he know that "the gallant prentice of London" has become "a pretty poet" (5.3.42–43 and 64). Touchstone and Quicksilver's master–apprentice relationship has been debased into a felonious debtor–creditor relationship; now it is primed for conversion into a patron–poet bond. Letters may not prevail with the goldsmith, but when he comes to the Counter and actually hears Quicksilver's performance, he admits that he is "ravished with his 'Repentance'" (5.5.115–16). This ought not to surprise anyone, since Quicksilver's "Farewell" brings the play right back to where it began. In a parodic imitation of Touchstone's fiscal policy as it was articulated at the beginning of the play, Quicksilver trots out precisely the sort of maxims that supposedly guide his former master:

> Seek not to go beyond your tether
> But cut your thongs unto your leather;
> So shall you thrive by little and little,
> Scape Tyburn, Counters, and the Spital.   (5.5.126–29)

His credit restored – he has "killed the desperate opinion" Touchstone had of his apprentice's "reclaim" (5.5.139–40) – Quicksilver is now worthy of admission into the fraternity of politic money-management. He now plays his part so well that we cannot be certain whether it is humility or fresh bravado that we are being asked to applaud. That we are being solicited, and that Quicksilver is now brokering on behalf of Chapman, Jonson, and Marston, is evident from the final lines of the play, Quicksilver's sales pitch to the audience:

> O may you find in this our pageant, here,
>   The same contentment which you came to seek;
> And as that [Lord Mayor's] show but draws you once a year,
>   May this attract you hither once a week.   (Epilogue, 7–10)[20]

Eastward Ho's version of debtors' prison requires of the play's chief plotter little more than a bravura gesture, a comic performance of humility. Something more abject was demanded of playwrights who

found themselves similarly incarcerated, if the distress of Thomas
Dekker, and that of Chapman and Jonson subsequent to their having
penned this particular play, may count as evidence. We know that Philip
Henslowe "lent unto the companey the 4 of febreary 1598 to dise charge
mr dicker owt of the cownter in the powltrey the some of fortie
shillinges."[21] Just short of a year later, Henslowe records a loan of £3.10s
"to descarge Thomas dickers frome the a reaste of my lord chamberlenes
men" (*Diary*, 104). From 1613 to 1619, Dekker was in the King's Bench
Prison for debt, and from this period of confinement there survives a
letter of supplication. The chapel at Dulwich College, founded by
Henslowe's son-in-law, the actor Edward Alleyn, was consecrated on 1
September 1616.[22] Dekker seems to have acknowledged the event with a
eulogy (which does not survive) for the benefactor shortly thereafter. He
then followed up on this "venture" with the letter that follows:

Out of that respect wch I ever caryed to yor Worth (now heightned by a Pillar of
yor owne erecting) doe I send theis poore testimonies of a more rich Affection. I
am glad (yf I bee the First) that I am the first to Consecrate to Memory (yf at
least you so embrace it) So noble and pious a Work, as This, yor last and
worthiest is. A passionate desire of expressing gladnes to See Goodnes so well
delivered having bin long in labour in the world made mee thus far to venture.
And it best becomes mee to Sing any thing in praise of Charity, because, albeit I
have felt few handes warme thorough that complexion, yett imprisonment may
make me long for them. Yf any thing in my Eülogium (or Praise) of you and yor
noble Act bee offensive, lett it bee excused because I live amongst the Gothes and
Vandalls, where Barbarousnes is predominant. Accept my will howsoever And
mee
                    Ready to doe you any service
                              Tho Dekker[23]

That Alleyn fully understood this "praise of Charity" to be a request for
relief is suggested by the first line of what seems to be a later, though
undated, letter from Dekker to Alleyn: "I give you thanks for the last
remembrance of your love."[24] That Alleyn, a man "of good credit,"
would have done something to relieve Dekker follows not only from his
vast wealth and philanthropy but from his demonstrated willingness to
forgive debts, such as one half of the £400 owed to him by a company of
players in March 1616.[25] Whether or not Alleyn *should* have done
something to relieve Dekker has everything to do with the era's conflicting attitudes toward indebtedness.

   Dekker's long years in prison left him with little sympathy for the
"noble-in-the-pound bankrupt . . . a voluntary villain . . . a golden
thief." Such "politic bankrupts," who "live safe to spend other men's
moneys," follow the route Quicksilver recommends to Sir Petronel. Put
your creditors in "sufficient sureties," he advises, then take up temporary

residence in prison, letting them choose which one, "either the King's Bench, or the Fleet, or which of the two Counters they like best" (2.2.288–91).[26] Dekker had deep sympathy, however, for the penniless prisoners in what he called the "Fourteen Golgothas environing one city." "The cry of these men is loud . . . it is the cry of sickness, of melancholy, madness, hunger, cold, thirst, nakedness, penury, beggary, misery." Dekker estimated that there were at least a thousand such debtors, each "pin[ing] in a gaol, his wife at home, his children beg, servants starve; his goods are seized on, reputation ruined, his name forgotten, health shaken, his wits distracted, his conversation blasted, his life miserable, his death contemptible." Nonetheless Dekker no more than his contemporaries knew whom to trust or where to place the blame for such misery: "[e]ither this must proceed from much cruelty in the creditor or much deceit in the debtor," he uncertainly concludes.[27]

Jacobean statutes betray a measure of the same puzzlement. 1 Jac. I, c.14, "An Acte for Recoverie of Small Debtes, and releevinge of poor Debtors in London," was supposed to free up the various courts in Westminster where plaintiffs were bringing suit to the great expense of debtors. Many were now finding themselves paying six times as much in court charges as their original debts amounted to, "to the utter undoing of such poore Debtors, theire Wives and Children, and also the filling of the Prisons with Poore so sued." At the same time, 1 Jac. I, c.15, "An Acte for the better Reliefe of the Creditors against suche as shall become Bankrupte," was directed against politic bankrupts (mostly merchants dealing in large sums) and took aim at their ears.[28] The first statute speaks to humility, to the "fiftie poore men" in "the hole in Wood-street Counter" who "humbly beseecheth" monied Londoners for relief some time in the latter half of the sixteenth century.[29] Still in 1644, there are seventy "poore prisoners in the hole of the *Poultry Counter*" (suffering "hunger, cold, nakednes, [and] noisome smels . . . in this our loathsome Dungeon") who "most humbly sheweth" their "lamentable estate."[30] The second statute speaks to bravado managed with art: "the practices of Bankruptes of late are soe secret and soe subtile as that they can verie hardelie be founde out" (1 Jac. I, c.15). Humility and bravado should not be very hard to distinguish from one another, but the drama suggests that they may be. So too, bits and pieces like the following from Dekker's biography: one of the playwright's creditors, the tailor Thomas Cator, sued in the Court of King's Bench, claiming that "Dekker had obtained a doublet and a pair of hose from him . . . and had since *repeatedly refused* to settle up."[31] Given that this was not the only such complaint brought against Dekker, are we to imagine cruelty in creditors or deceit in the debtor? In one of the chapters on prison life added to the 1616 edition of *English Villainies* Dekker, though himself an imprisoned debtor, writes that "[i]f creditors had not iron nets to fish for their money, all men in the world would still borrow but never pay" (270).

Humility and bravado also inform the second set of prison supplications to which I have referred. In his *Conversations* with William Drummond, Jonson is said to have recalled that "he was delated [*sic*] by Sr James Murray to the King for writting something against the Scots in a play Eastward hoe." Jonson and Chapman (though almost certainly not Marston, despite Drummond's report that Jonson had included him) were imprisoned and "the report was that they should then [have] had their ears cutt & noses."[32] In one of the prison letters to which I shall return, Chapman refers to "two Clawses" comprising the "chiefe offences" (218). Cancelled in Q, these clauses survive in two extant copies.[33] The gibe itself is part of an extended discussion about Virginia between the sea captain, Seagull, and two adventurers – Scapethrift and Spendall – who plan to accompany Sir Petronel on his voyage. Seagull avers that in Virginia there are no "sergeants, or courtiers, or lawyers, or intelligencers – only a few industrious Scots, perhaps, who, indeed, are dispersed over the face of the whole earth." He goes on to say that he "would a hundred thousand of 'em were there, for we are all one countrymen now, ye know; and we should find ten times more comfort of them there than we do here" (3.3.43–52). Mention of sergeants, the proverbial cue for arrest for debt, has as its sequel "industrious Scots," a token of the playwrights' bravado that turns out to have been an incitement to arrest for discrediting. Striking enough to have awakened what Chapman calls "the most sorrowe inflictinge wrath of his Excellent Majestie" (219), the gibe resurfaces in the next act in a reference to the notorious knighthoods (like Sir James Murray's) recently conferred by the King. Sir Petronel is himself either "one of my thirty-pound knights" or "one that stole his knighthood o' the grand day for four pound" (4.1.197–200). Quicksilver, his accomplice, aspires to leave the City to travel eastward (eastward ho!) "to the court" (2.2.62–63) at Greenwich.

Eastward Ho aligns itself with other plays, written solo by Chapman, Jonson, and Marston, which caution against depending upon the Court for accreditation.[34] But when push comes to shove and the playwrights find themselves in prison, they look with all due humility to the Court. Or so it appears. Turning a profit in the City (in the Blackfriars) has entailed loss of credit at Court and with the creditor of last resort, the King. In what are perhaps the least ironic and most poignant lines in the play, the punk Sindefy details the "injuries" one must "swallow" and one's inevitable "disgrace" (2.2.81 and 96) when sailing "court seas" (2.2.77). "What care and devotion," she asks, "must you use to humour an imperious lord, proportion your looks to his looks, smiles to his smiles, fit your sails to the wind of his breath?" (2.2.81–84). When Quicksilver quips that any journeyman can do as much, Sindefy responds:

But he's worse than a prentice that does it, not only humouring the lord, but every trencher-bearer, every groom that by indulgence and intelligence crept into his favour, and by panderism into his chamber. He rules the roast; and when my honourable lord says it shall be thus, my worshipful rascal, the groom of his close stool, says it shall not be thus, claps the door after him, and who dares enter? A prentice, quoth you? (2.2.87–95)

Like Quicksilver, the *Eastward Ho* playwrights were first bold, then discredited, then in prison, and, finally, repentant. Like Quicksilver, they make it difficult to determine the ratio of their bravado to their humility. If Sir Petronel represents an extended satire upon newly minted (Scottish) knights, then there is much bravado – what Sindefy calls "hazard" – in this play. But how much humility should we ascribe to Chapman's and Jonson's supplications, and does the uncertainty with which we respond to Quicksilver's "Repentance" bear upon our reading of the playwrights' letters?

There are a total of ten surviving appeals, three from Chapman and seven from Jonson. Each of them humors an imperious lord or a highly placed groom. In his letter to the King, Chapman presents himself and Jonson as "your two most humble and prostrated subjects . . . we cast our best parts at youre highnes feete" (218). To the Lord Chamberlain (Thomas Howard, Earl of Suffolk), he writes that "Off all the oversights for which I suffer, none repents me so much, as that our unhappie booke was presented without your Lordshippes allowance" (218). He and Jonson are "wth all humilitie enforc't to solicite the propagation of youre [Suffolk's] most noble favours to our present freedome" (219). Amidst much abjection there is a full measure of faith in their credit, an insistence upon "our poore reputations" (219). Chapman acknowledges his indebtedness to James's "Cesar-like Bountie" (218) even as he makes a case for self-accreditation. He reminds the King that "all Authoritie in execution of Justice, especiallie respects the manners & lives of men commaunded before it; And accordinge to their generall actions, censures any thinge that hath scap't them in perticuler; which can not be so disproportion-able: yt one beinge actuallie good, the other should be intentionally ill" (218). If the gibe has merely "scaped" them, and if intention is what Chapman would have the King judge, then we are not far from our experience of Quicksilver's "Repentance."

Jonson, another "most humble suitor," is also obligated on account of "former benefitts" and "Bountyes" (220–21; in this case, Robert Cecil, the Earl of Salisbury's, but former "Bounties" are also noticed in the appeal to Pembroke). Now bound in prison, he imagines himself eternally bound to Cecil once his lordship frees Jonson. To the Earl of Montgomery, Jonson writes that while his cause will not "discreditt" the "Most worthy Earle," he worries that "while I sue for favours I should be thought to buy them" (the Senecan discourse of benefits necessarily excludes purchase). Looking to the future, Jonson pledges the "forfayture of my humanitie . . . my fortune, Reputation, and Innocence" if it is determined that he has mismanaged the Earl's line of credit (224). Like Chapman, Jonson protests that anyone familiar with his writings would know "whether it be possible, I should speake of his Majestie as I have done, without the affection of a most zealous and good subject" (220). But Jonson himself calls attention to his previous run-in with the authorities due to his writing and he says only that since then, he has "attempred" his "stile" (221).[35] The same might be said of Quicksilver.

Predictably, neither Chapman nor Jonson has anything specific to say about the substance of the gibe that occasioned their imprisonment. The playwrights have been "misconstrued"; the complaints come from "enemies"; "*Rumor*" is to blame (219–20). "Trust us," they seem to say, even as they deflect attention onto their other, more successful writings and onto their intentions, which are invisible. Faulty management, or "stile," is both cause for embarrassment and that which must be improved. Successful amendment depends on expressions of humility which in turn lead to new obligations.[36] The alternatives for those who have been caught are endless imprisonment or dutiful acknowledgment of "favoures. . . done us" and "future services" owed (223–24). In a levelling comedy of socio-economic discriminations, where intentions, style, and gibes have variable costs and benefits, Chapman and Jonson (and Quicksilver) get themselves delivered from prison by calibrating the ratio of their submissiveness to self-assertion in performances marked by considerable artfulness.[37] The playwrights' prodigal wit puts them at the mercy of a testy creditor (King James) and leaves them scurrying after brokers who can help them put their credit relations with the Crown back in order.[38]

II

Humility and bravado are of course but two postures one might have assumed in relation to the demands of indebtedness. Another pair of stances may be described in terms of obliviousness and tenacity. These too allowed one to go about one's business, managing or mismanaging debt. To be oblivious to the consequences of one's obligations is to be cast to some extent as a dupe, with the important caveat that an audience's censure is held in check by the pleasure it derives from, perhaps even its envy of, a comic debtor's inattentiveness. When finally caught up short, the fully fantasized imprudent debtor magically rights himself, putting his house in order seemingly in spite of himself. Tenacity, even more than carelessness, arouses envy because while it is plausible, it strikes us that it demands more energy than we have to give. It is always someone else who succeeds with a stubborn, unflinching style of debt management that at once dodges the reproach elicited by bravado and yet allows one to get ahead, at least to get on, with one's estate or marriage planning. Tenacity answers well to what we feel it is reasonable to ask in the face of life, even if we doubt that we have the wherewithal to muster it. Obliviousness is tailor-made for comic plotting; no sooner does "reality" assert itself than a recovery commences.

Thomas Middleton's city comedy *Michaelmas Term* (1604–06) traces the fall and rise of Richard Easy – an exemplar of obliviousness to debt – in one of the few early modern English arenas where comic obliviousness was imaginable: the theatre. That the consequences of debt beyond the playhouse were too disturbing for sustained inattention to be deemed tenable is suggested by the career of a gallant in every way identical to Easy, with the exception of his provenance and his destiny. From the Wood Street Counter in 1616, William Fennor summoned up his outrage and moral indignation in order to describe how a "green gosling" or country gallant may be caught up in a scam engineered by some "goldsmith, haberdasher, silkman, woollen- or linen-draper," a citizen "commodity-letter."[39] Short on cash, the gallant accepts goods instead of gold, finds that he cannot sell the commodity, and soon defaults on his bond to the citizen. Instantly, "a brace (or more) of sergeants are not far from his shoulder, and, except he presently pay, he must presently to prison" (445). Thus far, Fennor has replayed *Michaelmas Term*. But now Fennor's gallant is hurried to the Counter, where "he shall lie two, three, four or five year, nay, a dozen or twenty years together, before he can get himself released" (446). No recovery, just "extreme misery for a prisoner to be indebted to a rich man" (447). Fennor's blend of prodigality and obliviousness ("These spells charms my poor prodigal" – 443) follows from a notion of indebtedness as victimization ("Is not this extreme and almost incredible villainy . . . thus to snare in the gentry of the land" – 444). Middleton's comedy suggests that something more fanciful was viable in a theatrical setting; but, even on stage, the rewards for obliviousness were limited.

When Chapman, Jonson, and Marston offer as their onomastic

comment on prodigality the name Quicksilver, they indicate a measure of self-conscious agency on the apprentice's part. He is mercurial, shifting, plotting, though he has still to contend with the goldsmith he frustrates.[40] At once compliant and credulous, Middleton's Easy enacts a very different sort of commentary on prodigality. While it is obvious to us that Easy is dissipating his patrimony by indebting himself to the woolen-draper Quomodo, we nonetheless find his easiness pleasurable.[41] To do one's ease is, among other things, to relieve one's bowels on a stool of ease. Although he lacks Quicksilver's ostentation, Easy calls to mind for us the apprentice's account of gentlemanly evacuation – "Wipe thy bum with testons, make ducks and drakes with shillings" (1.1.139–40). Because his bodily deportment, like the way he expends his riches (*Rich*ard Easy), is unthinking, it is unembarrassed. To be easy is also to be too ready to yield (an explicitly feminized orientation for a gentleman). In one and the same breath, Easy speaks of his being "easily possessed" and "free" (1.2.51) without any sense of contradiction occurring to him. "[S]omewhat too open" (1.2.57) is the way the aptly named Cockstone characterizes Easy's penetrability. Thus, even as he would distinguish himself from "those [who] live hinds" (1.2.52; like farm laborers), Easy's particular usage cannot help but call to mind his hind part.[42] Somehow, "shitting away" his inheritance is for Easy not only painless, it is easy, and it is pleasurable.

If such affect is not explainable in terms of prodigality, or reckless expenditure, neither is it entirely a consequence of another sort of recklessness: the inanities of a mere gull. This is because Easy also answers to a much more recent sense of his name, something we encode in the phrase, "I'm easy." Such easiness is a form of relaxed compliance, neither mindless nor prescient. It entails no more than an expectation that things will work out, an expectation borne partly of an obliviousness that occludes potentially dire consequences, partly of a history of calamities escaped, and partly of an absence of strong preferences. "I'm easy" is the insouciant, condensed biography of a gull never more than temporarily gulled, a gull who elicits our envy. In over his head and yet anxiety-free, he moves along with circumstances, hardly sweating, fully confident that one thing or one person or another will bail him out. This is Easy at cards, enmeshed in Quomodo's complex commodity scam, tricked out of his estate, coping with arrest, or down and out in London.

Easy's apparent passivity dodges the bemused disregard we reserve for a gull and escapes the censure appropriate to a prodigal because of the curious exercise of will it entails. On the one hand Middleton distinguishes Easy from Andrew Lethe, the play's noxious version of obliviousness. Lethe's forgetfulness is willful, strategic, and guaranteed to embarrass him in the end. On the other hand, though he stuffs his play from end to end with manic plotting on the part of everyone from Quomodo to his accomplices, his wife, and his daughter's suitors, Middleton places Easy at the still center of a scheming mania that requires merely his participation. What is attractive about Easy's will is its modesty. He has come up to London to live at "liberty" (1.2.52), but contrary to conventional expectations this does not mean riot, whoring, or drunkenness. Again, contrary to convention, his plans do not even include "wiving." He has it in mind simply to insinuate himself into the circuits of male camaraderie and capital expenditure. When he indebts himself, he does so because he does not want to disappoint his gaming companions: "I've already invited all the gallants to sup with me tonight . . . 'Twill be my everlasting shame, if I have no money to maintain my bounty" (2.3.140–44). When he marries, he merely responds to what Thomasine has instigated. Easy sidesteps the deep pains of abiding desire, both fiscal and amatory, by offering himself instead as a channel through which the wills of others may course. Thus able to conduct himself (although this may suggest more agency than Easy can fairly lay claim to) and still land on his feet, he represents a respite from a taxing consciousness of the frenzy of urban indebtedness and accreditation. Where Timon would forcibly exempt himself from round after round of obligation and where Gresham relies on finesse, Easy takes shelter in oblivion.

There are, of course, limits to Easy's nonchalance. While he may not appreciate the repercussions of debt, he quickly learns to worry about credit. "It stands upon the loss of my credit tonight," Easy tells Quomodo, "if I walk without money" (2.3.167–68). Here, as before, Easy imagines that the possession of wealth can be made to correlate solely with one's social and ethical, as opposed to economic, status. "[C]ourtesy" (2.3.306) preempts sufficiency (2.3.255).[43] He presumes that the financial burden he is about to undertake depends upon disparage-able worth ("I hope you will not disparage me so. 'Tis well known I have three hundred pound a year in Essex" – 2.3.284–85) and Quomodo responds in kind: "I will not disgrace the gentleman" (2.3.299–300). As long as Easy is preoccupied with his social value, what he calls his bounty, the only thing of consequence at stake for him will be the loss of his "credit against supper" (2.3.311–12). Easy can be caught up short and forced momentarily to acknowledge his own obliviousness. "I forgot all this. What meant I to swagger before I had money in my purse?" (2.3.324–25). However, he is instantly re-enmeshed in the niceties of indebtedness: who should sign his name first, "How like you my Roman hand"? (2.3.383), and so on. The fine print of the bond, not to mention the significance of the sequence of signatures, fails to register for Easy. At the moment of his arrest, when asked "Is not your name there [on the bond]?" Easy replies, "True, for fashion's sake" (3.3.42–43).

Easy's creditor, the "mercilous devourer" Quomodo, is said to have at least sixteen defaulted debtors "at this instant proceeded in both the Counters" and to desire not repayment but Easy's "body in prison" (3.4.80–82). This is the version of a merchant citizen that Fennor melodramatizes. In fact, were Easy to follow the sort of advice Quicksilver proffers to Sir Petronel, sheltering himself in prison to defeat his creditor, Quomodo would be foiled in precisely the fashion he has so carefully worked to prevent. Quomodo wants nothing less than for Easy to languish in prison. What Quomodo wants is Easy's land. He too wants to get off the city's fiscal treadmill and he would do so by escaping to Easy's estate in Essex. There is no usurer in *Michaelmas Term*, rather there is a merchant who aims to pass as a country gentleman.[44] Perhaps the most striking aspect of Quomodo's intimation of gentility is the degree to which he defeats our expectation that, given the chance, he would play the improving landlord. Instead, profit in a "goodly load of logs" gives way to "pleasant fruit" (3.4.15–16) which in turn gives way to a beneficent vision of foison, of "green fields" and citizens who "laugh and lie down," getting their wives "with child against a bank" (4.1.83–87). Quomodo would cultivate Easy's obliviousness as his own even as he gives the oblivious gallant "good counsel," teaching him how in the future to avoid becoming a "desperate debtor" (3.4.172): "a child must be broke, and a bond must not . . . the more you break bonds, the more they'll leap in your face" (3.4.150–53). Avid to engineer a chiastic transfer of rapacious desire for indifference, Quomodo imagines a more knowing Easy more carefully restructuring his debts while the draper himself gives over the cares of the city:

> Men may have cormorant wishes, but, alas,
> A little thing, three hundred pound a year,
> Suffices nature, keeps life and soul together.
> I'll have 'em lopped immediately; I long
> To warm myself by th' wood.   (4.1.72–76)

Even if we read this as thoroughly disingenuous, when coupled with Quomodo's subsequent rural holiday fantasia and his feigned death, it indicates a longing for ease.[45]

Meanwhile, with some prodding, Easy has begun to pay attention. Quomodo's wife Thomasine, who all along has served as a choric observer of Easy's unknowingness, reveals that she has sent Easy money. By the end of Act 4, if he has not quite begun to exert himself on his own behalf, Easy nonetheless acknowledges that Thomasine has "given the desperate hope" (4.4.77). And in the final act, with Thomasine's love as well as his "good deeds and bad deeds" (5.1.53–55; his mortgage and his bond) having fallen into his lap, Easy is finally on the road to recovery. The reaccredited Essex gallant makes a half-hearted and unsuccessful stab at saving his marriage to Thomasine. He is slightly more forceful and he is successful at reclaiming his wealth. That nothing more than the *status quo ante* has been achieved by the end of the main plot of *Michaelmas Term* suggests that Middleton was not prepared to reward obliviousness with something more generous than recuperation. The Counter has been avoided. All debts are settled. But the fantasy has its limits. Debt restructuring, as opposed to mere debt management, requires a more concerted exercise of will than Easy can muster. Perhaps a wider kinship network, able offspring, and a very different temperament must come together for one who is keen on not merely surviving, but thriving in the face of extensive debts and obligations.

III

Such a figure, whose affective adaptation to indebtedness I want next to speculate about, is James Burbage. As I have suggested, I imagine his experience of debt to have entailed an uncommon degree of tenacity. The very records which show Burbage losing his temper, bending the rules, even breaking them, disclose a man of unyielding persistence, stubborn in the face of manifold obstacles and obligations. One consequence of such steadfastness was the construction and operation of theatres in late-sixteenth and early-seventeenth-century London. For these enterprises were founded upon debt, that is to say upon the willingness of men and women like Burbage to capitalize on credit arrangements, to indebt themselves and indebt others, to borrow, lend, invest, mortgage, bequeathe, collude, and, with some frequency, deceive.

It is often noted that James Burbage and his brother-in-law John Brayne built the Theatre in 1576. The surviving documents which allow us to piece together the ownership and construction history of this edifice also provide us with a commentary on the fiscal profiles – the socio-economic sufficiency – of the two principals. Burbage, a joiner and subsequently a common player, appears to have had little of his own working capital in hand when he first began negotiations for the lease of property in Shoreditch from Giles Allen.[46] Testimony as to Burbage's worth is colored by each deponent's stake in the long series of suits that began in 1586 and carried over into the 1590s; however, not even those deposing on Burbage's behalf suggest that he was a man of much substance. The carpenter John Griggs reported that "James Burbage was not at the tyme of the first begynning of the building of the premises/ worth above one C markes in all his substance" (134). Henry Laneman, owner of the Curtain, agreed: "the comen speche went/ whan the said Theater was in building that it was Braynes money & Credit that builded the same/ and that James Burbage was at yt time verye unhable to Joyne therin/" (148). Most damning of all was the testimony of Burbage's chief antagonist, Brayne's strongest supporter and his widow's ally, the goldsmith Robert Myles. In 1592, Myles asserted that

he never knew him [Burbage] but a por man & but of small Credit/ being by occupacion/ A Joyner/ and reaping but A small lyving by the same/ gave it over/ and became A Commen Player in playes/ And further saith/ that he doth knowe/ that his Credit was suche/ as nether merchant nor Artificer would gyve him Credit for the value of x li unles his brother Braynes wold Joyne wt him/. (141–42)

The notary public William Nicoll confirmed Myles's estimate, deposing that Burbage "was not then worth a hundred poundes and as towching his credyt he thincketh it was but smale" (153).

Brayne himself was said to be "worth fyve hundreth poundes at the least and by commen fame worth A thowsand markes/ and A man well thoght of in london" (109). The grocer Edward Collins deposed that Brayne was "reputed emonges his neyghbors to be worth one thowsand poundes at the least" (137). And Myles says that while Burbage contributed about £50 to the construction costs, "the whole building of the premisses in effecte and the taking of the said lease/ was done at the onlye charge of the said Braynes by his own goodes/ & credit" (142). It was not long, however, before Brayne had exhausted his credit. Just why this should have been so was disputed. Myles claimed that

Braynes was dryven to sell his house he Dwelled in/ in Bucklers bery and all his stock that was left/ and gyve uppe his trade yea in the end to pawne & sell both his owne garmentes and his wyves & ren [sic] in debt to many for money to fynishe the said Playe housse/ & so to ymploye himself onlye uppon that matter/ and all whatsoever he could make/ to his utter undoing/ ffor he saith/ that in the end of the fynishing therof/ the said Braynes and his Wyfe the now compl. were dryven to labor in the said workes/ for saving of some of the charge/ in place of ii laborers. (141)[47]

Henry Bett, attorney, suggests that there may have been more to this story than Myles allowed. Deposing on Burbage's behalf, Bett claims that Brayne "did receyve more monye by a grete some then he laid out in the Theatre, and that yt could not be his undoinge" (87). He more ominously noted that

yt was a Comon thinge, wth the said John Braine, to make deedes of gifte of his good*es* and Chattelles, the reasone was as this depont taketh yt, to p*r*event his Creditors aswell before building of the Theatre, as since, for he beinge redie to be imprisoned for debt he would prepare sutch safetie for his good*es*, as he could. (86)[48]

Bett's "since" probably refers to Brayne's tactic for getting out from under the debts he and Myles incurred when building the George Inn in 1586. Wallace (a Burbage partisan) writes that Brayne "put all his property into the hands of others by deeds of gift to defraud creditors, and absented himself for a time, as also did Myles, so that when the bailiff went to levy on their goods and arrest them, they could not be found" (14).[49]

When Burbage secured his lease from Giles Allen, he and he alone signed the document. Allen was later to depose that

nether the said Jo. Braynes/ nor any other for him did ether make Sute to this depot at any tyme before the ensealing of the said lease, to be Joyned wt the said James Burbage in the said lease . . . in verye trothe the said lease was suewed for/ by the said Burbage & not ment any way to the said Braynes. (74)

But how could a cash-poor, poor credit risk like Burbage have effected such a deal? John Griggs and Robert Myles had an answer. According to the carpenter and the goldsmith, Brayne expected from the start that Burbage would assign half the lease to him for coming up with the cash that Burbage, the sole signatory, required. Although there appears to have been no written agreement at the outset of this venture, Griggs "did heare it crediblye reported/ that it was agreed betwene the said James Burbage/ and the said Brayne/ yt the said lease shuld be made in the name onlye of the same James/ and yet to the use of them bothe" (133–34). Myles asserted that Burbage himself had said he never would have undertaken the lease and building of the playhouse had Brayne not joined with him. Furthermore, Brayne told Myles that "he was advysed to suffre the said Burbage to take the said lease in his owne name and he to convey ov*er* to him the said Braynes his executors and assignes the moytie or half of all the profitt*es* growing by the playes & Rent*es* there" (140).

Whatever Burbage and Brayne had intended when Burbage set his name to the original lease, the two men had Nicoll draw up an "Indendure of lease" on 9 August 1577 that was to establish once and for all that Burbage "was willing to assure the one moytie of the premises to the said John Brayne" (151). But this lease, which seems to have been intended as an addendum to the original lease, was never sealed by Burbage. On 22 May 1578, Brayne managed to get Burbage to "seale and delyver as his dede" a £400 performance bond requiring Burbage to make a "good and lawfull lease graunt . . . of the moitie" of the Theatre property named in the original lease signed by Burbage (151). Burbage later acknowledged this bond, but he never did make the assignment of the lease. Finally, in July, Burbage and Brayne agreed to go to arbitration. That is, after once again adjourning to Nicoll's shop and after Burbage "did strike him [Brayne] wth his fist and so they went together by the eares" (152), Burbage signed a bond of £200 to the effect that he would abide by whatever settlement was worked out by the arbitrators. Predictably, this entailed making the two men equal sharers in the lease and in the profits "that shuld grow & ryse by the playes" as well as from the other tenements on the property (143). It was furthermore stipulated that all monies first accruing to Burbage and Brayne were to be used to retire whatever debts they had incurred to that point. According to Ralph Miles (Robert's son), not until Brayne had been "answered/ suche somes of money wch he had lade out/ for & upon the same Theatre/ more then the said Burbage had done" were rents and profits to be divided equally between them or was either man to have any profit to his own use (119–20). Perceived failure to perform one or another part of this arbitrated agreement fueled twenty years of litigation.

Mention of outstanding debts brings us back to Burbage's failure to seal the "Indenture of lease" drawn up by Nicoll back in August 1577. Nicoll deposed in 1592 that this lease was never sealed because the original lease (to which it would have been attached?) "was then at puwne for money wch was borrowed for the building of the said Theatre" (151). Already bound to Brayne, who was fronting most of the money, Burbage seems hastily to have obligated the two of them by mortgaging the lease to raise the cash they would need to proceed with construction. We know nothing more about this earliest pawning of the Allen lease, but if Nicoll's recollection is accurate then it would have had to have been redeemed shortly thereafter, because we know for certain that Burbage and Brayne were sufficiently in debt in 1579 that in September of that year they mortgaged the lease to the grocer, John Hyde.[50] According to Robert Myles, Brayne had "lade out of his owne purce & what upon Credit about the same" £600 or £700 (it was following this expenditure that he was forced to sell his house and stock).[51] Burbage, Myles deposed, was "nothing able ether of him self/ or by his credit to contrybute any like some"; although Myles also seems to have believed Burbage when the latter claimed "that all the charge wch he was at/ in the accomplishing of the premisses from the begynning to the end did not amount to the full value of one C li" (141). What with Brayne's enormous expenditures and Burbage purportedly "purloyn[ing] and filch[ing]" from the "Commen box" and thrusting playhouse gatherings "in his bosome or other where about his bodye" (142), it comes as no surprise to learn that both men were in need of more cash.[52]

A money-broker named John Prynne was able to secure £125 from John Hyde for the mortgage of the lease to the Shoreditch property. Burbage and Brayne were also required to sign a £200 obligation that bound them to redeem the lease within a year and a day or suffer the forfeit of both their lease and bond. Burbage and Brayne defaulted and Hyde "did therupon threaten to put the said burbage [sic] out of possession of the said Theatre" (54). For some reason this did not come to pass. Instead Hyde agreed to an extension, requiring that he be paid £5 a week until the entire mortgage was paid ("wt some reasonable consideracion for the forbearing of it" – 111). Burbage and Brayne made good on this latest agreement for four or five weeks but "they performed no more/ and so suffred ther lease to be ones againe forfetted" to Hyde (111). So in June 1582, Hyde "did cause the said James burbage to be arrested" (54). Again Burbage came up with some money – this time, £20 – and again he was released into renewed negotiations, or procrastinations.[53]

Although Burbage may not have been repaying Hyde (he "did complayne . . . that the said brayne [sic] had received and gotten in to his hands a gt porcon of money levied in the said Theatre at the play tymes" and that he, Burbage, could not "enforce hym to deliver ay [sic] part therof" – 54), he did improve his property. In 1582–83 he repaired and renovated buildings to the tune of £200. This figure answered precisely to the original agreement Burbage had with Allen to expend £200 within ten years on non-theatre property in return for a ten-year extension of the lease.[54] But wasn't the lease in Hyde's hands? With Allen, Burbage was proceeding as if the lease were still in his possession and its renewal his right. With Hyde, Burbage was soon trying a new tack. Burbage's son Cuthbert, a servant to Walter Cope (himself gentleman usher to the Lord High Treasurer), succeeded in 1589 in getting Cope to write to Hyde, suggesting a potential *quid pro quo* were Hyde to surrender the lease to Cuthbert. Hyde agreed, and Cuthbert borrowed at least part of the money required to repay Hyde (73). Thus it was finally Cuthbert Burbage who owned the Theatre (Brayne had died in 1586) and did so as a consequence of his credibility at Court and his willingness to indebt himself on his father's behalf. "[H]e affermed he would not have done [so]," said Henry Bett, "but only to have redemed and delivered his father, from many encombrauncces" (73–74).

Hyde was now out of the picture and the lease-renewal conflict with Allen occupied the background. The foreground was filled for Burbage with the operation of the Theatre and, not unrelatedly, his never-ending conflict with Margaret Brayne and Robert Myles over her (and subsequently his) moiety in the Theatre. As this is only indirectly a dispute over indebtedness (that is, insofar as the widow Brayne and Myles were not only trying to get title to half of the Theatre and so to half of its profits, but trying as well to enforce the two performance bonds that Brayne had been unable to get Burbage to sign), its progress may, for the purposes of my argument, be overlooked. However, since Burbage's temperament is my subject, it is worth digressing long enough to convey some sense of the man when his interests were threatened. Lengthy and colorful depositions conjure for us a sometimes comic picture of events at the Theatre when Margaret Brayne and Robert Myles appeared on the scene to demand their moiety. Here was Burbage, according to John Alleyn (innholder, player, and brother of Edward), shouting "hang her hor . . . she getteth nothing here" (100) and defying the Court of Chancery, "saying/ that yf ther were xx contemptes/ and as many Injunccions he wold wtstand them all/ before he wold lose his possession" (101). After Richard Burbage had turned away Brayne and Myles with a "Broome staff," the elder Burbage warned that "at ther next coming [he would] provyde charged Pistolles wt powder and hempsede/ to shoote them in the legges" (101–02). The soapmaker Nicholas Bishop heard Burbage call Myles "Rascall & knave" (98). "Burbage told the said Robert Myles/ that he had but A paper [the Chancery order]/ wch he might wype his tale wt/ and rather then he wold lose his possession/ he wold commit xx contemptes" (115). Moments later young Richard Burbage was "playing wt" Bishop's nose and threatening to beat him.

What with widow Brayne and Myles coming "Dyvers tymes to the said Theater" at start of the 1590s with an "Ordre of the Chauncerye" in hand (100), and Giles Allen either stalling or thwarting the renewal of the lease, first James Burbage and his sons, then the sons on their own, made preemptive strikes. In 1596, two years before the initial lease with Allen was due to expire, and perhaps flush with income from the sale of shares in the Curtain, Burbage purchased a building in the Blackfriars for the considerable sum of £600.[55] Burbage put £100 down. The Burbages borrowed the remaining money from George More, the son of the owner of the Blackfriars property, and then paid him off within six months. No sooner was this obligation met than Burbage was mortgaging more than £200 worth of property, probably to come up with the cash he needed to build a theatre in the Blackfriars.[56] Burbage's last preemptive strike, shortly before his death, was to make a deed of gift to Cuthbert of his personal property, and another such deed of the Blackfriars to Richard. Needless to say, both Myles and Allen would in short order be charging the heirs with fraud.[57] The most notorious tactical maneuver was left to

Cuthbert and Richard after their father's death: the removal of the
Theatre to a new site in Southwark.[58] Once again, money would have to
be borrowed to start up a new theatrical enterprise and, once again,
Burbages were in debt.[59]

In the "prologue" to his reconsideration of some of the "raw materials" from which we have for some time put together the "story" of the
building of the Theatre, William Ingram reminds us that the Burbage
who was for Charles William Wallace a collegial player, preparing the
English stage for the "full florescence of Shakespeare," was for E. K.
Chambers a profit-seeking entrepreneur, landlord, and rentier. Ingram is
wary of the "hazards of such schematizing," in particular because it rests
upon "authorial predisposition rather than upon data." Ingram also
finds it unsurprising that we have found less to admire in Brayne's story
of "impoverishment and early death" than in the "dash and verve" we
attribute to "antic young Richard Burbage . . . tweaking Nicholas
Bishop's nose, brandishing a broomstick in widow Brayne's face." It is
curious that Ingram's "let-the-facts-speak-for-themselves" narrative
should proceed from an understanding dismissal of "reductive" approaches to Burbage to not only a Brayne–Burbage schematization of its
own, but a Brayne–*Richard* Burbage contrast at that. Ingram offers up
the "disastrous adventures" of Brayne v. the "antic . . . reveling" young
Burbage.[60] What has happened to James?

In the course of retelling the Theatre story, Ingram and I cite Myles's
deposition to the effect that Burbage was stealing from the "Com*m*en
box" and thrusting in his bosom money that was properly Brayne's.
Ingram concedes that Myles "was certainly not a disinterested witness"
but concludes that the "picture he gives us of James Burbage is as
plausible as any other we might form from these documents."[61] But
plausibility calcifies into something akin to probability when Ingram,
while investigating the operation of the Curtain, writes:

[a]s we saw in the previous chapter, he [Burbage] seems to have found it easier to
be unscrupulous in his dealings and to be unmoved by the claims of the Brayne
faction that he filched money from the common box, or stuffed it down his shirt,
or otherwise attempted to deceive his fellows. If Burbage was growing more
reprehensible in his behavior, he was also growing more secure about being in
debt.[62]

"If" and "seems" have considerably less force in this version of Burbage
than does "plausible" in the raw material version. Burbage has become a
man of "growing ambition" about whose "good faith" one might
understandably be "chary" (Ingram, 228). But who in early modern
London lacked ambition and with whom might one have done business
without being "properly chary"? Just how much did Burbage trust

Brayne, or Brayne Burbage? How might kinship have inflected their dealings, given that Ellen Burbage was John Brayne's sister, and that Margaret Brayne was Richard's aunt? After whatever fashion, Burbage kept dealing with his brother-in-law Brayne; perhaps the exogamous Myles, coming suspiciously to widow Brayne's support, strained kinship affiliations. There was also inheritance to consider: to what extent was James building for his sons rather than for himself? And as for sentiment, how are we to know that Burbage was "growing more secure" about his indebtedness? Surely we cannot. As Ingram is the first to admit, this is but a story we might tell.

The litigants' claims that I have rehearsed I have selected mainly for their pertinence to my subject thus far: the affective experience of debt. Insofar as the Theater and subsequently the Globe and the playhouse at the Blackfriars are concerned, we have been attending to a comedy. Obstacles are overcome. Blocking figures are outsmarted, outmaneuvered, or defrauded. Most pleasurably of all, Shakespeare comes to pass. That James (not Richard) Burbage should turn out to be our comic protagonist, our antic, has everything to do, as Ingram shrewdly observes, with the fact that it is the Burbages who prevail. For our antiquarian delight, James provides evidence of procrastination, manipulation, fisticuffs, arrest, filching, default, negotiation, partial payments, escape clauses, small credit, non-performance, hard bargaining, and preemptive strikes. To my mind, this points to something less secure than Ingram's "secure," but not entirely distinct. Burbage comes off, I have suggested, as tenacious. His and his sons' conflicts with Brayne, with widow Brayne and Myles, with Allen, and with Hyde, represent an aggressive effort on the Burbages' part to hold on (*teneo*, to hold) to that in which they had invested so much. Burbage's indebtedness, giving up a mortgage here, signing a performance bond there, has as its motivation retention, not simply ambition. With a persistence that meets an Allen's or a Myles's own persistence head on, Burbage works his indebtedness, stubbornly making of it an enabling modality. The records conjure for us an unflagging expense of energy toward the perpetuation of an enterprise.[63] While something similar might be said about Quomodo's or Quicksilver's handling of debt restructuring, the Burbage plots include few easy marks (like Easy and Sir Petronel) and no foreseeable conclusion (only decades of litigation). Quomodo simply cannot defeat Easy, but because Allen or Hyde might defeat Burbage, tenacity might, for all one knows, have to suffice as its own reward.

The Burbage who becomes visible to us through court records thus comes into focus as one among a number of men and women whose indebtedness produced London's theatrical venues. The Swan theatre, to take another example, may be said to date back to the imprisonment of one Thomas Cure for debt. The land upon which it was erected, the manor of Paris Garden, came into the possession of the draper, alnager, and goldsmith (i.e. moneylender) Francis Langley when he offered Cure £850, all but £95 of which went toward releasing Cure from a variety of bonds, debts, and indentures.[64] Langley himself had had to take up most of the purchase amount "upon interest out of the Orphan's Court in London," since he too was already in debt at this time (78–79). Ingram describes Langley as having been in the nasty business of "cosigning bonds for defaulters in order to claim the penalty sum"; at least one contemporary said of him that he "had not any friend that would disburse any great sum of money for the good of the said Francis Langley" (79–80). It would later take the mortgaging of all of his Cheapside property as collateral for a loan of £1,650 before Langley could begin to develop his Bankside property, first with tenements and then with a theatre.

An extraordinary tangle of obligations, indebtedness, leases, and bonds underwrote the Boar's Head playhouse as well. The original entrepreneur in this instance was the haberdasher and moneylender, Oliver Woodliffe. With considerable understatement, Herbert Berry writes that Woodliffe, "like Francis Langley . . . preferred to make his way in the money market, especially by lending money to hard cases at the going rates of 8% or 10% or better and then vigorously achieving repayment."[65] Still, in 1596, Woodliffe had to borrow £66 that he might begin work on his playhouse. It was his intention to operate as a silent partner (shades of Brayne?), so he engaged the yeoman Richard Samwell to build and manage his playing space. The lease agreement between these two men, which never clarified the ownership of the inn yard (and which was crucially to become the theatre yard), became a bone of contention comparable to the Burbage–Brayne lease. At the Boar's Head, debt also played a pivotal role. When Samwell found himself in over his head, he first borrowed £100 from Richard Browne, the player-manager of his resident company (Browne was himself indebted to the scrivener/moneylender Israel Jordan). Shortly thereafter, Samwell applied that sum toward the sale of his lease to Browne. Woodliffe too was worried about capital and so he agreed to sell his property to none other than Francis Langley, for £100 down and three £100 bonds. The moves and counter-moves that followed, far too complex to summarize but many of them focused on the uncertain title to the yard, were all a result, as Berry summarizes, of "not enough capital and owners too eager for quick profits" (38). Woodliffe signs a £1,000 bond to guarantee the security of Langley's lease; Langley fails to pay Woodliffe the £100 that would redeem his first bond; Langley owes Woodliffe a £200 penalty; Browne stops paying the half profits he owes; Browne sublets to Worcester's Men whom Langley commences harassing for rent; Woodliffe turns to Jordan for more money; Langley dies in 1602 saddling his heir with debts, and so on. As at the Theatre, defaults and contested titles led to assaults, arrests, negotiations, and, of course, litigation. Another London playhouse, another testament to tenacity in the face of obligation.

IV

Richard Browne died of the plague in 1603. His widow, along with Woodliffe's widow Susan, were soon at peace and in control of the Boar's Head. When Susan Browne remarried, it was to Thomas Greene, the actor who took Kempe's place as the clown in the Queen's (formerly Worcester's) men. It seems to have been this Greene who played the part of Bubble at Court and at the Red Bull in still another play concerned with debt: Jo[hn] Cooke's *Greene's Tu Quoque, or The Cittie Gallant* (*c.* 1611; London, 1614).[66] Cooke's popular, if not particularly inspired play (by 1628, there appears to have been a third quarto already in print) brings home the extent to which indebtedness cramps agency and frustrates marriage plans. It also develops two versions of outrage, the last affective orientation toward debt explainable in socio-economic terms that I consider in this chapter. *Tu Quoque*'s chief debtors gesture briefly in the direction of humility; however, their primary response to their bankruptcy takes the form of outrage, a socially conditioned sense of affront that has the potential to instigate unexpectedly rancorous vengefulness. Whereas indebtedness might have been imagined to be enabling (for, say, a Burbage) in the same way as we do what we can to make our credit-card debt work on our behalf, it might as easily have been experienced as an indignity. Quicksilver trades on his obligations and, for Easy, they hardly register as such. *Tu Quoque* stages another possibility. It depends upon a gallant, Staines, and a citizen, Spendall, whose fiscal discomfort stimulates their own and perhaps Cooke's compensatory will to humiliate. The play's stunning, wholly unexpected burst of aggression follows hard on the heels of its one poignant moment of socially inflected abjection. While such plotting has been noticed for its generic confusion, its inability to fuse moral and satiric attitudes toward prodigality, it could also be understood as a coherent account of successive stages in the psychological progress of debt.[67]

The Staines plot commences with the conventional gallant having conventionally forfeited the mortgage to his lands to a "usuring rascall"

(175). Like Sir Petronel, he is afraid to walk abroad for fear of the sergeants; his "refuge is *Ireland*, or *Virginia*; necessitie cries out" (166). When his servant Bubble's uncle (the usurer who has supplanted Staines as landlord) dies and leaves his estate to Bubble, Staines changes places with his man and becomes Bubble's servant. Humiliation is not for Staines a direct consequence of his having indebted himself for three years to a usurer – this can be remedied by taking refuge abroad or turning pirate. The significant moment of humiliation derives instead from what we know to be a temporary, comic status reversal. The gallant must admit that his "case is desperate" and "beseech" his dimwitted former servant to take him into service, all the while confessing to being "humble in body, and dejected in minde" (266–69). Staines's predominant emotion, however, is outrage. In his fury he literalizes the indignities that *Eastward Ho*'s Sindefy imagines a servant at Court must "swallow": "That I should live to be a serving-man, a fellow which scalds his mouth with another mans porredge, brings up meat for other mens bellies, and carries away the bones for his own, changes his cleane trencher for a fowle one" (671–75). His tone turns sarcastic and his instinct is for revenge. "I shall fit you," he says to Bubble. "I serve my selfe, and not him . . . I'le carry things so cunningly, that he shall not be able to looke into my actions" (791–95).

Indebtedness has also cost Staines his place in the urban marriage market. For Sir Lionel, the father of the play's two marriageable women, he is economically unfit, having become "that unthrift *Staines*" (499). For the younger daughter Joyce, because Staines appears to her to be a servant, he is below caste (1,947–53). Insolvency, which has put him into "servile Roabes" (1,615), has also forced him into an unhappy likeness to Bubble ("a slave / Unto one worse condition'd then a Slave" – 1,601–02). The gallant's answering outrage sponsors his revenge plot ("I must cheat a little . . . I must vary shapes" – 798 and 802) and its attendant soft humiliations. Bubble is not only tricked out of the mortgage and rents Staines lost to the clown's uncle, but he is made to appear the fool he is. Staines schools him to a higher level of asininity than he achieves naturally and thereby scores the meager satisfaction of seeing Bubble brought low. This is a tempered humiliation because Bubble is too inconsequential to support anything profound. It must nonetheless address all of the clown's socio-economic pretensions, from his inane marriage aspirations to his preposterous miming of the discourse and *habitus* of a gentleman (1,411–29). Since Staines's debasement can be canceled only by Bubble's, the latter is predictably reinterpellated as the former's servant at the end of the play. Their social as well as their financial relationship operates according to the rules of a zero-sum economy: as Staines's joys "grow / To . . . full height, so Bubbles waxeth low" (1,664–65).

A fiercer rage and an altogether more hard-edged, nastier humiliation are evident in the Spendall plot. Having been put in charge of Sir Lionel's mercer's shop and already imagining himself Lord Mayor, Spendall proceeds to spend himself into bankruptcy. A seemingly conventional prodigal, he wastes his money on appropriately immoral vices like gaming and whoring. The familiar sergeants arrest him, he is imprisoned in the Counter, and he repents:

> . . . I was luld in sensualities
> Untill at last, Affliction waked me:
> And lighting up the Taper of my soule,
> Led mee unto my selfe, where I might see
> A minde and body rent with Miseries
>
> . . .
>
> O what a Slave was I unto my Pleasures?
> How drownd in Sinne, and overwhelmd in Lust? (2,106–10 and 2,150–51)

But the lesson Spendall learns is decidedly antisocial, even uncharitable:

> A man must trust unto himselfe, I see;
> For if hee once but halt in his estate,
> Friendship will proove but broken Crutches to him.
> Well, I will leane to none of them, but stand
> Free of my selfe: and if I had a spirit
> Daring to act what I am prompted to,
> I must thrust out into the world againe . . .   (2,462–68)

In Spendall's story, the debtor's progress commences with contempt for money ("A pox of money, t'is but rubbish" – 421) and a Timon-like bountifulness (he is "the liberall'st Gentleman" – 863–64), turns predictably toward moral self-reproach, then reorients itself with a new socioeconomic theory. Unlike Quicksilver's bravura repentance, Spendall's is a conversion experience. He has seen the light and is now armed (literally, it turns out) and ready to "thrust out into the world *againe.*" I emphasize "again" because it is an easily overlooked misrepresentation of what has gone before. The prodigal was no thruster. He was generous to a fault with his whore, her bawd, and her pander; even in his duel with Staines he was adjudged "charitable" (1,375). Something must happen to Spendall. Something must follow from his bankruptcy that explains his new-found creed of aggressive self-accreditation and Cooke's comic version of Marlowe's "You must be proud, bold, pleasant, resolute, / And now and then stab as occasion serves."[68]

In the Counter, Spendall has his first experience of the sort of humiliation that provokes outrage. He has just finished his first round of self-castigation when a prisoner enters, announcing the arrival of the "Bread and Meate man" (2,113). When the jailor, Fox, says that the food can "stay a little," the prisoner responds, "Yes . . . But you know our stomacks cannot stay" (2,114–16). What follows is a vaguely comic but (or because) mostly disquieting discussion over the almsbasket that Gatherscrap has brought on stage:

PRIS. I have a stomacke like *Aqua fortis*, it will eate any thing: O father
    Gatherscrap, here are excellent bits in the Basket.
FOX Will you hold your Chops further? by and by youle drivell into the Basket.
PRIS. Perhaps it may doe some good, for there may be a peece of powderd Beefe
    that wants watering.
FOX Heere sir, heer's your share.
PRIS. Heer's a bit indeed: whats this to a *Gargantua* stomack?
FOX Thou art ever grumbling.
PRIS. Zounds, it would make a Dogge grumble, to want his Victuals: I pray give
    Spendall none, hee came into th' Holl but yester-night. (2,119–32)

We are not quite done with "drivell," it turns out, but this is quite enough to suggest deprivation. This prisoner, who exemplifies Brecht's dictum that nourishment precedes morality, is no mindless Bubble. He knows his Gargantua even as he accepts his lot as a dog salivating over scraps. Perhaps his practical nature (putting saliva to good use), his feeling for self-reliance, and his sense of rough justice begin to make an impression on Spendall. But Spendall is "not yet seasoned" (2,135). Fox ignores the prisoner and proffers the almsbasket to Spendall. He refuses, saying simply, "I cannot eate, I thanke you" (2,134). Repentance does not lead to communion. Spendall's revulsion and his courtesy are, I suspect, his status-saving tokens of distinction.

If Sindefy metaphorizes service as swallowing injuries and Staines literalizes it as scalding his mouth with a gentleman's porridge, Spendall does not merely speak this humiliation, he gets a glimpse of it in action and is solicited to join in. Spendall moralizes his fall as the wages of his sin, but the disgust he feels at what he has been drawn into in the Hole smacks more of indignation than mortification. It runs entirely against the grain for him to conceive of himself as one who would fight over scraps. His potential participation in the culinary culture of the Hole sickens him:

> To such a one as these are must I come
> Hunger will draw me into their fellowship,
> To fight and scramble for unsaverie Scraps,
> That come from unknowne hands, perhaps unwasht:
> And would that were the worst; for I have noted,
> That nought goes to the Prisoners, but such food

As either by the weather has been tainted,
Or Children, nay sometimes full paunched Dogges,
Have overlickt . . .   (2,138–45)

The combination of shame and rage that Spendall feels in the Hole
prompts no more altruism or fellow-feeling in him than we see in the
starving prisoner. Instead, deprivation becomes the motive for thrusting.
After word reaches him that the widow Raysby has paid all his debts and
discharged his prison fees, there is no looking back.

Or so, at least, Spendall would have it. What he discovers is that his
humiliating imprisonment leaves its mark. The prodigal may be forgiven,
but the debtor represents an unresolved threat to comedy's requisite
marriage settlements. Thus, late in the play, when the recovered Staines
and his gallant companion Geraldine are half-way toward elopement
with Sir Lionel's daughters, Spendall finds himself still *persona non grata*:

My acquaintance scarce will know mee, when wee meet
They cannot stay to talke, they must begone;
And shake mee by the hand as if I burnt them.   (2,459–61)

Though a repentant debtor, Spendall is equally out of place in the
Counter and in the urban marriage-market. Incensed by the humiliation
he has suffered not merely in the Hole but in polite society, Spendall
"will leane to none of them" (2,465). Instead, he will strike out. His
objection modulates into a furious desire for compensatory humiliation
that has as its object the very source of both his solvency and his
marriageability: the widow Raysby. However, unlike Bubble, who is
crucial to Staines's financial well-being and marriage plans, the widow is
subjected to a violent, hardly comic assault.

Taking his cue from Lording Barry's *Ram Alley*, Cooke has Spendall
woo the widow with his dagger and threaten to strike her dead if she
refuses him. She agrees to his demands, but soon gets the upper hand and
binds him to her bed. When he refuses to curse the widow even though
she has gotten the better of him, she relents and offers her uncoerced
consent. Spendall has assumed that his strong back would convince the
widow that he, rather than old Sir Lionel, is her man. What she
represents for him is an end to the humiliation consequent upon
insolvency. "I will rather / Totter, hang in cleane Linnen," he tells her,
"then live to scrub / It out in lowsie Lynings" (2,528–30). Spendall's
experience of debt is consistently grounded in his vivid perception of
status infringements. The hand that others are reluctant to shake, the
fellowship of the almsbasket and, now, the thought of lousy under-
clothes, all ignite a sadistic rage that Spendall vents when he puts his
dagger to the widow, repellently tells her, "hold your Clapdish, fasten

your Tongue / Unto your Roofe" (2,523–24), and demands a kiss. She is "rich in Money, Lands, and Lordships, / Mannors, and fayre Possessions" (2,533–34); he is "desperate" (2,522). Cooke's solution to the problem of reintegrating Spendall into the copy-holding community (2,535), to quelling the former prodigal's outrage and salving his shame, is this offensive bit of self-reliant thrusting. But his altogether conventional resolution – marriage to the rich widow – gives the lie even to the pretense of standing "[f]ree of my selfe" (2,466) with which Spendall motivates himself. The citizen has simply been bound to a new creditor.

If debt, a species of obligation, signals dependence, then mismanaged debt denotes fault. Whether fantasizing himself Lord Mayor or in possession of the widow's estate, Spendall resists any such awareness. His repentance has less to do with culpability than with humiliation; indeed, the latter effaces the former, substituting a socio-economic reckoning for a moral reckoning. Spendall admits that he was "drownd in Sinne" but he stops short of an explicit acknowledgment of what he now owes to whom. The New Testament, which assumes that we are all debtors every bit as much as we are sinners, is unequivocal about our guilt, our dependence, and our obligations. In the Lord's Prayer, sin and debt are synonymous.[69] Or it might more precisely be said that sin is conceived of as debt. In the Geneva Bible we read, "forgive us our dettes, as we also forgive our detters" (Matt. 6:12) and "forgive us our sinnes: for even we forgive everie man that is indetted to us" (Luke 11:4). The King James versions of Matthew and Luke read, respectively, "forgive us our debts, as we forgive our debtors" and "forgive us our sinnes: for we also forgive every one that is indebted to us." If the God of the Hebrew Bible is a non-usurious deity (Leviticus 25:36–37; Deuteronomy 23:19–20; Ezekiel 18:8–17, 22:12; Nehemiah 5:2–3, 6–13), the God of the New Testament is a creditor with whom Christ intercedes on our behalf.[70] As Lancelot Andrewes explained, "*Forgive them*, because hee that taught us thus to *pray*, (our suretie) hath *paid* and discharged these *debts*."[71] Christ restores that which he never took, but "we cannot make satisfaction to God, therefore he must remit" our debts. The affect attendant upon this state of affairs is familiar to us: "consideration . . . [of our indebtedness] ought to work in us humiliation."[72] In our abjection, we must "confesse before God, that we are flat bankrupts and not able to discharge the least of our sins."[73] Till the day of reckoning, Christ must be our surety.[74]

When sin is conceived of as debt, theological discourse leans upon economic discourse. In a theological context, between, say, an individual and God, humiliation felt as a result of sin/debt may be resented but it is at least supposed to be tolerable, perhaps even something one can acknowledge as deserved. As it reminds us of our impotence, humiliation also enjoins us to charity and to forgive debts owed to us. When we talk about debt in a socio-economic context, charity is harder to summon and something like Spendall's indignity at what I have called status infringement proves closer to the heart of the experience of indebtedness. In London, where in the seventeenth century there were found "three or foure thousand prisoners, the greatest part for Debt, amongst which are divers Commanders, and men of good quality, and good endowments, who have done and are able to doe, good service to his Majestie and State," petitions against imprisonment for debt gestured toward the Bible, but their impetus was a juridically and socio-economically inspired sense of affront.[75] Thus the 1622 protest against imprisonment for debt from which I have just quoted (which Philip Shaw speculates may have been written by Thomas Dekker) begins with one chapter on the "Law of God" and moves on to six chapters on the law of man, the rule of justice, and so on.[76]

One source of outrage is the humiliation a debtor suffers upon being treated like a slave, not a free man.[77] "By *Magna Charta* . . . the body of a Free borne man, might not bee Imprisoned" (B1v). Imprisonment for debt "overthroweth a mans reputation" (B4v) and leaves him "open to every arrow of scandall or Calumny, that a malicious Adversary will shoote at him" (C1). Another insult derives from what the petition calls promiscuous punishment. Imprisoning all debtors, "as well frauders as *non* frauders," is tantamount to "thrust[ing] all kinde of Debtors into a Prison together in a heape, without respect to the different qualities of men" (B3 and B4). This was particularly galling because the petitioners believed that "non frauders" outnumbered "frauders" nine to one. Among all debts, "9 in 10 . . . are usurious Debts and Forfeitures, scarce one friendly and honest Debt of a hundred" (D4). Where nearly all debt was said to have been entered into usuriously, there was little possibility that it would have been understood, retrospectively at least, to have been enabling. The law permitted a creditor to keep a defaulter in prison "all the dayes of his life, upon a corrupt, and oftentimes causelesse or casuall Debt without any fraud" (C4v). From the petitioners' point of view, creditors who tormented debtors were more interested in humiliating them (causing them "disgrace and disreputation" – E3v) than securing repayment. As the petitioners reason, "[i]mprisonment no way inableth the meanes for payment of Debts, but many wayes wastes and consumes the Debtor and his estate" (E3). Debtors, not creditors, it is asserted, want to settle claims. When creditors thwart their efforts, they scramble to save face. One Dawley, who ran out of money just before he was able to win four years' respite from the last of his creditors, not knowing "how to keepe himselfe in prison, or his wife and children in life" (D2), hanged himself. "[W]ith shame and distemperature," the unhappy debtor dies (D3).

The displacement of blame wholly onto the shoulders of usurers suggests that the debtors' petition is in fact another in a long line of anti-usury tracts. It winds up by conjuring a land in which "[u]surious gaine were not," and in which "men would be carefull to reserve money by them . . . and free borrowing and lending would cause and encrease charity" (F3v). But the petition (like *The Merchant of Venice*) does not in fact place much stock in the feasibility of any such community of "Christian amity." Instead, it offers and repeats again and again a unique and seemingly reasonable corrective: that recovery be made only against a debtor's estate, not his body. The petitioners tacitly grant that such a policy would leave room for much that they deem usurious, but they argue that trade would better flourish and men's reputations would be better respected were debtors spared imprisonment. Their remedy delivers debtors from slavish indignities even as it permits them to continue to obligate themselves. In this regard, the petition aligns itself with the comedies of the previous decades with which this chapter has been concerned.

If debt restructuring occupied both petitioners and playwrights, it caught the attention of the Privy Council too. While it was less prone than the petitioners to assume that nine in ten creditors were usurers, or entirely to discount the maxim *Volenti non fit iniuria*, the Privy Council was cognizant of fiscal exigencies and debtors' reputations.[78] Consequently, when petitioned by debtors the Council sought to win for them an extension of time and a right to arbitration. Respite and composition were due those whom the Council's investigations led them to believe were being subjected to gross indignities, even if this meant an exercise of conciliar prerogative (or coercion) at variance with the law.[79] For common law offered less in the way of relief to honest than to dishonest debtors, and the Council had good reason to hesitate before it infringed on the legal rights of creditors. While the Elizabethan Council began, in 1576, to pass off the work of creditor–debtor mediation onto commissions, the dilemma faced by both Council and commissioners is evident in a letter from the former to the latter, written in April 1592.[80] The Council warns that "yf noe good perswacions or intreatie shalbe able to move them [creditors] to compassion," the commission should proceed against them with "severitie." This, however, turns out to be merely a threat that if "anye informacion shalbe broughte at anye tyme against them upon anye penall statute . . . they are to looke for noe favor but all extreamitie that may be used."[81] Meanwhile, the Council itself often sought to retard proceedings against debtors, first seeking a stay by consent, but not infrequently mandating that creditors restrain themselves. Whether acting through commissions or on its own, the Council meddled when it was confident that the "obstinacy" of creditors was such that a "man's case deserveth commiseracion and pitty."[82] For those in prison and especially for those already under execution for debt, a final protest against "disreputation" at the hands of obdurate creditors often depended upon the Council.

Thereafter, prisoners had to fend for themselves.[83] If we listen to what they have to say about their incarceration, we will hear little in the way of repentance and, unsurprisingly, much in the way of indignation. Thus Geffray Mynshul, a Gray's Inn gentleman imprisoned for debt in King's Bench, complains of "insulting" jailors who are

commonly either base tradesmen that have broken, and by a little money pared off from other men's goods, buy such offices; els are they lazy serving men, who beeing weary of carrying the cloake bagge, think it a brave life to come and command as good, and sometimes better men then their maisters, within the stinking precincts of a prison; or take the best choyce you can, they are but outworne soldiers, but indeed for the most part the very off-scum of the rascall multitude, as cabbage-carriers, decoyes, bum-bayliffes, disgraced pursevants, botchers, chandlers, and a rabble of such stinkardly companions; with whom no man of any reasonable fashion, but would scorne to converse . . .[84]

The thought of "noble, brave, and generous spirits," of "well descended" gentlemen "pinyond peradventure with leashes of keepers," their "oaths, faiths, honors, and reputations" gored, quickens Mynshul's outrage, drowning out his rather tepid hope that his readers will henceforth "be afraid to enter into debt any farther then necessity urgeth, and if they bee forced to borrow, to pay as soone as they can" (72–73 and 8). The indebted prisoner, once "a free borne generous spirit," finds himself in "bondage" to "petty insolent rakehells" (75–76). His "masculine courage . . . indures the braves of pesants" (76); though a lion, he is fastened upon by a "butcher's curre" (78). At every step along the way of the debtor's progress, Mynshul describes not so much financial miscalculation as status insult. Like Hotspur, for whom Mortimer's willingness to receive "deadly wounds" guarantees his innocence of "bare and rotten policy," Mynshul's commitment to a gentleman's honor makes any suggestion that he might be culpable irrelevant.[85]

The insult to an imprisoned debtor's prestige often registers on both the London stage and in the period's prison pamphlets in regard to prison fare and lodgings. The Counters consisted of three paying wards, the Master's Side, the Knight's Ward, and the Twopenny Ward. Those without any money resided in the Hole. Typically, the stage and pamphlet prisoner experiences incarceration as a graduated series of humiliations, a passage from the relative freedom and comfort of the most expensive quarters to the deprivations of the Hole. In *Greene's Tu Quoque*, Spendall has exhausted his funds, having sold even his clothes, and so can no longer pay the warden what he owes for his board and lodgings. Holdfast, the warden's assistant, confronts Spendall:

HOLD. If you have no monie
    You're best remove into some cheaper Ward.
SPEND. What Ward should I remove in?
HOLD. Why to the Two-pennie Ward,
    Is likliest to hold out with your meanes:
    Or if you will, you may goe into the Holl,
    And there you may feed for nothing.
SPEND. I, out of the Almes-basket, where Charitie appeares
    In likenesse of a peece of stinking Fish,
    Such as they beat Bawdes with when they are Carted.
HOLD. Why sir, doe not scorne it, as good men as your selfe,
    Have been glad to eate Scraps out of the Almsbasket.
SPEND. And yet slave, thou in pride wilt stop thy nose,
    Scrue and make faces, talke contemptibly of it,
    And of the feeders; surely groome. (2,060–74)

The "lowsie Lynings" that outrage Spendall could well derive from the "lowsie lodging" in the Hole that the formerly imprisoned merchant William Bagwell refers to. When a prisoner has no money and has exhausted his credit with the tapster, "when thou art brought to so much *disgrace*," Bagwell writes, "The Hole 'tis like will be thy dwelling place."[86] So it is that *Eastward Ho*'s Quicksilver "would be i' the Hole, if we would let him" (5.2.48–49). The apprentice recognizes that to commit himself to the Hole would be to advertise "a great deal of humility" (5.2.44). He also understands the Counter sign system every bit as well as does Spendall. Cooke's status-conscious citizen directs his scorn at the almsbasket. Quicksilver, no less alert to protocol, manipulates its significance: he "will eat o' the basket, for humility" (5.3.57–58). Whatever outrage the apprentice stifles he can displace into the petitions he is penning gratis for fellow prisoners (5.3.64–67), petitions which we might well imagine to combine a mixture of outrage and deference of the sort confected in the prison petitions produced by Chapman and Jonson subsequent to their arrest.

Imprisoned debtors were degraded and deprived. Whether their complaints were uniformly legitimate would have been of course no more easy to confirm about conditions then than it would be today, about prisoners' suits now. George Lee was a prisoner in the Fleet in execution for debt for £1,300. Lee complained that he had taken out a bond to guarantee his good behavior. The deputy warden, Alexander Harris, answered that Lee "broke that bond by many fowle abuses." Lee complained that he had paid "all fees of a Gentleman." Harris answered that although "he paid his fees at first, it is noe warrant to be irreguler ever after." Lee insisted that he had been held as a close prisoner for five months; but Harris said that he "had the use of six large roomes and a Court yard, and gon forth to drinke with and accompany his friends." Lee complained of confinement in the Fleet's equivalent to the Hole, a "loathsome dungeon, thorough which all sewers doe run." Harris explained that Lee's "last restraint is in a large but strong roome, which is noe otherwise then as any roome in the howse which is next the ground, and hath noe sewer."[87] And so it goes, in a miniature version of the extensive prisoner complaints and extraordinarily ample defense (660 pages) mounted by Harris in the main body of *The Oeconomy of the Fleete*.

From Harris's point of view, the prisoners' list of complaints was only apparently compiled in order to effect his "overthrowe." In fact, he argues, "theis nyneteen artic[l]es [the complaints] have a secret pointing": the prisoners simply "aim to have as many immunities as is possible" (13). Harris focuses on the economic as opposed to the social basis of the attack on his wardenship. He argues that the prisoners would extend their contention with him four or five years beyond the years they have already been at it so that "in the meane tyme the Warden may have no payment" (13) from them.[88] Furthermore,

their owne land and revenues may be inlarged, and their meanes swell to pay creditors, but it shall be noe more than ii. iii. or iiii.s. in the pound of their debts; reserveing and keepeing the surplusage for their posteritie. And this resolutely they determyne to obtayne or else lett their creditors take their carkasses when they dye, soe that it is an hazard counterpoysed whether the creditor or the debtor beareth the greater, for if the one dye in prison the other looseth the debt ... (13–14)

The House of Commons, however, while not unaware of the competing economic interests of imprisoned debtors and a warden who depended upon prisoners' fees to run his prison (and for profit), voiced outrage commensurate with the sensibilities of substantial prisoners. In 1621, apparently the same year Harris was writing the *Oeconomy*, a Committee of the Commons "resolved, never any such barbarous Usage of Poor Prisoners. – Lived in *Turkey*. – Hath gotten worse than the Qualities of a *Turke*." Sir Arthur Ingram took particular note of prisoners' complaints about extortion, irons, dungeons, and bribery.[89] Harris was called on the carpet and required to defend himself.

Prisoners responded to the humiliations and misery to which they were subjected by rioting, by petitioning the Commons and the Privy Council, and by inaugurating suits against prison officers. In the Hole in the Wood Street Counter, debtors who could not look forward to a comic reintegration into the larger community of mutual obligations were left to quiet their rage, to mitigate their abjection, and to manage their credit relations after their own fashion. According to Fennor, the Hole was administered by a Master Steward, the imprisoned debtors' analogue for a Lord Mayor.[90] "And as the City hath twelve companies that exceed all the rest for authority, antiquity and riches, so hath this place twelve old prisoners that help the Steward in his proceedings, who by the general voice of the house rule and bear sway over all the rest" (485). If status obsessions and attendant affronts in the extramural world stem from the entitlements of landownership, citizenship, family, or wealth, prestige in the Hole depends upon length of incarceration. Twelve *old* prisoners comprise the "council." "[P]risoners that have been of five or six years standing should have profit of it [legacies] before such as have been there but two or three months" (484). Denied re-entry into the world at large, the denizens of the Hole create "a little city in a commonwealth," complete with a constable, attorneys, a physician and tradesmen (485). When it comes to fiscal matters – precisely the sort of affairs that landed most inmates in the Counter in the first place – authoritarian procedures combine with communitarian assumptions to suppress self-regard or singularity. All legacies are put into "the Steward's disposing" (according to Bagwell, the "Lady of the Hole" among women prisoners), and the Steward then "carefully provides" for prisoners according to their "necessaries" (484–85).[91] Should a prisoner forswear himself, he must fine for it if he is able; "if he be not . . . [he shall] never have so much credit as run one penny on the tapster's score" (487). In the "little city" that is the Hole, centralized planning preempts individual credit and debt management, whatever one's social status may be. In an environment of controlled competition for scarce resources achieved in the teeth of profound deprivation (the almsbasket), neither humility nor bravado, tenacity nor outrage, affords an advantage. Instead, credit counter-intuitively accrues to those deepest in the Hole, to those who are perhaps deepest in debt or most oblivious to it. In this C/counter commonwealth, extensive indebtedness results in prolonged imprisonment which in turn confers prestige, power, profit, in sum, "that privilege the eldest ought to have" (484). Here, all inmates live their lives wholly, one would not want to be so foolish as to say happily, according to the dictates of that which this chapter began by affirming was common to all English people in the early modern era: debt.

3   Mortgage payments

In London, defaulting on a loan could result in imprisonment in a Counter. In the countryside, failure to repay on the appointed day could mean foreclosure. Indebted landowners, fearful of forfeiture, had good reason to detest their mortgage-holders. Then too, creditors often held mortgagors in no less contempt. While an improvident estate manager represented an easy mark, those who attempted to wriggle free of encumbrances, to convey property to third parties, or to appeal to Chancery, sharpened the animus of their mortgagees. The mortgage-holder had his (and it was generally *his*) own cause for, if not fear, then strain, since he himself was juggling borrowed money, trying to keep up with a rapid turnover of funds, defending himself in court, and enduring the opprobrium that inevitably was felt for a creditor. Nevertheless, merchants, moneylenders, and citizens succeeded or failed not in opposition to landowners but through them, just as landowners – powerful nobility in particular – were rarely the enemy of moneymen so much as they were their willing sponsors.[1] Putative borders were regularly crossed when merchants' daughters and merchants themselves married into gentry families and gentry daughters into merchant families; when nobles depended upon citizens to manage their customs farms and citizens built their own vast landed estates; when established peers underwrote the advance into government office of new men and were in turn serviced by these clients; and when landowners colluded with citizens in order more successfully to counter other landowner–merchant combinations with which they were in competition.

Within the early modern English economy, land was an estimable and a secure, if not especially profitable, form of investment. A landowner who met with bad luck, who had numerous daughters to provide for, who lacked an understanding of credit facilities or a competent steward, might easily be forced into mortgaging property. Even the savvy landowner bent on improvement, whether in the form of drainage or enclosure, new equipment or buildings, was dependent upon raising fines (itself a form of mortgage when coupled with low rents), savings (by no means easy to achieve), or short-term mortgages. Moreover, in an environment in which there was essentially no such thing as long-term credit, even a short-term mortgage was an improvement over the most common alternatives. Bonds and statutes (the former usually passed between friends for sums of no more than a few hundred pounds and enforceable at Common Pleas, the latter capable of guaranteeing loans of several thousands of pounds and recoverable at Chancery without the necessity of any suit at law) were usually due after a mere six months. Mortgages might run for a year or more and might be for very large sums. Thus among the various financial instruments that bound land to money and money to land, the mortgage was preeminent. However, prior to the 1620s a mortgagor who proved unable to repay his loan on the appointed day faced not only impaired credit and a diminished chance of finding short-term loans with which to cancel ancillary debts, but forfeiture. When a note was due, a landowner might have to choose between selling unencumbered property and forfeiture of mortgaged property, usually at a loss. The Earl of Leicester claimed that failure to clear a mortgage of £4,300 resulted in the forfeiture of property worth £13,000. Lords Grey of Wilton and Cobham "ostentatiously wrung their hands at the prospect of losing land they valued at £10,000 and £5,000 for mortgages of £3,000 and £600 respectively."[2]

There was no more obvious affective response to the economics of landownership than fear of foreclosure.[3] Predictably, there was a significant abatement of fear as protection from forfeiture became, progressively, an exception to the rule, customary, and then finally, in the 1620s, a legal right. This development, a fundamentally new way to pay old debts, took the form of an equitable right recognized in Chancery to redeem mortgaged land after the day fixed for repayment – a right known as "equity of redemption."[4] The social and economic contexts of this legal development stand quietly beside the raging affect that in this chapter I discuss in terms of both mortgage payments in Philip Massinger's *A New Way to Pay Old Debts* (1625) and the business dealings of Sir Lionel Cranfield (1575–1645) and Sir Arthur Ingram (1565–1642). An unprecedented volume of land sales and purchases as well as a sharply increasing frequency (and level) of indebtedness in the early seventeenth century goes some way toward explaining the fortunes of an Overreach, a Welborne, a Cranfield, or a Hicks. In some counties, 60, 70, even 90 percent of the landowning gentry were of relatively recent tenure. They and those whom they displaced were equally eager to convert their primary asset, their land, into a long-term security. Once a debtor could be confident that he retained possession of his land beyond the expiration of his mortgage – that is, once he was assured that upon payment of principal, interest, and costs, he could redeem his property – indebtedness not only lost much of its urgency but became positively enabling. The mortgagor now had "time to devise a gradual process of recovery, without resorting to sale of land. There was time for economy and retrenchment, time for the slowly accruing profits from his estate gradually to reduce his debt."[5] One could now improve one's estate or borrow to provide for children without having to face the ruinous prospect of foreclosure. Creditors, for their part, could now assign a mortgage, or secure a Chancery decree that would fix a date after which a defaulted landowner could finally be foreclosed of his equity of redemption and forced to convey the property in question to the mortgagee.[6]

The pent-up need for more flexible credit mechanisms at a moment when many among the peerage were deeply in debt, and when both middling and lesser gentry were buying ever more land, helps to explain the establishment of a maximum legal rate of interest in the Act of 1571. The late-sixteenth and early-seventeenth centuries then witnessed a marked rise in the supply of money available for loan. Not only rich London merchants but lawyers and scriveners, not to mention officers of the Crown with exchequer funds passing temporarily through their hands, were putting their money out at interest. The Privy Council was also, as we have seen, responding to the credit crunch by protecting debtors who fell prey to merciless creditors or to the common law itself. And so it is not surprising that the Chancellor stepped in to offer relief to mortgagors by asserting his jurisdiction precisely where common law would have required forfeiture. Turner notes that the Court of Chancery seems first to have addressed the issue of mortgages in the reigns of Henry VI and Edward IV.[7] When a debt had been paid or satisfied out of rents or profits, but the property was not redelivered, relief in the form of reconveyance was offered on grounds of conscience, as was typical of Chancery law. Where fraud or oppression on the part of the mortgagee was evident, relief was granted. Later, under Elizabeth, Chancery began to offer relief to mortgagors who failed to pay on the date named. But special circumstances, such as hardship or fraud, still had to be proved. As causes of hardship multiplied and the Chancellor allowed more and more special circumstances, cases in which no relief was afforded were themselves soon the exceptions. Finally, by 1625, relief was uniformly extended

to forfeitures of mortgages in general, irrespective of fraud or other special circumstances as the ground of relief. What is more, the relief has soon not only become general in the sense that it can be given apart from special circumstances, but it has come to be looked upon as a definite rule of the Court that such relief shall always be given. Very soon the mortgagor considers that he has a right to redeem in Chancery, although the day is passed for such redemption at law.[8]

In *Emmanuel College* v. *Evans*, it appears that Chancery is assuming that a mortgage is simply a security for a loan, not the transfer of property rights. Relying on conscience, or what Turner calls "equitable conscience," the Chancellor was moving steadily toward what would become a principle of law after the Restoration.[9] In the meantime, whether because of Chancery's aggressive efforts to expand its jurisdiction (efforts that came to a head in the triumph of equity and of Ellesmere over Coke and the courts of common law in 1616), or because of a genuine desire for fair dealing in the midst of a turbulent land market, between 1615 and 1630 the grounds for relief available to a mortgagor in default were greatly expanded.

I

When Portia defeats Shylock by insisting on a still stricter interpretation of his bond with Antonio than even Shylock has imagined, part of our enjoyment of the moment derives from our sense that a credible way out of an intolerable situation has been found. Whatever our feelings about the sequel to this solution, a folk-tale crisis is plausibly resolved by legal acumen. Massinger's *A New Way to Pay Old Debts* turns this process around: when "certaine mineralls" (5.1.330) are deployed to counter Overreach's sharp practice – a triumph by means of "chemical reaction" – we may find the solution to the crisis "less [than] satisfactory" because something akin to magic appears to be the only relief available in all too familiar circumstances.[10] In *The Merchant of Venice*, everyone's nightmare version of a creditor is foiled by a character who passes for a doctor of laws operating within the rules of what may pass for the law. Massinger's plot also relies upon a man with a keen understanding of the law, a "publike notarie" (5.1.205); but even a corrupt "Tearme-driver" (*dram. pers.* 7) like Marrall lacks the legal wit to trip up Overreach. Instead, he depends upon what may pass for alchemy – "mysteries / Not to be spoke in publike" (5.1.329–30). Hocus pocus, what looks like a "deale with witches" (5.1.194), is alone capable of providing the necessary solvent.

What is it that is defeated in the person of Overreach? And what accounts for the remarkably bitter tone not only of his defeat, but of so much of the dealings between characters in this play? It has been argued that Lord Lovell's and Lady Alworth's sponsorship of the victory of Tom Alworth and Welborne represents the triumph of the patriarchal status quo (a "morality of 'benefits'") over a "cash nexus" (a "morality of contract"). A "commercial and domestic Tamberlaine," a tyrant, and a "gangster," Overreach is said to be the "hyperbolic embodiment of avarice and ambition threatening a relatively settled traditional social fabric."[11] In two thoughtful companion essays, Martin Butler takes issue with such arguments. He steers away from readings which turn the play into "a hysterical document of class anxiety" and argues instead that variant forms of patriarchy are at odds in *A New Way*. According to Butler, Massinger pits Lovell, the benevolent patriarch, against Overreach, the tyrannical father. Rather than an encounter between an ideology of rank or status and a bourgeois ideology founded on thrift, the play stages tensions *within* the ideology of deference and advocates "controlled social change." Massinger allows that money may after all be "tacked on to blood without the hereditary elites feeling it has damaged their authority."[12] I quote at some length from Butler's shrewd analysis of this "tacking on" by means of scapegoating:

Overreach's power is provided by his daughter and his cash: as objects of aristocratic desire, they enable him to establish control in the aristocratic environment. From Overreach's point of view, it is only because the social elites are led by the drives for sex and credit that these opportunities open themselves for him . . . In return for their indebtedness to him, Sir Giles assumes the guilt, being content to be blamed for avarice so that aristocrats may have their lavish spending without the imputation of dishonour . . . It is thus made to appear that the moral responsibility for genteel indebtedness rests not with the debtor but with the lender, since aristocratic desire is only called into being by a preceding civic desire: the citizen's wish to lend eggs on the gentleman's wish to spend. Overreach is thereby made the scapegoat for the vices of his debtors . . .

Of course, Lord Lovell holds Overreach in contempt even though any sex or credit drives he may have have nothing to do with Sir Giles. And, as Butler acknowledges, the play cannot quite get Welborne off the hook by making Overreach the scapegoat. In what Butler describes as "the play's crucial ideological manoeuvre," Welborne's gentility, not Overreach's desire, excuses his riot.[13] In the end, Butler argues, guilt and responsibility do lie with Overreach, but only at one remove. The demon that Lovell and Welborne exorcize is one that they themselves have created, and Massinger is hard put to reconcile himself to the demystification he himself has accomplished ("Overreach's ambitions have been brought into being by the society which disclaims him").[14] Unlike Marlowe, who goes eagerly out of his way to insist that the scapegoat the Maltese externalize in the person of Barabas is in perfect accord with the venom within them, Massinger takes no pleasure in even a measured critique of polite society.

If we consider that Overreach's needs can be met only by means of the play's greater and lesser gentry and, conversely, that they depend on him, then several conclusions may follow. First, the play is structured not in terms of land versus wealth but land *and* wealth (that is, land in search of, dependent upon, or as a token of wealth). As I have already suggested, moneylenders worked *through* landowners and vice versa (and moneylenders were landowners, just as landowners loaned money) – there was usually no alternative.[15] Second, responsibility or blame for one or another sort of ambition in *A New Way* ought not to be assigned either to an Overreach who stimulates desire or to gentry who beat him to the punch. Both parties have a share. They collude. And, third, the unavoidable interdependencies that the relations among all of play's characters reveal explain the remarkable animus felt at every turn. They despise one another because they are bound to one another, because a Welborne or a young Alworth can no more fulfill his desires without affiliating himself with the Overreach family than the latter can satisfy their ambitions apart from Nottingham's Welbornes, Alworths, and Lovells ("All my ambition is to have my daughter / Right honorable, which my Lord can make her" – 4.1.99–100). There is an abundance of reciprocal contempt here, but not enough to clog the circulation of accreditation.[16] On the one hand, Welborne anathematizes "*Cormorant Overreach*" (1.1.131) and wishes he would cut his own throat, Furnace would like to roast Overreach's heart, and Marrall taunts the "mad beast" (5.1.335) who beat and humiliated him. Early on, Overreach himself pauses to comment on the "strange Antipathie" between his sort and "true Gentry" (2.1.88–89). On the other hand, they cannot seem to make do without one another. Welborne first depends upon Overreach to extend him credit in the form of "mortgages, statutes, and bonds" (1.1.50) and then to lend him £1,000. Overreach, for his part, married a Welborne, would now marry Lady Alworth, and acknowledges his dependence on Lovell's name and "reputation" (4.1.88) to make his grandson a credible "young Lord" (4.1.102). Margaret praises Lord Lovell's "bounty" and thinks of herself in his "debt" (4.3.6–7). Lovell in turn makes it possible for his page Alworth (whose father's debts to Overreach almost consumed his estate – 1.3.100 and 4.1.205–06) to recover his patrimony by inheriting the "[p]olluted, and unholsome" (4.1.199) Overreach estate, that is, by marrying (perhaps even becoming) Sir Giles's "undoubted heire" (5.1.385).[17]

Contempt for the mortgage-holder is the preeminent but by no means the most virulent example of antipathy between creditors and debtors in this play. In the raucous and angry opening scene, Tapwell and Froth deny a drink or a smoke to "tatter'd, louzie" (1.1.17) Welborne. His "credit not worth a token," Welborne "grew the common borrower" and is now no better than "the beggers on high wayes" (1.1.54–57). Tapwell delivers a condensed version of *Eastward Ho*'s Touchstone's history of thrift and modest "profit" (1.1.63), as well as Golding's progress toward civic fame:

> . . . poore *Tim Tapwell* with a little stocke,
> Some forty pounds or so, bought a small cottage,
> Humbled my selfe to marriage with my *Froth* here;
>
> . . .
>
> The poore Income
> I glean'd . . . hath made mee in my parish,
> Thought worthy to bee *Scavinger*, and in time
> May rise to be *Overseer* of the poore;   (1.1.59–61; 65–68)

Tapwell concludes that if he is indeed given responsibility for the poor, he "may allow you [Welborne] thirteene pence a quarter" (1.1.70). Welborne's furious response – beating and kicking Tapwell – follows from his conviction that Tapwell's success has little to do with what he has insinuated in his hypocritical rehearsal of industry and everything to do with Welborne's generosity – his "gift" (1.1.24). In other words, Welborne rewrites his prodigality as bounty ("Am not I Hee / Whose riots fed, and cloth'd thee?" – 1.1.26–27) and Tapwell expresses his contempt for Welborne by imagining himself his parish benefactor. Have Tapwell's whores and canters stimulated Welborne's appetite for "Mistrisses / Of all sorts, and all sizes" (1.1.45–46), or is it Welborne who has made "purses for" Tapwell, his former "under-butler" (1.1.75 and 43)? Tapwell would have it that he labored for ("glean'd") his £40. Welborne says "'twas I that gave it, / In ready gold" (1.1.79–80). Each works through the other and despises him for this necessity. The alehouse-keeper takes pleasure in lording it over the former "Lord of Akers; the prime gallant" (1.1.42) and then Welborne humiliates his tormentors, insisting that they creep off stage on their knees after he has beaten them.

Massinger dwells at some length on Welborne's physical degradation. "[T]atter'd, louzie" from the start, Welborne himself speaks of having been "vomited out of an Alehouse / And thus accoutred" (1.1.178–79). Furnace would have him confined to a "piggestie" (1.3.48) and Lady Alworth's women are repelled by Welborne: "what a smell's here . . . A creature / Made out of the privie" (1.3.53–54). When Lady Alworth enters, she is advised to keep her glove to her nose until her chambermaid has had time to fetch perfumes. In *A New Way*, monetary indebtedness defiles. When money tacks on to blood, it hurts. Not just indebtedness, but any fiscal exigency takes its toll. Yet such exigencies are pervasive, almost inevitable. For some reason, good old Sir John Welborne, even though he "kept a great house" (1.1.36), countenanced his sister's marriage to Overreach. Sir John's son can recover himself only through further indebtedness to Overreach. "Want, debts and quarrells / Lay heavy on" Lady Alworth's "late noble husband" (1.3.101–02 and 96). Now Tom Alworth finds himself having defensively to distinguish between the "conditions" of Margaret Overreach and "the base churl her father" (1.1.149 and 151). What is at stake is one's purity, in the case of Lord Lovell, his "immaculate whitenesse" (4.1.95). Thus Welborne would rather die than accept "eight peeces" from Alworth; he would "want . . . ever" before he would "borrow six pence" from Lady Alworth, let alone the £100 that she offers him (1.1.171–85 and 1.3.119–22). Monetary transactions can be imagined only to tarnish these generation-old relations, just as marriage to Margaret would "adulterate" (4.1.223) Lord Lovell's blood. To endorse such an alliance would be to condone "rubbage [being] powr'd into a river / . . . that was pure before" (4.1.196–98). And yet Welborne will bait his trap for Overreach with the Alworth lands and Lord Lovell lends his prestige to secure Margaret's hand for Tom.

The gentles persuade themselves that they are tricking and defeating Sir Giles, or bringing his better part into their fold; but there is no path around Overreach, only through him and his wealth. He holds the Welborne mortgages, stands behind the Alworth debts (4.1.205–06), and controls Margaret's dowry. Only the Lovell estate stands entirely free of the encumbrances with which Overreach thwarts all and sundry. Only Lord Lovell can afford the luxury of refusing the "Queene of flowers, the glory of the spring" (1.1.146). This, Massinger's more "crucial ideological manoeuvre," represents the play's greatest mystery that cannot be spoken in public. Standing free of any fiscal necessity, Lovell enacts a more full-blown fantasy than even the admittedly prodigious predator that is Sir Giles Overreach. Surely it would have been more difficult to imagine an unfettered Jacobean nobleman than a creditor like Sir Giles. Remarkably, neither Lovell the landowner nor Lovell the "Courtier, and a Soldier" (3.2.106) stands in need of the cash Overreach represents. It may be that the play ends unexpectedly with Welborne redeeming his reputation by serving under Lovell's command, although we have been given to understand that it is Alworth who aims to "follow / The path my Lord markes" (1.2.84), because Alworth now suffers from the contamination Lovell could not tolerate for himself. Having deigned to consort with Sir Giles and Margaret – even if only to conspire on Alworth's behalf – Lovell in the end must be insulated from an alliance that he sanctioned. Welborne is given the opportunity to be made "right agen" (5.1.399) but it is not clear that in Lovell's mind this is still possible for an Alworth allied to an Overreach. Alworth's "integrity" regrettably may suffer from having been "sullied with one taint" (4.1.96–97). While Alworth issue may be "one part skarlet / And the other *London*-blew" (4.1.225–26), Lovell makes clear just how unimaginable this would be for a "young Lord *Lovell*" (4.1.102).

A New Way tempers the Lovell fantasy of immaculate whiteness, obliging Lovell to work through Overreach. If a little soiled in the working, Lovell, like Welborne, can still redeem himself on the Continent. Responsive to generic expectations, the play most emphatically disrupts the Overreach fantasy of omnipotence in the final scene. However, Overreach's delusions of singularity (typically articulated in the assertion, "I must have all men sellers, / And I the *only* Purchaser" – 2.1.32–33; my emphasis) are undermined throughout. From first to last, Sir Giles can comprehend his own identity only in relation to the "true Gentry" (2.1.89) from which he is excluded but through whom he must work. His "maine worke" is to "insinuate" himself into Lovell's "knowledge" (2.1.68 and 72). Aware that he is an *arriviste* ("'tis my glory, *though* I come from the Cittie" – 2.1.81; my emphasis), Overreach tacitly acknowledges that he himself can never be one of "them." His best chance of securing his family's prestige lies in Margaret, but he cannot imagine even a "right honorable" daughter without the conspicuous presence of those once above her now beneath her, confirming her elevation. The children of those whom he has undone will kneel to Margaret "as bond-slaves" (2.1.83). "Ile not have a Chambermaide / That tyes her shooe . . . / But such whose Fathers were Right worshipfull" (2.1.84–86). Knights and ladies will offer up their "eldest sonne / To be her page, and wait upon her trencher" (4.3.136–37). Such table-turning, premised upon the oppression of the "Lady *Downefalnes*" and the master Frugalls of the world, is evidence of genuine power. It also reveals Overreach's fierce dependence on the "unthrifts" he "squeeze[s] . . . into ayre" (2.1.3) no less than the gentles who will ennoble his daughter.

The sadistic pleasure Overreach derives from Lady Downefalne's humility, from "[t]rampl[ing] on her" and imagining her howling in the Counter (3.2.42–48), must be set against the masochistic pleasures to which Sir Giles disciplines himself. A life of haling down curses upon himself culminates in his critical interview with Lord Lovell. Confident that his own "wealth / Shall weigh his [Lovell's] titles downe" (3.2.104), Overreach begins their conference by inventorying the "lands, or leases, ready coine, or goods" (4.1.55–87) that will come to his future son-in-law. In short order, however, Overreach is offering to shoulder "any foule aspersion" that might otherwise sully Lovell's "unquestioned integrity" (4.1.90 and 96). The opprobrium that follows from ruining "[t]he Country to supply your [Lovell's] riotous wast," coupled with the "darke / And crooked wayes" by which Overreach arrives at his wealth, afford him "more true delight" than could any imaginable expenditure (4.1.109 and 135–37). After a perverse fashion, Lord Lovell's participation in Overreach's grand scheme would permit him to satisfy his two abiding desires: to continue to play the tyrannical "Extortioner . . . Cormorant, or Intruder / On my poore Neighbours right" (4.1.123–24) and abjectly to stand bare before his honorable daughter (3.2.176–77). He unnervingly derives pleasure from his self-hatred as a submissive father fused with a pleasurable contempt for both extortionate mortgage-holders and poor mortgagors. Equally satisfying are the seemingly contradictory desires to promulgate the "utter ruine" (2.1.7) of the gentry and to supply their waste. If Overreach exploits the familiar logic of accreditation, reaccreditation, and then ruination to bring down Welborne, in his pitch to Lovell Overreach envisions wreaking havoc with the country expressly to support its very exemplar.

The compulsion to prop up and to fell the Nottinghamshire land-owning class may explain what must be Overreach's momentary mis-recognition of Lovell for Welborne in the conference in 4.1. When Sir Giles explains that he will supply Lovell's "riotous wast" in order to spare him the "scourge of prodigalls" (4.1.109–10), surely it is Welborne, not Lovell, who is on his mind (it was, after all, Welborne's "loosenesse" that Overreach had "suppli'd" – 1.1.51). Or is it that Overreach simply cannot subscribe to the play's fantasy of a self-sufficient landowner? That *A New Way to Pay Old Debts* is itself in partial denial of the liabilities of its gentry is best illustrated by Massinger's handling of Welborne's obligations to Overreach.[18] In the first scene of the play we learn that Sir John Welborne left his son Francis an estate worth £1,200 a year. This, the conventionally prodigal heir wasted. Uncle Overreach then stepped in with "mortgages, statutes, and bonds" (1.1.50). We have every reason to believe that this means that Welborne encumbered his estate in order to fund his hunting and whoring, and that when he had run through the cash he had been advanced, he was forced to sell his mortgage. First Tapwell explains, "Your land gone, and your credit not worth a token, / You grew the common borrower" (1.1.34–35). Then Marrall: "*Welborne* was apt to sell, and needed not / These fine arts Sir to hooke him in" (2.1.49–50). It was Welborne the "common borrower" who contributed to the decay of 4.2's vintner, tailor, and surgeon.

The cycle seems to start up again when Welborne trades on the apparent prospect of his lordship over the Alworth estate to induce his uncle once again to loan him money. But this time Overreach advances the cash before receiving "security / For his thousand pounds"

(4.2.115–16). Sir Giles is left to demand "good security . . . by *Mortgage*, or by *Statute*" (5.1.128–29) after the fact. In his remarkable reply, Welborne insists that his uncle either restore to him his land or face recovery of a debt of his own for £10,000. This figure, which Welborne got from Marrall, is said to represent money Overreach withheld from his nephew upon the sale of the latter's land. But precisely what is at issue is never made clear. On the one hand we know that Welborne was running through his cash at an unseemly rate, and that he was both prepared to mortgage and "apt" to sell. On the other hand Marrall claims to have been involved in the "sale of your [Welborne's] land . . . When you were defeated of it" (4.2.119–21). Of what did this "defeat" consist? Did Overreach, the mortgagee, illicitly assign the property or somehow defraud Welborne? Did he undervalue it by a factor of ten? Granting sharp practice (Overreach certainly boasts of his technique and the play refers to his cheating no fewer than three times), what sort of sharp practice was this and how complicitous was Welborne? If Welborne did sell his land, and he does admit to having been a "riotous foole" (5.1.163), how can it be that Overreach is indebted to him? Overreach's stunned query, or exclamation – "I in thy debt!" (5.1.160) – goes a good way toward expressing our sense that the entire socio-economic environment that we assumed these characters were inhabiting has been overturned. Suddenly the "worldly" (3.3.50), city-born money-lender is in debt to the profligate heir. To meet a debt with a wholly unexpected counter-claim of indebtedness must be to have found a new way to pay old debts.

As if sensitive not only to Overreach's amazement but to our own, Welborne sets out to explain the matter, or to hedge, or to lie. He now refuses to acknowledge that there ever was a deed of sale, granting only that there was a "trust," for a period of "a yeare, or two" (5.1.167–68). There is little conviction in that "or two" and there is little reason to imagine that Marrall was referring to a trust each time he spoke of Welborne's "sale" of his land. Even if on the basis of Overreach's reputation for outrageous duplicity we are disposed to credit Welborne's account, we soon discover that he has played fast and loose. With Overreach out of earshot, Welborne asks Marrall to "discover the quaint meanes you us'd / To raze out the conveyance" (5.1.328–29). A written document by means of which the legal transfer of property is effected, a conveyance was also a form of underhand dealing or jugglery (*OED* 7 and 11b). Be this as it may, whether we are dealing with a mortgage, a statute, a bond, a deed, a trust, or a conveyance, none other than Lord Lovell reserves judgment as to Welborne's claim to the land. "[F]or your land master *Welborne*, / Be it good, or ill in law, I'le be the umpire"

(5.1.383–84). The jury is out; Welborne's right to redemption has not been established.

In the closing moments of *A New Way*, the linguistic overtones of credit – at once social, economic, legal, and theological – are all audible. Welborne, who has been attentive to Alworth's "language" (5.1.388), chooses his words carefully as he prepares to ask Lovell to confer a company on him so that he may restore his credit:

> there is something else
> Beside the repossession of my land,
> And payment of my debts, that I must practise.
> I had a reputation, but 'twas lost
> In my loose course; and 'till I redeeme it
> Some noble way, I am but halfe made up.   (5.1.389–94)

I am confident that Massinger's writing *circa* 1625 about land, debt, repossession, and redemption is largely coincidental with the extension of full equity of redemption to mortgagors *circa* 1625. Still, Massinger was the son of the house-steward and agent to Henry Herbert, the second Earl of Pembroke. He was himself imprisoned for debt in 1613, and as recently as 1624 he was embroiled in a suit in Chancery concerning a modest debt.[19] Massinger might well have been alert to legal matters pertaining to land and emanating from the Court of Chancery. His play patently reflects the urgent need for some sort of relief in the face of fearsome creditors. It stages the contempt which creditors and debtors felt for one another, an enmity based not so much on difference (though differences there were) as on the vexing recognition of mutual dependence. And it conjures two make-believe reactions, each in its way driven by animosity. Lovell's hardly imaginable autonomy inoculates him against loathsome contamination. No financial need or exigency bears down upon him, even if the same cannot be said for his client, Tom Alworth. Still, even Lovell proves susceptible to Overreach's poison. At the end of their stunning interview, he finds himself "bath'd all over / In a cold sweat" (4.1.152–53). Welborne's scorn for Sir Giles corresponds to his more grievous infection, which he treats with an altogether more powerful antidote than Lovell requires. "[M]ysteries / Not to be spoke in publike" turn out to have the strength both to dissolve Welborne's bonds and to drive Overreach to Bedlam. Of course, the force of his recognition that the son of one of his former debtors (probably a former mortgagor) will inherit his estate serves only to aggravate Overreach's fever. One way or the other, *A New Way to Pay Old Debts* confirms that the gentry went about their business by means of the great Jacobean moneymen, and vice versa. Overreach's plans to amalgamate the Alworth estate with his own in order to pass it on to Lovell and his heirs are simply reversed when, in his confinement, he is forced to tolerate the consolidation of his own estate into that of the Alworths.

II

Near the end of my discussion in chapter 1 of the Earl of Suffolk's corrupt practices, I included a very brief discussion of the sorts of collusion one might find between a powerful noble and a canny financier like Arthur Ingram. A good deal more can be said not merely about the intertwined relations among nobles, gentles, and moneymen (who themselves had often progressed from the city to landed estates), but about mortgages and the affect consequent upon them, by pursuing more closely Ingram's career, and that of his patron, partner, associate, and sometime friend, Lionel Cranfield. Like Overreach, Ingram and Cranfield were bred in the city and rose to extraordinary wealth and considerable estates. While Ingram, like Overreach, was knighted, Cranfield was created Earl of Middlesex in 1622.[20] Unlike Sir Giles, Ingram was never toppled, although he did experience at least one severe financial crisis. Cranfield *was* brought down. Buckingham engineered the Lord Treasurer's high-profile fall in 1624 and the scandal was still eliciting comment the next year, when Massinger wrote *A New Way*.[21] I do not want to advance either Ingram or Cranfield as a source for Overreach; however, I do want to consider a small portion of their complex financial activities in order to document the ways nobility and landed gentry worked in necessary if often uneasy concert with moneymen (again, moneymen who had acquired at least the pretense of gentility). Their dealings were characterized by considerable stress, intimidation, and contempt, with land sales or purchases consistently providing a venue for heightened affect. Thus in 1624, when Ingram sought to win for himself a grant out of lands in the possession of the Prince of Wales, he turned to Thomas Wentworth (later Earl of Strafford) for help. Anthony F. Upton, Ingram's biographer, writes that an "operation of this kind was only possible if there was complete mutual trust between Ingram and Wentworth." He then quotes from a letter Wentworth wrote to Ingram in which the former professes "how plain I am with you, but I doubt not but you will rightly interpret me, the inwardness of friendship betwixt you and me assuring me that it can admit no bad one."[22] In 1635, when asked by Archbishop Laud for his opinion of Ingram, Wentworth wrote in response a letter of reference Lord Lovell might have written for Overreach:

I know well his avarice is sordid howbeit his wealth prodigious: of an insolent vainglorious nature, no honesty or rule to be had further than stands with his own gain, which is far nearer to him than any obligation or conscience: a man of no virtue or ability, take him out of the tract of making of bargains and broking in business which he ever defiles and sullies in the handling. (*AI*, 51)

The same Wentworth who needled Ingram for his failure to "hazard one night ill-lodging with your friend"; who relied on Ingram to help negotiate a new farm of the Irish customs and later, the grant of the alum farm; who got the farm of the recusancy fines in the North of England through Ingram's intervention, and then deputed its administration to Ingram; who, in sum, depended on Ingram as "a kind of steward, solicitor, and banker" (*AI*, 153 and 213–16) and in turn used his own great power to requite Ingram for these services, this same Wentworth was prepared to drop his "loving, kind, true friend" Ingram when the client/broker brought his patron's credit into question (*AI*, 225). But whether Wentworth's break with Ingram was due to the latter's having cut into the former's profits in recusancy fines, or as Wentworth would have it, due to Ingram's having impugned Wentworth's "integrity, or ability" (*AI*, 227; Wentworth to Ingram) by suggesting to the Lord Treasurer that Sir Edward Osborne, Wentworth's supervisor of the collection of fines, was dishonest, it is impossible to say. Tom Alworth profits from the Overreach estate even as he helps to crush its proprietor. High-minded, self-righteous Wentworth pulls the carpet out from under Ingram even as he continues to enjoy the fruits of the nasty farm of the recusancy fines which Ingram helped him cultivate in the first place. There is no doubt much that speaks ill of Ingram; but anyone familiar with *A New Way* will not be surprised to find that the very same hatred expressed in the gentry response to the creditor Overreach surfaces in what Upton describes as "the withering contempt" of Wentworth's dismissal of Ingram: "I can highly scorn to enjoy a much better profit . . . rather than to borrow it from your good nature (forsooth) and gentleness" (*AI*, 228). Of course, Wentworth has his gentleness and his profit too.

Most of the energies of men like Ingram and Cranfield were devoted to court business, whether brokering farms, arranging land purchases, lending money, or securing lucrative contracts for courtiers, for city syndicates, for one another or for themselves.[23] Each such activity stimulated appetites and quickened emotions. Mortgage transactions, though but a small part of this sprawling economy which I will take up shortly, nonetheless represent a particularly emotionally charged component. It could hardly have been otherwise when a single financial arrangement brought two crucial markers of early modern English identity – land and credit – into such precarious proximity. When a man like Cranfield was flying high, he could write to Ingram,

no reckoning ever [shall] breathe any discontent between you and me . . . if God preserve me in my right will. One rule I desire may be observed between you and me, which is that neither of us seek to advance our estates by the other's loss, but that we may join together faithfully to raise our fortunes by such casualties [debts and forfeitures] as this stirring age shall afford.[24]

When, after his impeachment, Cranfield was himself furiously struggling to pay his fine and satisfy his creditors, he did everything he could to avoid mortgaging or selling land and to maintain face as a peer. Still, he was forced to sell his estate at Ebury in 1626, to mortgage Shering in 1627 (and so lose £313 in annual income to cover a debt of £800), and to mortgage Pishobury in 1634. With debts as high as £13,850 and often hovering at £8–9,000 in the late 1620s, Cranfield, though just before his fall flourishing with an income of over £25,000, came to know the humiliations of forced mortgages and the embarrassments of land sales (C, 477–97 and 420). The predatory mortgagee might turn vulnerable mortgagor; the powerful office-holder might turn "bored, ill, and cantankerous . . . always trying to make economies, watching the bills, harrying his stewards, counting sheep, calculating rents" (C, 545). Though far from poverty or ruin, Cranfield's income of £5,000 a year after 1635 represented a very great falling off, perhaps less than a fifth of what he once could count on.[25]

Cranfield's aspirations suggest why it makes only limited sense to conceptualize early modern English socio-eonomic tensions in terms of land versus wealth, aristocracy versus new men, or virtue versus profit. Such schema certainly were brought to bear against men like Cranfield and Ingram. Suffolk was prepared to accept an Ingram or a Cranfield as a client, but when confronted with the prospect of Cranfield as his under-treasurer, balked at being "matcht and yoked with a prentise of London."[26] John Chamberlain thought that Cranfield was out of his "owne element" at Court and that for Ingram to agree to serve as Cofferer of the Royal Household was for him to set himself up for "publike obloquie and disgrace."[27] However, Ingram fought tenaciously to maintain his position at Court and Cranfield could ingenuously set out to serve the state by reforming the Crown's finances, cleaning up corruption and reining in the King's bounty, even as he expected to profit handsomely from reform. Though city bred, he did everything he could to preserve his earldom and the state proper to it. Cranfield the hard creditor, ever prepared to foreclose or renegotiate to his own advantage, spent more than half of his life acquiring land or fighting to hold onto it. A fantastic bogeyman like Overreach can appear to have no terrors of his own, being "frighted" merely "as rocks are / When foamie billowes split themselves against / Their flinty ribbes" (4.1.111; 113–15). Cranfield, however, did not merely inspire contempt – he felt it as well. When Cranfield (then Middlesex) informed Prince Charles that his marriage plans ought to depend solely on the "good and honour of the kingdom," the Prince is reported to have replied that Cranfield should "judge of his merchandizes, if he would, for he was no arbiter in points of honour" (*C*, 426).[28] Needless to say, Cranfield was judging of his merchandises. Viewing foreign policy through the lense of domestic finance, he had been counting on the Infanta's dowry to help balance the royal books. There was no easy way to be of the court and its auditor – its profit-taking auditor – too. Even James understood that any man who sets out to reform the household and curb the king's bounty must make enemies. "[A]ll Treasurers," the King told the Lords just two days before the impeachment commenced, "if they do good Service to their Master, must be generally hated" (*C*, 448).[29] Although tepid, this may be understood to have been the royal defense of Cranfield's concern for the "good and honour of the kingdom" and an explanation for the hatred such service provoked. If his enemies held him in contempt, it was not for his opportunism, self-righteousness, or grasping, so much as it was for the way these traits got in the way of their own gain.[30]

Unlike Cranfield, Ingram never operated at the highest echelons of Court. Yet he too must be understood as a "contact man" (*AI*, 8) and not in terms of an imagined ideological antagonism between aristocrats and proto-capitalists. As Upton has written, "Ingram's fortune was grounded on the opportunities which government service, and the good offices of his patrons opened up for him." His "success was to be his ability to bring together the courtiers, who had grants to exploit, and the business-men who had the capital to exploit them" (*AI*, 5 and 8). His career was a testament to the interdependencies of landed and mercantile interests and to the animosity which such confederations might provoke. As often as not, Ingram was pitting mercantile syndicate against mercantile syndicate on, say, Cecil's or Cranfield's behalf. Or he was out-maneuvering another contact man or his patron on behalf of his own benefactor, thereby managing intra-aristocratic competition. If he profited from exploiting customs farms, he was able to do so only within the larger context of administering them on behalf of profit-seeking courtiers. If he profited from the sale of Crown lands, he did so in the course of negotiating contracts instigated by a king desperate to reduce his debt. Much the same might be said of the mortgages he bought up – these were often advances paid out to landowners trying to clear themselves of other

debts. Like Cranfield, Ingram was despised as much for the aristocratic
desire that he underscored by servicing as for his sharp practice, his city
origins, his astonishing sanctimoniousness, and what Tawney calls his
"shameless exhibition of appetites." There can be no doubt that Ingram
"knew the way to aristocratic hearts," and pockets too. But Tawney, as
he almost concedes, resorts to caricature when he proposes that men like
Ingram were "predatory animal[s]," "capitalists," "professionals"
duping "amateurs" who were mere "aristocratic statesmen . . . at sea."
Collaboration, not predation, better describes the relations between men
like Cecil or the Howards and men like Ingram and Cranfield. The
former were perfectly willing to open both their hearts and their pockets
to the latter.[31]

It is also a mistake to imagine that a man like Ingram was always in
control. Upton writes that "Ingram lived from day to day and month to
month" (*AI*, 183). His papers reveal that at one point he was involved in
twenty-one lawsuits simultaneously (*AI*, 205). A combination of sharp
practice and patience at law must have brought Ingram considerable
profit, but at considerable cost. Moreover, Ingram was probably borrowing as often as he was lending. He mortgaged property, raised cash on
royal letters patent, borrowed on short terms, and often – intentionally –
let debts stand, their interest unpaid. Appeals to Cranfield for what must
seem, in the context of Ingram's overall wealth, paltry sums typically
suggest urgency and Ingram's precarious liquidity. The clock is always
ticking. On 15 December 1605 he writes,

I was loth to trouble you, in regard I made bold unto you so lately, but my
present urgent occasion makes me so bold as to entreat you to lend me 100*l*., the
which concerns me to have ready by to-morrow eight of the clock . . . If you have
it not ready, if you call Mr. Cullimore to come along with you, he will do it of
money at my house of the which I dare be no further bold.

Three weeks later, Ingram "kindly salute[s]" Cranfield, "being sorry that
my occasions be such as that I am enforced to be over-troublesome with
my friends. Many I desire not to be beholden to, and to those I do
specially make choice of I will make as near as I can full requital. The
effect of what I write for is for 100*l*. . . . I must entreat your favour, as it
may be sent by noon." Three weeks later, Ingram is again writing to
Cranfield, for a mere £50.[32] Much of the capital Ingram put to use was
borrowed at a rate of 10 percent. Anything less than a healthy profit
from his speculations and transactions would have impaired his own
ability to borrow. At various moments, we can hear Ingram weighing his
credit, his reputation, and his wealth, worrying the value of one or the
other, of one at the expense of the other. Thus in the midst of his one real

financial crisis, when he seems to have gotten caught short while speculating in Crown lands with borrowed money, Ingram appears to panic. Writing to Cranfield, he laments,

[m]y poor reputation is at stake and I protest before God I know not how to help myself but by your good means. Now when I should pass all things in such sort as might every way stand with my reputation and credit and settle myself in quiet, now I am in present danger utterly to overthrow my credit. (*CP*, 251; cf. *AI*, 36)

Because he goes on to assure Cranfield that he is certain that very shortly he will have "good means come in," solvency seems to be his predominant concern. But there is no easy way here to separate solvency from reputation. In the event, the Court stepped forward to guarantee Ingram's reputation and the City stood surety for his debts (inviting creditors to make their claims and receive full payment at Ingram's house in Fanshawe Street). As Chamberlain reported, with more than a touch of disappointment, "Ingrams credit was repayred the last weeke by bills set up in the exchaunge, and shewed in Poules, subscribed by three or fowre principall counsaillors, with ther addition of esquire, and this attestation that they held him for an understanding officer, a goode cittisen, and an honest man."[33] Mere self-interest prompted these principal councillors – the Lord Chancellor, the Lord Treasurer, and the Lord Privy Seal – to close ranks with urban financiers in defense of Ingram.

Often it is difficult to ascertain which variety of credit – monetary or a less tangible sort – Ingram was preoccupied with. At the height of his credit crisis, Ingram indicated his readiness to defend his credit/honor: "I ride this afternoon . . . I will wear no other weapon but my rapier and dagger" (*AI*, 36). While this may indicate an intention to duel, it is nevertheless part of a note that was never sent to an enemy. Rather, it was included with another letter to Cranfield and so may have been intended, as Upton speculates, "to play upon the anxiety of Cranfield and his friends to avoid any open scandals . . . and induce them to prop up his credit" (*AI*, 36). As is the case with Overreach's brandished sword, which Martin Butler reads as evidence of Sir Giles's aristocratic deportment, it is difficult to say whether Ingram and Overreach were committed to defending their honor or were engaged in posturing – miming aristocratic investment in reputation.[34] In 1625 Ingram had to contend with the aftershocks of Cranfield's fall; the loss of what little favor he may still have had with Buckingham, not to mention the new King; the loss of his seat on the Council of the North; and, importantly, his having been thrown out of what looked like and subsequently proved to be an extemely profitable venture – the alum farm. In this instance, Ingram made his priorities somewhat more clear: "I would this [loss of his seat on the Council] had been all that had fallen unto me, for then it had *only* touched me in point of reputation, which, I confesse, is dear and precious unto me, but that which I have suffered in the alum business hath given a *great*[er?] wound to my poor estate and fortune" (*AI*, 103; my emphasis). Upton unsentimentally concludes that "while Ingram's reputation and prestige were dear to him, his money mattered more, and if driven to a choice between the two, he would choose money" (*AI*, 104).

Still, any calculation of a ratio of prestige to profit is difficult, and this is very much the case for a man like Ingram, or a character like Overreach. Higher place could, after all, mean greater profit. Is Overreach's single-minded commitment to his daughter's honor motivated by a desire to secure for himself a reputation he covets but knows he can never achieve, or does it represent the only thing his ruination of the country can buy?[35] Overreach's willingness to endure "complaints / Breath'd out in bitternesse . . . Widdowes cries, / And undon Orphants . . . teares" (4.1.121–27), if this will unite his daugher with Lovell, suggests that he desires prestige, if after a perverse fashion, every bit as much as money. Ingram's Cofferer affair suggests something similar about credit, shame, and profit.[36] The ostensible basis for the Howard–Carr sponsorship of Ingram for this post in 1615 was that the latter, purportedly well-equipped to ferret out what Bishop Goodman would later call "the cunning craft of the cozening merchant" (*AI*, 70), could supervise the fiscal reform of the royal household. That profit and the opportunity to confer favors were legitimate perquisites, no one ever doubted. Nor could anyone have doubted that the promotion of a man like Ingram would escape energetic opposition. For not only was he deemed an upstart (whose advancement would contravene the King's own recent promise to observe rules of seniority), but he was bound to upset the profit-making arrangements already in place. Protests were lodged with King James as soon as word of Ingram's installation leaked out. According to Chamberlain,

all the officers in court even to the blacke garde seemed to take yt to hart, that such an indignitie shold be offered, and such a scandalous fellow set over them as they paint him out to be. Wherupon the green-cloth and some others pressed to the King and had audience, where they behaved themselves very boldly or rather malapertly . . . [and] told the King that yt shold have ben lesse grevous to them yf he had sent a warrant to hange them at the court-gate then he shold dishonor himself and go from his hand and word. The King gave them goode wordes and gracious, assuring them that he did not remember what had passed, but that all shold be redressed . . . They got the Quene likewise and the Prince on theyre side who told his father that there was discontentment enough otherwise . . . but for all this he [Ingram] was established in his place . . . so that I am of opinion that for all this contradiction he will not be so easilie removed as most men ymagin . . .[37]

Here it is important to note that while Somerset backed off in the face of this protest, not only Ingram, but the Howards, too, held the line (Chamberlain writes that Ingram was "loth to dislodge, or leave his hold" – I.590). There must surely have been some very fine calculations as to potential monetary profits and loss of reputation, since even after the officers of the household *and the King* had worked out a plan for Ingram's quiet removal from office and reimbursement, he was keeping his table and furnishing his lodgings at Court.

When Ingram forced the issue and sent for his diet, according to Chamberlain, officers of the household refused him. Ingram complained and King James allowed that he "deserved better of him then to be sent away utterly discountenanced" (Chamberlain, I.590). Although Chamberlain thought that opportunities to leave town either on business (the alum works) or for pleasure (a German spa) had been provided for Ingram, it appears that he was in fact operating as Cofferer for several months in mid-1615. It was thus months before Chamberlain was able to report that the King had "quite cashiered Sir Arthur Ingram out of the court, where he was so well backed that he kept his hold, and with much ado was put out of possession" (I.606). No wonder Chamberlain wrote to Carleton that

yf this busines of Ingrams had not ben I know not how we shold have entertained ourselfes, for this whole moneth together yt hath filled both court and citie, with dayly newes and discourse . . . Ingram himself is anatomised in every part, and so canvassed too and fro, that he had ben a hundred times better to have ben without this new honor. (I.590; cf. *AI*, 76)

It is reasonable to imagine that the Howards would have been the subject of comparable scrutiny, even amusement. Upton notes that according to Anthony Weldon, at least, Ingram's "setback marked the beginning of the downfall of . . . Somerset, and the whole Howard influence. He claimed that the king had welcomed the opportunity of administering a check to that influence, and had incited the household officers in the course which they adopted" (*AI*, 77). While neither Bishop Goodman nor Chamberlain takes this line, it is fair to say that credit was expended in this affair and that Ingram, for one, was bruised. At the time, he could hardly have been thankful that he had escaped the far more grievous wounds that Cranfield, who did successfully get himself installed in high court offices, was to suffer. Ingram's Overreach-like tenacity met head on with status-based resistance such as Lord Lovell might have organized. But Ingram's defeat was only temporary: unlike the Nottinghamshire gentry who imagine themselves capable of supplying their own riotous waste, the Howards recognized that they, if not the King, could ill afford to cashier Ingram. He was actively servicing their financial desires right up till the moment of their disgrace in 1618.

III

Such service regularly took the form of loans and mortgages. In one instance, in late 1608, Ingram plays the part of the good cop, Cranfield the bad. In a letter to Ingram, which Ingram enclosed with his own letter to Cranfield on 5 December, Lord William Howard evinces what by now ought to be a familiar concern with word and bond, reputation and finances. Howard writes:

Because I borrowed 70*l.* of Mr. Cranfield upon my word, which I esteem more than any bond, and have not as yet paid it at the time which I promised . . . I have thought to write unto you earnestly to pray that you will make my excuse unto Mr. Cranfield for my not payment of it . . . I have thought good also to desire you to mind this unto him that whereas Mr. Trevor hath of late bought the one half of the last mortgage of 300*l. per annum* and gave for it 600*l.*, and that the other half remaineth to be redeemed by myself in January next, because I have ever found Mr. Cranfield to deal kindly with me, I have thought good to offer unto him by you that if it please him to let me have 30*l.* now which will make my debt 100*l.*, either that he shall have his 100*l.* before Christmas next, or else if he and I can agree for the mortgage, I had rather he should have that than a stranger
    (*CP*, 175)

In his own accompanying letter to Cranfield, Ingram professes that he "could be very well content my lord would be his own messenger himself, for I know these things be no way pleasing to you" (*CP*, 174). Lord William and Ingram are equally, if differently, unhappy to find themselves dealing with Cranfield. The Lord Admiral's impecunious son uses Ingram as a buffer. Ingram then blames his aristocratic patron for the nuisance he now causes Cranfield. If this epistolary flurry generates in the end a mere £30, none of them could have but loathed the expenditure of time and tact for so little profit. It was no less awful to have to turn to Cranfield when the threat of forfeiture hung over Lord William's head. In 1612, he wrote directly to his creditor, acknowledging that he was going to have to "try" their "friendship." £550 is due Cranfield in nine days; most of this consists of a mortgage taken out on Howard's Donington castle and park. Lord William at first writes that he is prepared to sell land worth more than £1,400 at a £200 loss, rather than forfeit Donington. A moment later, however, he is suggesting that Cranfield "make up the 550*l.* which is due unto you . . . to be 1000*l.* for 5 months longer, for the which you shall have for your security the same which you have already of Donington and that of Barstable . . ." (*CP*,

262). Two days later, Howard has been forced to sell Donington. Whatever "friendship" there was between the two men was tried and found wanting. Still, neither of them would let this particular rub terminate their relationship. Just over a month later, Lord William was again writing to Cranfield, was again acknowledging his indebtedness, and again proposing a scheme for repayment and then further indebtedness (see *CP*, 267).

In his transactions with Peter Frobisher (the explorer's nephew), Cranfield resembles the Overreach who was eager to supply Welborne, even to deal with him after he has been "lodg[ed] . . . / Into the Counter" (3.2.47–48).[38] In 1609, Cranfield's agents in Yorkshire alert him to the possibility of acquiring Altofts, the Frobisher manor in Yorkshire which adjoined an estate Cranfield had just purchased at a bargain price from yet another impecunious gentleman. Hume Burdett writes to Cranfield that he can find Frobisher "at the sign of 'The Reindeer.' I pray you send for him and if you bid him to dinner and supper often and a pipe of tobacco you may prevail much." For "it [the manor of Altofts] is a thing that he knoweth not what is" (*CP*, 192). At the same time, Ralph Sorocold advises Cranfield that if Frobisher "but pawn it [Altofts] to you, take it, for that will make such work with him for ever" (*CP*, 193). He also notes that there already exists a mortgage on the property to the tune of £1,200 and that Cranfield should keep in reserve that much to stay clear of the mortgagee. Cranfield's local informants keep him posted as to his competition – there are others who would like to get their hands on the Frobisher estate – and they mention that they have hired a "cunning workman" of their own in order to estimate the value of the Frobisher coal mines: "but let not Mr. Frobisher know but that you hold it [the mines] a thing of little value. Yet it is a good thing . . ." (*CP*, 194; also *C*, 77). Cranfield purchased Frobisher Hall in 1610; but Peter Frobisher made quick work of the proceeds and was soon using what remained of his property as security for loans from Cranfield, then selling piecemeal one portion after another.

Frobisher sounds consistently desperate – though he never seems to bottom out. In March 1610 he writes to Cranfield, "[A]s ever you do respect a gentleman, as ever you would have any to respect you or yours hereafter, in this cause relieve me, for my cause is lamentable without measure" (*CP*, 195). The cause in this instance is £60 that Frobisher owes one Mary Masterson. But what Frobisher has in mind is not so much that Cranfield bail him out, as that he avouch to Masterson's people "that there is another statute [bond] before theirs of 1000*l*. which is already extended, so that if I go to the prison, she is like to have nothing at all . . . I pray you help me both your words, your counsel and your purse" (*CP*, 196). In June, Frobisher says he is now "going to the Counter." He tells Cranfield that he will agree to sell off his property at whatever prices Cranfield "will in conscience give to the value of the same" (*CP*, 198). From the Wood Street Counter in 1611, Frobisher writes, "I pray you as ever you tender or can pity a gentleman, let me be delayed no longer, for if I should be four days more here, I shall die with the cruel and noisome stenches in this prison." According to Frobisher, £70 will get him discharged. "For God's cause fail me not," he begs Cranfield, "for you have good security for your money and my word is and shall be ever as good and better . . ." (*CP*, 200). Three days later, still in the Counter, Frobisher writes, "[f]or God's love help me out of this miserable and hateful prison of the Counter. You did trust me upon my word for 1400*l*. and I made you the security you desired with better. Therefore, I pray you, let me have 80*l*" (*CP*, 201). In 1612, Frobisher is reduced to asking Cranfield for £5, "if ever your heart could have remorse" (*CP*, 202). But it is worth noting that for all that Frobisher was in and out of prison, and imploring Cranfield for £20, £10, or £5, even 40 shillings, he was no mere pauper. Like Welborne, who can work his connections with Lady Alworth and Lord Lovell to his own advantage, the same Frobisher whom Menna Prestwich describes as "uttering the anguished cries of the ruined gentleman" (*C*, 77) was able to secure a place for himself with the King at Royston and thereby obtain "his Majesty's reference in my suit" (*CP*, 202). It was to cover his Royston expenses that Frobisher was asking Cranfield for 40s.

Although he paid just over £2,000 for Altofts, Cranfield valued it at some 50 percent more. In short order, Cranfield's tenant, Hume Burdett, was improving the estate on his landlord's behalf. Rents were raised, new tenants were fined, ditches were being dug, coal mined – and "inhabitants" grew testy (over rents, common rights, killing deer, and taking wood). Cranfield got the best of Frobisher, but making his new estate profitable was to prove perhaps more difficult than extracting repayments from Peter. Overreach boasts of driving people off their land, but we never see Sir Giles the estate manager. On the back of one of Cranfield's notes written shortly after he has taken possession of Altofts, we read: "Innovations are *Conceptu laeta Tractatu difficilia Eventu tristia*" (*C*, 78). In time, Altofts would pass into the hands of none other than Arthur Ingram, despite the fact that this small portion of a much larger land deal may have been included only because Cranfield fraudulently overvalued rents at Altofts (and adjoining Wakefield) by more than a third. Meanwhile Frobisher, although he was consistently at Cranfield's mercy, continued to come back to him again and again, even as late as 1618. It may be that at the outset bait had been set and

Frobisher hooked. However, every time the fish was thrown back into the water, it rose up for one more bite. Or, in a different register, "[i]f it were not for need of some present money I could come to your house, and stay like a porter in the hall twenty days more, for patience is a virtue" (Frobisher to Cranfield, 28 June 1612; in *CP*, 267).

The above-mentioned land swap between Cranfield and Ingram, first talked about in 1622 and finally settled in 1624, sheds light on the dealings of both men with improvident gentlemen like Sir Edward Greville, and with one another. All three were for years closely bound up with one another – whether in their desire for land, for cash, or for credit – and each man deeply distrusted, even despised, the others. Cranfield's holdings at Altofts were attractive to Ingram because they complemented his already extensive Yorkshire properties. The most attractive asset that Ingram could make over to Cranfield was the estates of Sir Edward Greville. As far back as 1607 Greville, a Warwickshire gentleman and the younger son of Ludovick (the father was a convicted murderer, the son accidentally killed his older brother when playing at long-bow), had entered into several business arrangements with Ingram and Cranfield. The three men were part of a syndicate formed to speculate in rectory lands. Soon thereafter they came up with a scheme to make starch from bran. They chartered a monopoly company (the Starchmakers of the City of London), secured protective tariffs on imported starch, and succeeded in having issued a proclamation forbidding the making of starch from edible grain. This venture, like so many others satirized by playwrights like Ben Jonson, was a complete failure.[39] By 1610, Greville had lost £900 and was stuck with sixty unsaleable barrels of starch (*C*, 70). He was also in debt to Cranfield and Ingram (*CP*, 156–57).[40]

In 1615, Ingram and Greville came up with a new way to settle Greville's old debts – debts to Cranfield and to others, the "major share" of which, however, had fallen into Ingram's hands (*AI*, 157). Greville's daughter Mary would become Ingram's third wife. In return for this favorable marriage into a Warwickshire gentry family, Ingram would effectively float a mortgage on the Greville estates. He would come up with £21,000, partly to pay off Sir Edward's debts, partly to settle on his new wife, and partly to allow Greville an annuity of £900 chargeable on the estates at Milcote. Upon the death of Sir Edward and Lady Greville, the estates were to become Ingram's. Here was a low-cost way to support Greville's riotous waste. Indeed, that cost was soon spiraling downward, to the point where borrowing against his annuity in combination with ancillary debts drove Greville's annual payment to as low as £100 to £200 per annum. When Greville was not trading on his annuity, he was handing over additional parcels of his estate to satisfy Ingram. At the time of the land exchange with Cranfield, when Greville was drawing an income from his family estates well below what they might have generated, Ingram valued the property at almost £3,000 a year (*AI*, 157–58). Still, Greville should not be underestimated or imagined as merely the financiers' victim. Thomas Catchmay, Cranfield's agent at Milcote after Cranfield had taken over the payment of Greville's annuity, deemed Greville "full of imagination and invention" but "void both of religion and moral honesty" (*C*, 402). Greville could not help but despise the likes of Ingram and Cranfield, to whom he kept indebting himself even as they made up his debts and further tightened his leash. And Cranfield, who as late as 1631 was complaining of his "hard bargain over Sir Edward Greville," could only have held his testy pensioner in contempt (*C*, 404). But this was not simply a case of collusion on the part of moneymen at the expense of a reckless gentleman. While Ingram may have been out to get the better of his father-in-law, the numerous recriminations passed back and forth between Cranfield and Ingram in the course of haggling over the swap indicate that each creditor was fully prepared to gouge the other. Even as Cranfield was leaving to defend himself at his impeachment hearings in the House of Lords, Ingram appeared at Chelsea House armed with a bond for £1,000, an unpleasant bit of blackmail that Cranfield recollected was "ready prepared for me to seal, affirming it was the just sum I owed him remaining upon the exchange of the land" (*C*, 406). The portion of the deal pertinent merely to the Greville lands saw Ingram failing to clear prior claims on the manor at Weston-on-Avon. Cranfield had budgeted £1,000 for this encumbrance, but the claimants – the Shirley family – were still awaiting payment in 1625. Cranfield first began to complain of "the shortness of the valuing" of the Greville lands in 1623; he was still insisting that their worth had been overestimated by more than £6,000 in 1631 (*AI*, 158–59; *C*, 406–07 and 409). Cranfield's biographer writes that "[e]ach knew the other too well to trust him fully" (*C*, 403).[41]

Not long after the Greville estates were under his control, Cranfield set to work to remove Sir Edward from Milcote. The latter agreed to take up residence at Cranfield's house in Pishobury, but this was to cost him £500 a year from his annuity. In short order, Greville was in debt to Cranfield as he had been in debt to Ingram (and before that to Cranfield) and so further abridged his annuity. This is in turn occasioned his removal in 1631 to a less grand house in Fulham (and made it possible for Cranfield, who as has been noted was himself in need of cash, to mortgage Pishobury). But at every step along the way, Greville dragged his feet, resisted Catchmay's improvements, and made himself a miserable thorn in Cranfield's side. Greville had been a wretched landlord who countenanced deceit on the part of everyone from his bailiff to his shepherd's son; now, while pretending to help patch up differences between his son-in-law and Cranfield, he did his best to insinuate that Ingram had indeed cheated Cranfield insofar as the Warwickshire properties were concerned. Amazingly, as late as 1632, there was still talk of trust and credit. When Cranfield sold Greville's annuity to George Lowe, the latter wrote that Greville was "much discontented with the strictness of the reckoning which your lordship doth hold him unto and the little trust and credit that you give him in anything" (*C*, 534).

Watching her father foam and bite the earth (5.1.375–76), Margaret Overreach reacts with pained concern. Tom Alworth, Overreach's new son-in-law, counsels patience on her part. Upton does not record Mary Ingram's response to her husband's dealings with her father, Sir Arthur's father-in-law (and I have not consulted the Ingram Papers in Leeds). Upton does, however, make clear his own response: "Sir Edward was squeezed dry, and then cast aside when there was nothing left" (*AI*, 158). It might be imagined that Mary Greville, like Margaret Overreach, was no more than an instrument taken to hand to facilitate the designs of Arthur Ingram. But even as we see Margaret Overreach doing what is in her power to do to marry Alworth, Upton is constrained to note "that personal compatibility [between Ingram and Mary Greville] was a condition of the conclusion of the bargain" Ingram made with Greville (*AI*, 73). Furthermore, there is no mention of Mary Ingram coming to her father's widow's (her mother's?) aid when, shortly before her death, she pawned her household effects for £27 (*AI*, 158). There is, however, a note in 1642 from Mary Ingram to Cranfield in which the former explains that her husband has died, but that her purpose in writing is to see to it that Cranfield pays a rent in Yorkshire "now due to me from you" (*C*, 537). We might also join Upton in imagining that Greville was merely a sponge, incapable of resistance, little more than a dupe. However, on this score too, we do well to keep in mind Massinger's play: while they certainly are squeezed, neither Alworth nor Welborne proves incapable of serving his own interests in his dealings with Overreach. And while Greville never turned the tables on Ingram or Cranfield, neither did he roll over.[42] As we have seen, he was able to mortgage what was left of his annuity and so still must have represented a plausible "investment" for an experienced creditor like George Lowe as late as 1632, two years before Greville's death. Intricately and persistently intertwined with one another, the Ingrams, the Cranfields, and the Grevilles, like the Alworths, the Welbornes, and the Overreaches, depended upon one another for credit and for profit. But their propinquity undermined affection and proved an incitement to unexpectedly acute resentment. Greville's class-inflected discontent at being afforded "little trust and credit" by a parvenu like Cranfield (then Earl of Middlesex) betrays much the same rage and self-pity as does a note in Cranfield's hand at the bottom of an Ingram letter demanding money as a result of disputes already more than a quarter of a century old: "Sir Arthur Ingram most unjust and unreasonable" (C, 536).

IV

The imbrication of affective and property relations among Sir Edward Greville, Mary Ingram, and Sir Arthur Ingram commences with a mortgage. Another, still more ingrown triangulation occurs in Shakespeare's Sonnet 134, which not only includes the unique mortgage in the Shakespeare canon, but turns as well upon forfeiture, surety, statute, bond, and use.

> So now I have confessed that he is thine,
> And I myself am mortgaged to thy will,
> Myself I'll forfeit, so that other mine
> Thou wilt restore to be my comfort still.
> But thou wilt not, nor he will not be free,
> For thou art covetous, and he is kind;
> He learned but surety like to write for me,
> Under that bond that him as fast doth bind.
> The statute of thy beauty thou wilt take,
> Thou usurer that put'st forth all to use,
> And sue a friend came debtor for my sake;
> So him I lose through my unkind abuse.
>   Him have I lost; thou hast both him and me;
>   He pays the whole; and yet am I not free.[43]

As is the case with Welborne's and Alworth's credit relations with Sir Giles and Margaret Overreach, there can be no easy distinction of necessity from desire from contempt in this sonnet. Having acknowledged that he has mortgaged himself to the lady, the speaker is loathe further to confess what he has for his mortgage: the use, or abuse, of her will (*pace* Booth, *her* wishes, lust, and willfulness, but perhaps also her *will*, her William – the speaker's friend). As long as she has him (the self he has mortgaged to her), he must have something of hers – else why the mortgage in the first place? The suppression of the *quid pro quo* intrinsic to any mortgage reinforces the speaker's ability to cast the lady in the role of the hard-hearted, cruel and covetous creditor. She sues; like a usurer, she enforces her statute.[44] Her will is satisfied while his comfortless heart groans (133.1). Just what she, the mortgagee, has gotten from him, the mortgagor, is also temporarily obscured. For although the speaker says she has him ("I myself am mortgaged to thy will"), she does not seem to have even this much, or to want it either. What has become hers, for having credited the speaker with her will, is the young man.

If, according to the metaphysics of the sonnets, the speaker and the young man are one ("I love thee in such sort / As thou being mine, mine is thy good report" – 96.13–14; "Think all but one" – 135.14), then the sonnet progressively reveals in its narrative sequence what we should have suspected from the start. The "myself" that the lady holds as security for the mortgage is the speaker's "next self" (133.6), that is, his "other mine," the "friend came debtor for my sake."[45] The mortgage is profitable for the lady because of the use to which she can put the speaker's security. By means of this mortgage, both the mortgagor and the mortgagee aim to put forth to use the young man ("the comfort still") who secures their bond. Such usage follows darkly from the speaker's conviction that the friend's "sweet love . . . such wealth brings" (29.13); it exemplifies both her covetousness and the speaker's "unkind abuse." She deals with the speaker to "bind" his friend to herself and the speaker uses his friend to secure his mortgage to the will of the lady. No wonder she "wilt not" accept a forfeiture on the speaker's terms. Were he entitled to avail himself of the equity of redemption, he (on his own initiative) would be able to "restore" to himself his friend. She, however, would end up with the only thing he truly has or can forfeit: himself, the self mortgaged to her will. It appears that she is either none too interested in this, or, again, that she desires it only because he, like Greville in relation to Ingram, is but a means to the consolidation of her estate in both him *and* his friend: "thou hast both him and me" or "Both find each other, and I lose both twain" (42.11).

Just as the speaker, in his never-ending pursuit of a win–win advantage, would forfeit what he has signed over and yet hold his ground ("thou wilt restore"; at 30.14, "All losses are restored"), so he would both have and use his friend and the lady too. But agency and temporality frustrate the latter desire every bit as relentlessly as economic principles thwart the former. To (ab)use his friend is to guarantee his loss ("he is thine"; "Him have I lost"). When it becomes apparent that he must use himself ("Myself I'll forfeit") – when he sets out, that is, to bargain with his own self and not his "other mine" – he discovers that he not only cannot dislodge his friend (now fast bound), but that his friend, who now "pays the whole," "will not be free." The "kind" friend turns out to be no less entangled in and enraged by this triangle founded upon interest and contempt than the speaker or the lady. Formerly at one with the speaker and now bound to the lady, the friend gives every indication that he has deflected the enmity and use value designated by the speaker for the lady back in the direction of the speaker. "[M]y unkind abuse" must refer, as Booth's predominantly linguistic analysis suggests, to what the speaker occasions as well as to what he suffers. The friendly guarantor has himself become a mortgagor; he turns out effectively to have mortgaged – "surety-like" – the speaker. He has become a "debtor" seemingly with the intention of provoking the lady's suit ("sue a friend": pursue, woo, bring suit against). His kindness cruelly consists of his predisposition to act according to his kind. Spitefully ready to forfeit himself and to pay for the "whole" affair (writing "under" with his pen, he pays the lady's hole), the friend can disguise his advantage as a lose–lose scenario.

Sonnet 134's mortgagor, mortgagee, and the one mortgaged (to the extent that the speaker, friend, or lady occupies any of these positions with any consistency) are all abusurers who make monetary and sexual use of one another. Here, the laws of love and land use are such that all players can, like a Cranfield, a Greville or a Welborne, lament their victimization even as they act on their own behalf and form alliances to the disadvantage of now one and then another among them. Ingram and Cranfield began their relationship pledging themselves "faithfully to raise our fortunes" on the back of their age's "casualties"; but each of them regularly complained that the other was "unjust and unreasonable." "But wherefore says she not she is unjust?" (138.9) asks the same speaker who believes his love "is made of truth" (138.1). Complaint, the note of self-pity, the badge of victimization, and the ensuing hatred, these are all evident in Sonnet 134, in the Cranfield and Ingram records, and in *A New Way to Pay Old Debts*. If Massinger even partially sanctions these sentiments and the evasive self-exculpations that accompany them, Shakespeare the sonneteer comes off as cool, clinical, and detached – precisely as Keats has taught us to expect. We find ourselves confessing that *our* selves are mortgaged to his will, offering ourselves in forfeit, and hoping that he will restore our comfort still.

4   Venture capital

In *The Trumpet o[f] Fame: Or Sir Fraunces Drakes and Sir John Hawkins F[are]well* (London, 1595), Henry Robarts, Devonshire sailor turned London poet and pamphleteer, robustly celebrates the sort of commercial adventure (which would soon be called "privateering") that led in 1595–96 to the disastrous West Indian expedition that cost Drake, Hawkins, and many others their lives:[1]

> You Gallants bold, of *Albions* fertile soyle,
> For Countries fame, on land and seas that toyle,
> Searching with paine, the Confines of the earth,
> Whose painfull toyle, all Nations admireth:
> By whom enriched is your Countries store,
> And some made rich, which earst was held but poore:
> To you brave minds, whose thoughts doth reach the s[kie]
> And scorne at home, like sluggards for to lie:
> To you that fetch more woorth, then *Iasons* fleece,
> To you I do my rustike Pen addresse,
> For Countries honor, that spareth not your blood,
> But ventures all, for Commons publike good . . .   (A3)[2]

Signficantly, Robarts expands his encomium to include John Watts, an exemplary city merchant who financed voyages like Drake's and Hawkins's:

> [B]e not omit, our Merchant of renown:
> [F]or *Londons* honor, where he of worship is,
> [A]n Alderman of credit great I wis,
> [F]amous *Wats*, whose forward readinesse,
> [I]n all attempts was never knowne to misse:
> [W]ho in this fleete to quaile the enemies pride,
> [F]oure gallant ships for warre he doth provide . . .   (B2v)

It is the proximity of a number of terms in a handful of Robarts's lines that attracts me to the otherwise banal, unstinting boosterism of the man Louis Booker Wright described as a "patriotic propagandist." In *The Trumpet o[f] Fame*, toilers scorn sluggards, merchants share credit with

110

gallants, and adventurers venture all for both the public good and for private profit ("The gaine is yours, if millions home you bring" – B3). Again and again, Robarts returns to toil and to hazard – commending the privateer William Grafton, whose "actes are such: / As fewe I knowe will hassard halfe so much" – as if labor and risk alone could justify such "quick returne, and so much store of wealth" (B3).[3]

Just as the law depended upon evidence of risk to distinguish a lawful lender from a usurer, so an adventurer's *bona fide* consisted in his willingness to put himself at "fortune's hazard" in the course of "his travaile on the Seas."[4] Not only the spectacular prize that a golden fleece represented, but venturing itself seems to have required legitimation, if not mystification, in the form of apprehensiveness, sweat, and public benefaction.[5] In this chapter, the evocation of structures of feelings answerable to the hazard and the profit of venturing will occasion a re-examination of *The Merchant of Venice* and a look at Walter Ralegh's role in the capture of the great Portuguese carrack, the *Madre de Dios*, as well as a consideration of *The Alchemist*, at least partly in terms of holding shares in the Children of the Queen's Revels and the King's Men.[6] Whether "painfull toyle" is a mere by-product, or whether it serves as an anticipatory (or an *ex post facto*) testimonial to character and intention, venturing consistently exacts a toll. Ralegh hopes to validate his first venture to Guiana by virtue of his "labour, hunger, heat, sickness, and perill." The "labour" that an empty-handed Ralegh hopes Elizabeth "will yet take . . . in gracious part" was already evident to Robert Cecil four years before, when he noted of Ralegh that "he can toil terribly."[7] In Shakespeare's Venice Antonio, the merchant adventurer, wants to be seen to have been "bated" (3.3.32) and the venturing gallant Bassanio must "hazard all he hath" (2.7.16).[8] The prospect of instant wealth, a fleece or mine either hazarded for or won (but perhaps thought not to have been earned) by gallant and merchant alike, requires compensatory evidence of dexterity, of effort, better still, of strain. Moreover, the destabilizing energy that fuels hazarding generates an off-setting desire for risk management: late-sixteenth-century piratical privateers became legitimate East India Company "committees," or directors; men-of-war were re-outfitted for lawful trade; Face resumes service as Jeremy; and Lovewit takes Dame Pliant as *his* prize.[9]

Adventuring sovereigns, nobles, gentry, merchants, and lesser sorts from mariners to the likes of Subtle were bound together in shared risk-taking and financial obligation. "The magic word," writes Michael Nerlich, "in which the interests of the different classes and strata seemed to converge was 'adventure.' The knightly adventure, the cooperative trade enterprise, the manly deed, the life of employees, of entrepreneurs who no longer went on trade journeys themselves, even the dangerous enterprise and the goods themselves – all went by the same name, adventure." But this convergence of interests "superficially concealed (if at all)" what Nerlich at once recognizes as "class antagonisms" and as "differing motives and . . . different purposes."[10] A commercial adventurer's affiliation with a gentleman willing to hazard all he has garners for the former a certain social cachet – potentially, an even more durable social entitlement.[11] A bold gallant or a plotting rogue in turn depends on the capital, the credit, more generally, on the wherewithal (for instance, Lovewit's Blackfriars house) that derives from a merchant or aristocratic financier.

Affiliation may be more precisely described as manipulation when a courtly adventurer like Ralegh tricks a financier like William Sanderson into returning to him the "Acquittance and Release" Ralegh had given him prior to setting sail for Guiana in 1595. Sanderson had good reason to believe that if either of them owed the other anything, it was Ralegh who was still in debt to Sanderson. But without Ralegh's release in hand (it had been given to Thomas Hariot, ostensibly for safe keeping), Sanderson was later to find himself fighting from a precarious perch – a debtor in the Fleet – with those among Ralegh's friends who had been granted the administration of his estate following his attainder. Suits over financial mismanagement (of some £60,000 for which Ralegh claimed Sanderson never fully accounted), debt and forgery proceeded in Chancery and Star Chamber, but beneath the charges and countercharges lay a dispute over credit and credibility, and protestations of toil. In a memoir written in defense of Sanderson, it was asserted that Sanderson

did mannage his [Ralegh's] affaires all the tyme of his prosperity; And did . . . stand bound for the said Sir Walter Raleigh for more then a hundred Thowsand pounds starling; And also for meere debt more then sixteene thousand pounds at one tyme taken up in London most part thereof at Usury upon his own bond, such was his Credite and Reputation in those dayes . . .

However, John Shelbury replied on Ralegh's behalf that it was Ralegh's good name and connections that attracted capital, that in fact Sanderson falsely "doth arrogate unto himselfe a kinde of credite that . . . Raleighe should be beholdinge unto him for his countenance or credite . . ." We have neither Chancery nor Star Chamber determinations in these cases – judgments may never have been handed down – but Sanderson appears to have been the abused party. Even Shelbury admitted that Sanderson "was [so] careful and provident that he kepte continually five booke of Accompte the one for Receipts and the other for disbursements everie daie settinge downe what was recevied and what disbursed and for what cause and by what warrante . . ." Sanderson himself would insist on his "painfull endeavour" and "great travell" on Ralegh's behalf, at one time or another standing bond with Ralegh, borrowing money at his own risk for Ralegh's use, even investing his own money, to the tune of £50,000 at one point, £30,000 at another. Venturing with Ralegh – which in 1590 entered Sanderson, on Ralegh's behalf, into negotiations (and later litigation) with John Watts over a combined voyage for Roanoke relief and privateering – proved onerous for Sanderson.[12] But of course venturing was no less hazardous for Ralegh himself. While he may have set out on his first voyage to Guiana with a courtier's sense of satisfaction at having just trumped his merchant creditor, when he set sail on his second and final voyage to Guiana it was King James, the creditor of final resort, who stacked the deck in his own favor. Matters were then arranged so that whether Ralegh succeeded or failed, James alone was guaranteed the advantage.[13]

I

The familiar horizon of understanding against which Antonio is customarily placed extends from classical or Christian notions of (self-sacrificing) friendship on one side to his mercantile identity as merchant adventurer or "royal merchant" (3.2.238) on the other. My reading of *The Merchant of Venice* at the beginning of chapter 1 assumes Antonio's generalized mercantile function and focuses on his commitment to extricating himself from it, even if this means death. An equally generalized sense of Antonio as creditor, as opposed to adventurer, underwrites my reading of his relationship with Bassanio. There are, however, grounds for imagining Antonio a good deal more specifically as a *privateering* merchant like Watts, working in concert with (or, like Sanderson, standing surety for) Bassanio, a bold gallant adventurer, "a scholar and a soldier" (1.2.109) like Ralegh. The great Elizabethan privateering merchants were men engaged alternately, or simultaneously, in trade and plunder.[14] We have several warrants for conceiving of the play's chief Venetians in this way, the better known being Bassanio's hope that by "adventuring" in Belmont he can bring as "hazard back again" a "lady richly left . . . like a golden fleece" (1.1.143–70). As Gratiano later boasts: "We are the Jasons, we have won the fleece" (3.2.240). John Russell Brown notes in his Introduction to *The Merchant of Venice* that "Sir Francis Drake returning from his voyage round the world was said to have brought back with him 'his goulden fleece'" (lv). For "fleece," the *OED sb.* 2b. offers, "A share of booty"; *v.* 3., "to plunder, rob." Sir George Carey's 130-ton privateer the *Jason* (alias the *Bark Burr*) was set on fire and "blown up" by a Spanish patrol off Cuba in 1591.[15] Hard on the heels of the play, in 1598, the *John* (also known as the *Jason*), a ship belonging to John Davies, a Londoner whose business was privateering, seized a Bayonne ship bound for Spain.[16] Attempting to date the play, John Russell Brown has suggested a second reason for thinking of Antonio in terms of plunder. Salerio (or Salarino), who first conjures Antonio's argosies "on the flood" (1.1.9–10), goes on to imagine "[w]hat harm a wind too great might do at sea" and to "think of shallows and of flats, / And see my wealthy Andrew dock'd in sand" (1.1.24; 26–27). In this regard, Brown notes that "'Andrew' is in italic type in the quarto" and that the Spanish galleon *St. Andrew* (*San Andrés*) was a prize captured at Cadiz in 1596 (xxvi). Indeed, writes Brown, the *St. Andrew* had not only been captured while run aground but, having been brought back to England, "she nearly ran aground again among the sands and flats of the King's Channel off Chatham" (xxvi).[17] The Lord Admiral, Essex, and Ralegh all failed to seize the outgoing Indies fleet or the incoming treasure fleet at Cadiz, but the *St. Andrew* did fall to them (to Ralegh, in fact), and within a year it would be refitted as a troop carrier to support further privateering during the unhappy Islands voyage of 1597.[18]

Finally, it is difficult to make sense of a late-sixteenth-century Venetian merchant trading in Tripoli, the Indies, Mexico, and England (1.3.16–18), not to mention having ships in Lisbon and Barbary too (3.2.267–68). But it certainly would have been possible in the 1590s, in the heyday of trade combined with plunder, to entertain such "Elizabethan ambitions for London" and its great privateering merchants.[19] Backed by four such merchants, an experienced captain like Christopher Newport could set out in early 1591 on a voyage whose first leg was trade to Barbary, then take prizes in the West Indies in May, only to return to England with hides and sugar worth £500 in August.[20] Salerio's mention of "spices" and "silks" (1.1.33–34) reminds us not only of the centuries-old Venetian import–export trade, but of the luxury commodities sought by English privateers at the precise moment of *The Merchant of Venice*.[21] To conceive of an Antonio who, according to Salerio at least, ought to be concerned about the return of a prize ship like the *Andrew*, or about his far-flung trade and privateering ventures, is to imagine the merchant of Venice according to an altogether different structure of feeling from that which neurotic nostalgia entails. Nonetheless, I think that privateering and the potential for overnight, golden fleece-like prizes pertain in their own, distinctive way to both Antonio's sadness and his penchant for self-displaying self-martyrdom. These are predictably nuanced Shakespearean inflections of Henry Robarts's "painfull toyle." Antonio's melancholic self-surrender epitomizes an affect and ethos that anticipates Portia's declaration, "I stand for sacrifice" (3.2.57): the merchant's and perhaps the heiress's discomfort at once tempers and sanctions the gallant's gain.

Part of our problem evaluating the affective component of Antonio's venturing has to do with its possible affectedness – with what we mean by affectation. If earlier I explained Antonio's sadness in terms of a reactive dismay at what he has become, and a desire to be without desires realizable only in death, I want now to suggest that the merchant of Venice's sadness may also be productive.[22] I take my cue from Gratiano's little-remarked-upon, seemingly unkind words of caution to Antonio: "fish not with this melancholy bait / For this fool gudgeon, this opinion" (1.1.101–02). Gratiano warns against affecting sadness in order to be "reputed wise" (1.1.96). But Shakespeare does not offer Antonio any alternative to playing this particular "part" (1.1.78). What his play can show, whether or not it "knows" it, is that the appearance of a constitutional sadness lends *gravitas* to one who, it is evidently assumed, must be anxious only because he has ships at sea. A defining existential disquiet is considerably more dignified than temporary money trouble. Sadness does the work of much-needed ballast, given the Venetian gallants' effervescence. Antonio's reserve, his caution ("My ventures are not in one bottom trusted" – 1.1.42), and his mysterious sadness contrast markedly with their cocky self-assurance. Their social privilege may disguise his status handicap, yet his temperamental austerity grounds their frivolity.[23] Initially, Antonio's adversity will be confined to his credit ("That shall be rack'd even to the uttermost" – 1.1.181), to a mostly painless torment, though one still more stressful than what Bassanio experiences while he "live[s] upon the rack" (3.2.25).[24] Later, when Bassanio and Gratiano head off to Belmont to "hazard all" and to bring Antonio's "hazard back again" (1.1.151), Antonio's sadness will modulate into a carefully scripted self-martyrdom according to which, *pace* Robarts, you "spareth not your blood."

There is, then, good reason to compare Arragon's and Morocco's postures *vis-à-vis* adventuring not only to Bassanio's – as we customarily do – but also to Antonio's commitment of his "extremest means" (1.1.138; Antonio pledges his "person" well before there is any talk of a pound of flesh). Antonio anticipates and then reconciles himself to distress, not risk. By contrast, Morocco is at first all swagger.[25] His expectation of success is couched in terms of the pain he has inflicted on others ("by this scimitar / That slew . . ." – 2.1.24–25). Even when he tries to imagine himself choosing the wrong casket, it is as Hercules; he will rage, but Lichas will feel the pain. Of course Shakespeare is engineering a set-up, but is it any more of a set-up than Antonio's deportment? One venturer comports himself according to a gauche ethos of success, another, Arragon, according to an overblown sense of desert. The "royal merchant," however, belittles himself as a mere "tainted wether of the flock" (4.1.114). To the extent that we understand Antonio to be in competition with the play's princes – it is Antonio's "means" which enable Bassanio "[t]o hold a rival place" (1.1.173–74) with Morocco and Arragon – the play endorses the merchant's painful toil, not the Moroccan prince's scorn for any "weak disabling of myself" (2.7.30) or Arragon's contempt for the "barbarous multitudes" (2.9.33). The spoils go to the risk-taker, Bassanio, backed crucially insofar as ideology is concerned by one who suffers on his behalf, "one in whom / The ancient Roman honour . . . appears" (3.2.294–95).[26] Neither Morocco nor Arragon has such a partner or such an affidavit.

In relatively neutral economic terms, Antonio accredits Bassanio by standing surety for him. In more emotive terms appropriate to the play's moral economy, Antonio may be said to provide sweat equity. But just as literally from line one he advertises his sadness in a highly public register, and thus intimates its utility, so Antonio takes advantage of every opportunity he has to blazon the ongoing challenge to his stamina. Antonio's artful manipulation of Bassanio's feelings of guilt – what in the first chapter I read as an iteration of Bassanio's monetary indebtedness – may be understood, oxymoronically, to be the fanfare that heralds Antonio's silent suffering. For Bassanio's benefit, prior to his departure for Belmont, there is Antonio's "[s]lubber not business for my sake" (2.8.39). Once at Belmont, there is the letter from Antonio with its announcement that his "estate is very low" (3.2.315). For Solanio there is the self-display of the "bated" Antonio, whose "melancholy bait" has taken its toll: the merchant can "hardly spare a pound of flesh" (3.3.32–33). For the Duke there is Antonio's reassuring insistence that he is "arm'd / To suffer with a quietness of spirit" (4.1.11–12). Then there is the avowal that he is "Meetest for death, – the weakest kind of fruit / Drops earliest to the ground, and so let me" (4.1.115–16). Finally, and again on Bassanio's behalf, Antonio is "arm'd and well prepar'd" (4.1.260). "What we have," René Girard has written, "is a masochistic and theatrical self-pity."[27] Less self-pity, I think, than an exhibition of self-inflicted misery calculated to achieve as much profit as pleasure. What I previously read as an embrace of death, a flight toward interestlessness, may in this context be recognized as tactical, as anything but a retreat. Antonio's sufficiency enables him to stand surety for Bassanio by making "waste of all" (1.1.157) he has for his venturing friend. His distress is Bassanio's ethical surety; and it must be known to be at the root of Bassanio's triumphant quest if the gallant is to avoid the signs of indiscretion or audacity evident in the princes' hazarding. Robarts's already vaguely mystified "painfull toyle" is psychologized in the person of Antonio, whose blood never flows and whose pain is psychosomatic only. Not that it is any less real, less felt, or less efficacious for being located in the mind, as opposed to a limb or pound of flesh. Antonio submits himself to what Bassanio calls a "happy torment" (3.2.27). To the merchant falls the effort and endurance that support the gallant's folktale hazarding and fleecy prize.

In his allegorical reading of *The Merchant of Venice*, Michael Nerlich casts Bassanio as "the representative of the victorious bourgeoisie," victorious in that he "triumphs over fate: subjugates Fortune [Portia]."[28] Given Portia's astonishing control over every event from the moment Bassanio chooses the lead casket until her surprise announcement about Antonio's ships, it makes more sense to say that Portia triumphs over Bassanio, or, at least, that her interests and his are made to coincide. Moreover, it is arguable that relations among Bassanio, Portia, *and* Antonio represent a complex convergence of interests along the lines Kenneth R. Andrews draws when he classifies some privateers as "amateurs" and others as "great merchants."[29] According to this schema, Bassanio would not have been recognizable as anything like what we now denominate as bourgeois. His are the contours of an amateur/gallant whose adventuring derives from what Nerlich identifies as one of the historically important goals of *aventure* – "a good match, a rich marriage" – while his *modus operandi* has a more contemporary source.[30] Andrews's account of what set the amateur privateer in motion bears a striking resemblance to what transpires in *The Merchant of Venice*:

[l]anded gentry who busied themselves in London to the neglect of their estates would soon find their real incomes declining as prices rose. This was a favourable time for money-lenders. In circumstances of this sort there was always a temptation to gamble, and to men fed upon notion of chivalry one form of gambling seemed especially attractive – the sea venture.[31]

The 1590s were cluttered with such bold gamblers, perhaps none more famous than George Clifford, third Earl of Cumberland, whose "first privateering venture in 1586," Andrews writes, "was undoubtedly undertaken in the hope of meeting . . . debts – an extension of his gambling operations to a new and larger sphere."[32] Prior to 1593, Cumberland's privateering ventures were carried out by his own and Queen Elizabeth's ships. But beginning in 1594, and right through to his twelfth and last voyage to Puerto Rico in 1598, Cumberland was in partnership with London's great merchant promoters. From 1595, Thomas Cordell of the Mercers and the Levant Company, and a large-scale shipowner, regularly served as Cumberland's creditor. Cordell and John Watts, among others, invested their money and ventured their own ships in the Puerto Rico expedition.[33]

Bassanio's relationship with the merchant of Venice, his "disabled . . . estate" (1.1.123), his willingness to hazard all, even the "lady richly left" (1.1.161) for whom he ventures, all mark him as one of Andrews's late-Elizabethan amateurs. There remain, of course, differences between Bassanio and Cumberland. For one thing, Shakespeare makes the great Elizabethan courtier's fantasy realizable in *The Merchant of Venice*. Bassanio succeeds in his "quest" (1.1.172) for Portia, in whom prize and wife coincide. Cumberland's mistress, Queen Elizabeth, was unavailable. This particular dedicatee of *The Faerie Queene* had to content himself with tilting as the Queen's champion and venturing on her behalf, her Knight of the Garter in search of Spanish treasure.[34] Then too, the merchants to whom Cumberland turned were at once his partners and his creditors. Shakespeare allots these functions more or less separately to Antonio and Shylock, perhaps, as Walter Cohen has argued, insulating Antonio from the taint of usury.[35] Nonetheless, merchant and usurer are bound and unbound, coupled then uncoupled, and so are the play's merchant and gentleman. In their partnership, Antonio is cast in the unappealing role of the sad toiler, while Bassanio enjoys the glamour and the risk that go with fleece-chasing. Something of Morocco's bravado may surface in Bassanio's belief that the lead casket "rather *threaten'st* than dost promise aught" (3.2.105; my emphasis). Something of Cumberland the tilt champion and privateer may be heard in Bassanio's concern not to wrong Portia by "underprizing" (3.2.128) her, and in his conceit that he is

> Like one of two contending in a prize
> That thinks he hath done well in people's eyes,
> Hearing applause and universal shout,
> Giddy in spirit, still gazing in a doubt . . .   (3.2.141–44)

Something even of Antonio's uneasiness may be audible in Bassanio's fear of failure (which sounds very much like a fear of success): "that ugly treason of mistrust, / Which makes me fear th'enjoying of my love" (3.2.28–29). This Bassanio prefigures Romeo and, more perilously, Othello. Insofar as venturing is concerned, these lines disclose the misgivings that any voyage of plunder could have awakened in a gentleman. Ralegh thought that it "sorted ill with the offices of Honor

... to run from Cape to Cape, and from place to place, for the pillage of ordinarie prizes."[36] Having "lost [at least] one shaft ... by adventuring" (1.1.140–43), Bassanio has good reason to pitch this "quest" (1.1.172) as the big one. In his comic play world, Bassanio prevails. His profit and success rehearse the ongoing drama of late-Elizabethan privateering and what was to prove its long-term payoff.

The passage from Antonio's *status quo ante*, his "fortunes ... at sea" (1.1.177), to the merchant's final disposition, three of his "argosies / ... richly come to harbour" (5.1.276–77), depends on his sufficiency, on Bassanio's hazarding all, and on Portia's golden fleece. Portia is the object or the prize, and she is the solvent. She bails out the venturers. Robarts celebrated an analogous fusion of toil, risk, and prize-taking as he watched Elizabethan traders with Venice and Turkey convert their merchantmen into men-of-war, and invest in their own or gallants' privateering schemes throughout the war against Spain. This in turn facilitated the incorporation of technical and financial gains, the organization of the East India Company, and the development of an array of new trading patterns.[37] As Carole Shammas has suggested, the late Elizabethan marauders' inclination toward quest and conquest, gold and El Dorado, gave way to a Jacobean "commercializing of colonization," with an emphasis on markets and trade.[38] Privateering primed the market for luxury goods and expanded the import trade more generally. It stimulated the construction of costly ships suitable for long-distance trade and it filled the pockets of great merchants who then organized trade to the east and developed colonies to the west. All of which is to say that its anarchic and unpredictable energies were soon harnessed. In the minutes of the East India Company, it is clearly noted that "ther is noe intention to ... make anie attempte for reprisalles but onlie *to* pursue the voyag ... in a mchauntlike [*sic*] course."[39] In 1595, Cumberland built the *Malice Scourge*, a very large, 600-ton man-of-war designed expressly for privateering. Two years after the Puerto Rican voyage in 1598, Cumberland's merchant-creditors brokered the sale of the *Malice Scourge* to the East India Company.[40]

To construe Bassanio's career as a rehearsal of the drama of post-Armada privateering and its Jacobean consolidation is not to say that *The Merchant of Venice* is a prophetic allegory. Portia does not "represent" a Spanish carrack and Antonio will not return home to take his place on the board of the Venetian counterpart to the East India Company. The play has its own narrative and generic obligations, including folk material and multiple marriages, not to mention Shylock and the trial scene. But Portia is first introduced as the consummate prize, as she whose "worth" attracts rivals "from every coast"

(1.1.167–68), and Antonio, though Venetian, is a "royal merchant" (3.2.238) who backs an "adventuring" (1.1.143) gallant. The plot itself turns on hazarding all one has and on profitable commitment to sacrifice on the part of a "sad" merchant and a weary heiress (1.2.1). Throughout the play, a sometimes somber, sometimes elegaic, sometimes ominous shading imbues commercial capital, the romance of risk, and the possibility of windfall profit with a gravity and an authority the basis for which is neither aristocratic nor mercantile alone. This, along with the unexpected conjunction of affective elements like distress ("meetest for death" – 4.1.115) and "mistrust" (3.2.28) in *The Merchant of Venice*, leaves us hard pressed to align the play ideologically with Marx, Smith, or Weber. Because in the person of Shylock he mostly sequesters, then dispenses with, what Aristotle condemned as the "unnatural" function of money, Shakespeare is free, even bound, to articulate a more nuanced structure of feeling responsive to what Bassanio calls "thrift" (1.1.175).[41] This is primarily an affective and not an epistemological endeavor, amenable to the theatre if not to a mercantilist pamphlet or a Baconian essay. For while there may as yet have been few tools that could produce an accurate knowledge of the capacities of wealth, money, or capital, characters on the popular stage might still act out a felt experience of venture and thrift.

II

The capture of the huge 1,600-ton Portuguese carrack, the *Madre de Dios*, in August 1592, constituted one of the great English triumphs in the privateering war with Spain.[42] The cast of characters who took part in this drama on land and at sea included Queen Elizabeth, Ralegh, Cumberland, Cecil, Charles Howard (the Lord Admiral), Sanderson, and Watts. Like *The Merchant of Venice*, it is a story of self-dramatized toil, of hazarding all one has, and of prize-taking that points in the direction of more enduring profits. Unlike the play, the *Madre* episode reveals something of the underside of venturing, the squabbling, opportunism, and rapacity that Shakespeare either finesses or attempts to contain in Shylock (but that Jonson blazons in *The Alchemist*). The English fleet included the Queen's *Garland* (under Sir Martin Frobisher) and her *Foresight*, Ralegh's *Roebuck* (under Sir John Burgh), Ralegh's brother Carew's *Galleon Ralegh*, Watts's *Alcedo* and his *Margaret and John*, Sir John Hawkins's *Dainty*, and the Lord Admiral's *Lion's Whelp*. Ralegh himself set out with the fleet, but was soon called back to Court by Frobisher. This seems to have been part of Ralegh's plan from the start, or so at least his letter of 10 March to Robert Cecil suggests: "I have

promised her Majestie that, if I can perswade the Companies to follow
Sir MARTEN FURBRESHER, I will without fail returne; and bringe
them but into the sea but sume fifty or thriscore leagues . . . which to do
her Majestie many tymes, with great grace, bedd mee remember."[43]
Whatever his initial intentions, Ralegh was at sea long enough to obtain
information that Philip had stayed the Spanish West Indian flota. He
therefore abandoned plans to sail to the West Indies, and before
returning to England he divided the fleet in two. A squadron under
Frobisher was to cruise the Spanish coast. Sir John Burgh led the other
ships to the Azores. Meanwhile Ralegh returned to Plymouth, but in the
place of a rendezvous with his expectant Queen, he either married or let
slip knowledge of his marriage to Elizabeth Throckmorton. On the
Queen's orders, he was imprisoned in the Tower with his new bride in
early July.

Ralegh's fleet was not the only one to sail from Plymouth for the
Azores in 1592. Cumberland's *Tiger*, *Samson*, *Golden Noble*, *Phoenix*,
and *Discovery* were also launched. When the Earl's squadron attacked
the *Santa Croce* off Flores, it was joined by Burgh's crew. The purser on
the *Santa Croce* revealed under torture that three more carracks were
approaching the Azores; from the islanders Burgh learned that the
Madre de Dios would soon be upon them. At this point, Burgh joined up
with still two more ships, Captain Newport's *Dragon* and the *Prudence*
(these were owned by a syndicate of shareholding London merchants),
which had stopped at Flores on their way back from the West Indies.
Burgh now assumed command on the Queen's behalf of the entire
combined fleet. As for spoils, Burgh entered into consortship with the
two London captains (agreeing to share prizes "jointly and severally, in
sight or out of sight, ton for ton, and man for man"). Cumberland,
though himself not present, would later allege that his squadron had also
entered into consortship with Burgh – a claim Elizabeth was none too
willing to credit.[44]

The *Madre de Dios* was first sighted on 3 August by the *Dainty*, whose
crew began its attack at about 11.00 a.m. Newport's *Dragon*, a more
substantial ship than the *Dainty* but still only a fraction of the size of the
Madre, joined the fray some three hours later. In November 1592, John
Estridge, a 49-year-old Limehouse mariner, deposed that Newport
rallied his men after a fashion that might have appealed to Shakespeare's
Henry V: "m*aste*rs nowe the tyme is come that eyther we must ende our
dayes, or take the said carricke & wisshed all the company to stande ato
theire chardge like men and if eny displeasure were amongst eany of
them to forgett & forgive one an other, which every one seemed willinge
unto."[45] By about 4.00 p.m., Burgh in the *Roebuck*, and then some three

hours later, the Queen's *Foresight*, were fully engaged in the assault on the *Madre*. By 10.00 p.m. that night, after considerable loss of life and damage to ships, the *Dainty*, the *Foresight*, and the *Roebuck* had for all intents and purposes defeated the carrack. It remained for Cumberland's men on the *Samson* and the *Tiger* to arrive after midnight and to join in the plunder.

Though he was the commander, Burgh himself was too preoccupied with keeping his own ship afloat to board the carrack until the next day. Cumberland's men took advantage of the power vacuum, furiously pillaging the *Madre* as they stepped over the bodies of Portuguese sailors heaped on the decks.[46] They very nearly blew up the ship when one of its cabins, in which powder cartridges were stored, caught fire. Burgh's appearance on board at first had little effect on Cumberland's nearly mutinous seadogs – it was only his shrewd decision to claim the entire prize in the Queen's name that allowed him finally to take control. As Bovill writes, "[m]erchant adventurers were fair game, but to rob the queen was a very different matter."[47] It took Burgh until 7 September to bring the enormous prize ship into Dartmouth harbor, though by then nearly every privateer that had taken part in the spoil had hightailed it back to one or another English port to dispose of spoils before the Crown's commissioners could intervene.[48] The scene in Dartmouth must have been extraordinary, what with reports of 2,000 London merchants ("like [at] Bartholomew fair," according to an eyewitness quoted by Edwards) ready to do business with anyone who had anything to sell, not to mention a very real threat that the ship's entire cargo would be plundered before investors were satisfied. Robert Cecil wrote to his father of "[e]very one he met within seven miles of Exeter, that either had anything in a cloak, bag or malle which did but smell of the prizes at Dartmouth or Plymouth (for he could well smell them almost, such has been the spoils of amber and musk amongst them) . . . [t]here never was such spoil . . . desperate ways, nor more obstinate people."[49] Having failed to take control of the seamen in port (Cecil feared "the birds be flown for jewels, pearls, and amber"), Sir John Hawkins got Burghley to convince the Queen that no one but the still imprisoned Ralegh, whom the sailors trusted, could restore order. So it was that Burghley sent first his son, and then two days later Sir Walter (with his gaoler), to Dartmouth to protect the Queen's stake in the prize. Both men were on board the carrack when Cecil witnessed the mariners' shouts of joy upon seeing Ralegh. It was then, Cecil wrote to Thomas Heneage, that he realized that Ralegh's "heart is broken; as he is very extremely pensive, unless he is busied, in which he can toil terribly" (*CSP Domestic 1591–1594*, 273).

With a cargo worth £150,000, there was much at stake for the Queen, for the City, for Ralegh, for Cumberland, and for anyone else who could make a case for a part of the action. Looting, which had begun at sea, continued on land. The Mayor of Exeter found "in the custody of the said Alunso Gomys, 320 sparks of diamonds, a collar of a threefold roll of pearl, with 6 tags of crystal garnished with gold, a small string of pemell, with a pelican of gold," and the list goes on. The master of the *Susan* was said to have taken 150 diamonds; his mate "had one packet of diamonds, which was sent to the Cardinal [the Archbishop of Toledo], the same being in quantity as big as his fist." Some who were caught red-handed cut deals with the Queen's commissioners, informing on London goldsmiths and jewelers who were already trafficking in *Madre* booty. Thus Francis, at "'the Bottle' in Fenchurch Street . . . hath good store of fair rubies and diamonds" and one "Robert Brocke, in Lombard Street, hath in his hands and hath sold divers diamonds."[50] Rumor had it that a great jewel had been or was still to be found. Then too, besides the "spices, drugges, silks, calicos, quilts, carpets, and colours," the "elephants teeth, porcellan vessels of China, coconuts, hides, eben-wood as blacke as jet, bedsteds of the same, cloth of rindes of trees very strange" that Hakluyt reported, there was a vast shipment – some 300 tons – of pepper on which the Queen had set her sights.[51] Thomas Myddleton, the Queen's Receiver of Customs, was charged with overseeing the tranship-ment of the pepper from Dartmouth to London. Were bags better because they would allow Myddleton to keep freight charges low, or should he employ casks and so cut down on pilferage? Bovill cites Myddleton writing "despairingly to Cecil: 'We do all that is possible for us to further the common benefit, yet for my own part I expect no thanks.'"[52] Here as so often in this business, despite the huge profit that was in hand, the note of hard work and sacrifice was sounded.

Surely this was pensive, broken-hearted, exhausted, and sad Ralegh's part: disappointment without even the offsetting financial rewards enjoyed by nearly everyone else who survived the capture of the *Madre*. Before the successful adventure, in March 1592, Ralegh wrote to Cecil that "I have layd all that I am worth, and must do, ere I depart on this voyage. If it fall not out well, I can but loose all, and if nothinge be remayning, wherewith shall I pay the wages?"[53] Edwards assumes that Ralegh could have raised the sums necessary to outfit the expedition only by borrowing on usurious terms. In September, after the prize had been won, Ralegh wrote from the Tower to Lord Burghley: "Before I heard of the taking of the Carack, I thought not worth the labour [to compute the account of the Voyage]. And myself being the greatest Adventurer, I was contented rather to smother my loss, than labour to publish an hopeless overthrown estate, &c." "[A]rm'd" like Antonio "[t]o suffer with a quietness of spirit" (4.1.11–12), Ralegh trumpets his comparable insistence that "injury [be done] to none but myself, I hope it may be thought that it proceeded from a faithful mind, and a true desire to serve Her . . . And if Her Majesty cannot beat me from my affection, I hope her sweet nature will think it no conquest to afflict me." Just as desire is triangulated in *The Merchant of Venice*, so the steadfast "affection" expressed in Ralegh's letter could have been understood by Burghley to refer as easily to Elizabeth Throckmorton as to Elizabeth the Queen.

Given the magnitude of the prize, Ralegh's reasonable expectation that the largest share of the profits ought to have been his, and the Queen's extraordinary windfall, it is not surprising that the courtier could have convinced himself that he had magnificently sacrificed nearly all for his sovereign. "I that adventured all my estate, lose of my principall . . . I tooke all the care and paines . . . and they only sate still." "I was the cause that all this came to the Queen," Ralegh wrote to Burghley. "Fourscore thousand pounds is more than ever a man presented Her Majesty as yet. If God have sent it for my ransom, I hope Her Majesty of her abundant goodness will accept it." Here too, something of *The Merchant of Venice*'s amalgam of risk and toil (adventure and pain) and of Antonio's blend of renunciation and blackmail is audible. Ralegh effectively offers his rightful share of the *Madre* profits in return for release from the Tower ("[m]y promise was not to buy my bondage, but my liberty," he had told Sir George Carew). "The queen's favor was everything to Ralegh," Stephen Greenblatt has written. "More than anyone of stature in the court, Ralegh was committed in his whole being to that strange, artificial, dangerous, and dreamlike world presided over by Gloriana, the world of adulation so intense that it still has power to shock us."[54] If service, even affliction, were second nature to Ralegh, it was nonetheless the case that he had a keen sense of what was rightfully his own and what were his own rights.[55] His unauthorized marriage could hardly be construed as royal service. His push toward dominion in Ireland, in Virginia, and in Guiana might be undertaken in her or his majesty's name, but Ralegh aimed for a healthy share of whatever power, glory, and profit might accrue.[56] While there is much to be said for thinking in terms of Timias and Belphoebe, we ought not to lose sight of the degree to which Ralegh's relationship with Elizabeth also consisted of hardnosed bargaining and protracted negotiation. The Queen wrangled for her part of the prize, and she cut Ralegh no slack. As Burghley wrote to his son Robert on 7 December 1592, "[y]ou shall understand that her Majesty is laboured to accept my lord of Cumberland's offer, which I hear is for her Majesty *de claro 80,000* . . . Thereupon her Majesty hath asked me twice or thrice whether Sir Walter Raleigh's offer be better, which I said I thought it might be."[57] The faerie queen was ready to adventure and merchandize; her bold courtier and gallant was something of a thief operating with a writ of mart. In Epigram 126, John Harington wrote that

> Proud *Paulus* [Ralegh] late my secrecies revealing,
> Hath told I got some good conceits by stealing,
> But where got he those double Pistolets,
> With which good clothes, good fare, good land he gets?
> Tush, those he saith, came by a man of warre,
> That brought a Prize of price, from countries farre.
> Then, fellow Thiefe, let's shake together hands
> Sith both our wares are filcht from forren lands.
>   You'll spoile the Spaniards, by writ of Mart:
>   And I the Romanes rob, by wit, and Art.[58]

There is not a shred of legitmating affect in Harington's account, no weariness, no pensiveness, no painful toil. If Ralegh was fishing with "melancholy bait," Harington, who deeply resented Sir Walter's relationship with his godmother, was not biting.

We can only guess what Lord Howard and Sir Robert Cecil, or for that matter Queen Elizabeth, made of Ralegh's pose. Cecil's comment about Ralegh's ability to "toil terribly" suggests both admiration and mockery. His Ralegh is at once capable of exhausting labor and is potentially comical – in the way Hercules might be deemed comical.[59] Such toil is, for a Cecil, daunting and demeaning. One cannot help but sense that the clerk's fear and dismissal of the sword is at work here (there is, as well, the fact that Ralegh lacked Cecil's pedigree). In *The Discoverie*, in his dedicatory epistle to Howard and Cecil, Ralegh insists for the first but by no means the last time in this tract on his willingness to make sacrifices in order to ensure future profit. "I could have laid hands and ransomed many of the kings and . . . have had a reasonable proportion of gold for their redemption: But I have chosen rather to beare the burthen of poverty, then reproch, and rather to endure a second travel and the chaunces therof, then to have defaced an enterprise of so great assurance." In his dedication "To the Reader," Ralegh counterbalances his expected "profit and honor" with the "perilous and chargeable labors and indevours" he suffered in Guiana.[60] Fifteen years later, still trying to convince Cecil of his credibility and of the value of a second travel/travail, Ralegh assured the Lord Treasurer that the King could have the Guianan mine for merely "this hazard of a Reede, for the Adventureinge of an ould, and Sorrowe-worne Man, whom'e death would shortlye have delivered."[61] Years of bitter confinement in the Tower might well have rendered Ralegh "meetest for death." But short of the ultimate sacrifice, and whether he was privateering or in search of El Dorado, Ralegh seems to have felt that domestic exigencies (gold for the royal coffers) and foreign policy (advantage over Spain) could never offer sufficient justification for the profits he aimed at. An ethos of toil and self-sacrifice, which is to say, the affect attendant upon pain and peril, could alone complete the authorization and accreditation of an adventuring gallant bold. That someone like Cecil could not imagine maintaining his credit while engaging in such activities is evident from a letter dated 12 January 1603, in which Cecil suggests that Ralegh and Lord Cobham join him in investing in a privateering voyage. "I pray you as much as may be conceal our adventure, at the least my name above any other. For though I thank God I have no other meaning than becometh an honest man in any of my actions, yet that which were another man's pater noster would be accounted in me a charm." Kenneth R. Andrews, who cites this passage, concludes that it "would be difficult to make a declaration of innocence sound less convincing."[62]

Still, it is important to remember that privateering, like credit, was taken up by English people up and down the social hierarchy – mariners, mates, captains, soldiers, merchants, Ralegh, Cumberland, Lord Howard, Cecil, and Queen Elizabeth too. The venturing alliance formed by Antonio and Bassanio, and eventually preserved and joined by Portia, enables distinct but complementary legitimations. Similar alliances from among the likes of Elizabeth, Ralegh, Watts, Howard, Burgh, and many others enabled the transformation of pillage into commerce. What men like Ralegh sanctioned in the 1590s by means of perilous labor, men like Watts certified after the turn of the century by means of shares in the initial offerings of the East India Company. As I have noted, rumor had it that a great jewel was taken along with all the rest of the spoil from the *Madre de Dios*. Though never found or even confirmed, it was said to have been meant for the Archbishop or for King Philip himself. One Anthony Moon wrote in October 1592 to John Bedford, the master of the *Roebuck*, "that the great jewel which is wanting and is had in so high a price, was delivered unto a Portingall that dwelleth in London . . . It is reported . . . this jewel is worth 500,000 ducats." That same month, the commissioners for the carrack informed Cecil that with most of the pepper now in bags, "they hope to see the bottom [of the *Madre*], and to find what is hidden therein, wishing it may prove as they expected, but fear the contrary, for that the like hath not been seen, neither any of the Portingals here, that can speak of any such matter."[63] What did surface, however, "'enclosed in a case of sweet cedar wood and lapped up amost [*sic*] an hundredfold in fine Calicut cloth, as though it had been some incomparable jewel', [was] an account of China and its riches, written in

Latin by a certain Duarte Sande. With it were a 'Register of the East Indies' and various maps, including one of the Moluccas."[64] History was of course to prove this the real "great jewel," for with it we pass from the spoils of privateering to the profits of commerce, from an era of cloth export to an era of luxury imports, and from the Elizabethan plunder of precious stones and spices to the Jacobean organization of eastward-looking trade. Bovill shrewdly gives Richard Hakluyt the last word on the significance of the capture of the *Madre*:

And here I cannot but enter into the consideration and acknowledgement of Gods great favor towards our nation, who by putting this purchase into our hands hath manifestly discovered those secret trades & Indian riches, which hitherto lay strangely hidden, and cunningly concealed from us; whereof there was among some few of us some small and unperfect glimse onely, which now is turned into the broad light of full and perfect knowledge. Whereby it should seeme that the will of God for our good is (if our weaknesse could apprehend it) to have us communicate with them in those East Indian treasures, & by the erection of a lawfull traffike to better our meanes to advance true religion and his holy service.[65]

Bassanio's fleece hunt, which among other things was meant to enable him to repay his debts to Antonio, eventuates in a grand consolidation of interests in the form of aristocratic, gentry, and merchant capital. Having wived wealthily in Belmont, Bassanio can afford to watch as Portia jettisons the instrusive affective burden that is sad Antonio by restoring to him his ships and his Venetian mercantile calling. It is not just that Antonio's melancholy jars with the wit of the newlyweds, it is that his pain and toil are no longer needed. They have no more work to do. With the mercenary venture – hazarding after a "lady richly left" – now forgotten, there remains nothing for which to compensate. Ralegh's original West Indian designs turned into the plunder of an extraordinary prize ship; this in turn offered a glimpse of the "erection of a lawfull traffike." Though licensed by letters of reprisal, privateering ventures were only nominally lawful. As Andrews notes, the "sea war degenerated into an indecorous scramble for private profit."[66] Once privateering – ships, captains, and all – was assimilated into lawful traffic, however, there would be no need for even the pretense of self-sacrifice or terrible toil that we have seen in Ralegh.

Now men like John Watts, Robarts's "merchant of renown," could come fully into their own. Watts, born mid-century, married the daughter of a London clothworker who would become Lord Mayor in 1574–75. After admission to the Clothworkers' Company, Watts worked as a factor in Spain for his father- and brother-in-law. By 1585, he was immersed in Iberian trade to the extent that when Spanish confiscations began, he and his partners put their losses at £15,000.[67] Letters of reprisal in hand, Watts's career in privateering began. He was one of the promoters of the Cadiz expedition in 1587, he was aboard his own *Margaret and John* when it attacked the *San Lorenzo* in 1588, and in more years than not between 1590 and 1598 his ships were taking prizes on the Spanish Main, in the Azores, and in the West Indies.[68] In 1600, Watts was invited to become a "committee" in the East India Company "in respect of the great experience of Mr Alderman Watts [he was a London alderman from 1594 to 1616] in shipping and other directions in voyages" and in 1601, he was elected governor of the company.[69] Watts was knighted by King James and elected Lord Mayor in 1606–07; he died in 1616. The trajectory of Watts's career led from legitimate Iberian and Levant trade to the rapacity and indecorum of privateering; then it resumed, or was consolidated, in the East Indies and in Virginia. Such an arc is also traced by the careers of the mercer Thomas Cordell and the grocer Paul Bayning. As Andrews writes, their privateering "served to irrigate all trade."[70] Although I cannot get at the affect attendant upon Watts's adventuring (Andrews, who seems to have read through nearly every High Court of Admiralty document for this period, notes that Watts's "personality . . . even as a business man, escapes us"), I do see a structural homology between his and Antonio's, the merchant of Venice's, career paths.[71] It may or may not be reasonable to assume a straightforward, great merchant pre-play past for Antonio. If we allow the evidence of the *St. Andrew*, then he had a fictionalized promoter's part at Cadiz nearly a decade after Watts. The Antonio who racks his credit on Bassanio's behalf is unmistakably involved in prize-hunting. The post-play Antonio is also left to our imagining; however, the return of his ships and, as we might expect, his return to Venice, seem to put him in a good position to bring his recent experiences in venture capitalization to bear on future enterprises. In their planning and conduct, ventures carried out by ships like the *Hazard* and the *Poor Men's Hope* and the *Why Not I?* were sanctioned by risk, sacrifice, and toil. Years of plunder and profit gave way, however, to normalization and commercialization. Perhaps Bassanio can set sail again, the spoils of a casket, if not a carrack, in hand, capitalized by his friend's argosies and his wife's inheritance.

III

Venturing, as we have seen in both *The Merchant of Venice* and the capture of the *Madre*, typically depends upon partnerships. Bassanio needs Antonio's backing, and eventually Portia's too. Ralegh was far from alone in financing the fleets that set out in 1592 to cruise the Spanish coast and the Azores. The promoters of the East India Company who petitioned the Privy Council in 1599 for a charter explained that "trade so far remote cannot be managed but by a joint and united stock." Large capital outlays, capital locked up for longer than was common in European trade, and considerable uncertainty all called for new ways to share both risk and cost.[72] The joint stock company was, then, not merely a regulated company, an assocation of traders who made separate investments. It was instead an "association of capital" designed to facilitate collective trading.[73] As such, the East India Company had to find ways to discipline its partners; it had to develop managerial procedures that would maximize confidence and continuity from one venture to the next.[74] Inital investors ventured their capital in new undertakings only after securing their profits from previous voyages. A full thirteen years of trade that could boast nine out of ten profitable voyages were alone sufficient to prompt the East India men to give over terminable stocks (capital raised for and delimited to individual voyages) for a quasi-permanent or revolving joint stock assignable to successive voyages.[75] And even then, the company "carefully avoided the insecurities of long-term capital investments in 'development.'"[76] Such caution seems to have derived not only from the dangers of eastern trade and an unwillingness to risk fixed capital, but from the uncertainties of partnership and so of managing pooled capital.

The first meeting of what would become the East India Company took place on 24 September 1599, with fifty-seven adventurers present. Fifteen subscribers were elected to serve as committees, or directors, at a minimum subscription of £200. When a charter was finally signed late in 1600, the company was organized under a governor and twenty-four committees.[77] It has recently been argued that the company was "modern because of its command structure rather than its investment." Its success was due to a "sophisticated administrative structure that paid attention to details, and a mandate that everyone understood as being focused on trade and profit [as opposed to privateering]." The records of the company reveal a history of careful administrative surveillance, careful record-keeping, company court debate, and numerous rounds of voting.[78] Even before their charter was awarded, the subscribers "thought it meet to direct them selfes by certan Rules and orders."[79] They also demonstrated a marked sensitivity to the social status of key employees. When Sir Edward Michelborne solicited employment as principal commander of the first voyage, the company's Lord Treasurers let it be known that they "purpose not to imploy anie gent in any place of charg." The generality would "not indure to hear of such a motion . . .

and yf they shuld be ernestlie prest therin they would wthdrawe ther adventures."[80] Neither were run-of-the-mill employees ignored; "ordi-narie mariners" were offered two months' wages before the first voyage set sail. Still more striking is the stake these sailors were offered in the company: "for the better advauncemt of his sallarie . . . everie the said mariners shall have two monethes wages *in adventure* as his stocke."[81] In order to satisfy everyone with a share in the enterprise, auditors were commissioned to examine and certify the pursers' accounts, and to report their findings to the committees. What with more than half a million pounds having been invested in the company in its first twelve years, and an average profit in excess of 150 percent, there was a very great deal at stake.[82]

Ben Jonson's *The Alchemist* (King's Men, 1610) begins in the midst of its own disciplinary crisis among the directors of its "venter tripartite."[83] Each of the scam artists claims to have been the first to accredit the other: "I ga' you count'nance, credit for your coals . . . lent you, beside, / A house to practise in" (1.1.43–47); "I've ta'en thee out of dung" (1.1.64). The desire for particular profit, for "primacy in the divisions" (1.1.131), has disrupted joint proprietorship, what Dol refers to as "[a]ll things in common . . . [w]ithout priority" (1.1.135–36). "[C]ivil war" (1.1.82) has broken out. Moreover, because from the outset rank among the adventurers is called into question, it comes as no surprise that origins are thoroughly inspected. In short order, Face is revealed to be no more than a "plain, livery-three-pound-thrum" (1.1.16) and Subtle's wretched, Pie-corner past is laid bare. Of course Jonson, a bricklayer's son, could hardly divorce himself from a desire for singularity and status, especially if it were predicated upon toil; and there is some irony in the poet's concern that his own dedicatory letter to Lady Wroth (pronounced "worth") might look less like the work of a "zeal[ous]" sacrificer than that of "one of the ambitious *faces* of the time" (ll. 2 and 12, my emphasis). Notoriously resentful of partnership, whether with the likes of Inigo Jones or with audiences, and yet enmeshed in a cooperative industry that put him at the mercy not only of audiences, but of fellow actors, entrepreneurs, and printers, Jonson – like Subtle at odds with ambitious Face – validates his particular art in terms of travail. Subtle "ever murmurs, and objects his pains, / And says the weight of all lies upon him" (1.1.143–44). Jonson proclaims, "Who casts to write a living line, must sweat."[84] Ralegh toiling terribly, Sanderson in great travail, Robarts's painful toil, Antonio "arm'd and well prepar'd" (4.1.260), Jonson sweating, and Subtle objecting his pains: time and again, hazard is discursively aligned with effort, strain, or labor. Risks which might eventuate in noteworthy profits must be seen to entail toil.

Any reader of, or spectator at, plays like *Volpone* and *The Alchemist* cannot help but notice the expenditure of sheer energy in pursuit of gain. In the earlier play the division of labor may suggest that Volpone, the brains or imaginative faculty, can sit back while Mosca, the worker, feverishly activates the plots. But it is the fox who is most fully committed to action. Not long after Volpone sends off Mosca praying that "heaven your *labor* bless" (3.9.63, my emphasis), the exhausted parasite is ready to give up: "We must here be fixed; / Here we must rest" (5.2.12–13).[85] Stasis, however, has both an ethical and a more prosaic valence for Volpone. Leg cramp and palsy diminish not only outcomes but *virtu*. So Volpone wills himself to set in motion again: "I *must* be merry / And shake it off . . . / I *shall* conquer" (5.1.7–13, my emphasis). The anxiety-induced "sweat" (5.2.37) of the momentarily entrapped fox must be allowed to signify normal effort ("A little in a mist" yet "Never but still myself" – 5.2.40–41). Although he has been sentenced to "lie in prison, cramped with irons" (5.12.123) and ordered off stage, Volpone jauntily steps forward at the end to solicit applause. In *The Alchemist*, the breathless machinations of the cozeners, their endless plotting and the farcical stage business are inordinately and equally labor intensive for all three of them. When Dol commands Subtle to "cozen kindly" (1.1.137), to "labor kindly in the commune work" (1.1.156), she picks up two threads crucial to their endeavor. "[K]indly" and "commune" speak to the management of resources and to the deportment, or what I have called discipline, appropriate to "stock-affairs" (5.4.93; joint-stock enterprise). "[L]abor" and "work," like Antony as "workman" in *Antony and Cleopatra*, are the less aggrandized reminders of the sweat such travail exacts. In the course of *The Alchemist*, possibly at the Blackfriars theatre, a Blackfriars house is transmuted not only into an alchemical workshop and a dream machine but into a sweatshop. Face, Subtle, and Dol all labor strenuously, even if the fruit of that labor is given over in the end to Lovewit, the absentee landlord.

Given the ease with which it can be said that alchemy "makes a neat metaphor for nascent capitalism," it bears repeating that neither alchemy, such as it is in the play, nor nascent capitalism, such as *it* is, is meet for the idle.[86] Speculative investment on the part of a Dapper or a Drugger depends upon what they are led to believe are the projectors' onerous and finely calibrated exertions. For all the smoke and mirrors, the theatre audience never loses sight of the extent to which even display, the mere pretense of technique, demands toil. Many words are strung together to conjure the illusion of a laboratory in Lovewit's house, but as is the case with *Volpone*, elapsed real time in the theatre is measured according to the hectic back and forth, on and off stage movement that sustains the plot.[87] From the moment the bell rings in the first scene, a nearly frantic pace is set. "Who's that? One rings. To the window, Dol" (1.1.180).

DOL COMMON	O, let him in.
SUBTLE	Stay. Who shall do't?
FACE	Get you
	Your robes on. I will meet him, as going out.
DOL COMMON	And what shall I do?
FACE	Not be seen; away! (1.1.194–96)

"To . . . let . . . Stay . . . Get . . . meet . . . going out . . . away" – nothing illusory is signified in either the here of the Blackfriars house or of the raised stage itself, and there is only the barest of Jonson's celebrated linguistic invention in this. Instead, there are the markers of effort and action.[88]

In *The Alchemist*, passive investment is discredited. It is not so much fantasy or desire that Jonson is impatient with as the conviction that advantage can be had without effort (Lovewit is an obvious exception, but, crucially, he lacks the *expectation* of easy profit). Those who are convinced that they can get ahead not by exertion but by purchase are ranked first among the play's dupes. Their untroubled sense of entitlement allows Subtle effectively to manipulate them and prompts us to find them by turns outrageous and ridiculous. "You may be anything" (3.2.53) at trivial cost, Subtle advertises, and the investors empty their pockets. Sir Epicure thinks that he can simply buy the stone, free of the strain of "pious, holy, and religious" life (2.2.98). "I buy it. My venture [not taxing piety] brings it me" (2.2.100–01). Ananias protests that the Brethren "will not venter any more" (2.5.65); their £120 expenditure already should have procured them the projection. Tribulation similarly thinks it sufficient to "[t]hrow down their purse before" Subtle (3.2.18). Dapper is another thoroughgoing dupe, but he wins at least a measure of our sympathy because we either see him or know him to be toiling terribly. Although like the Brethren he is a speculator, Dapper must truly endure "a world of ceremonies" (1.2.144):

> You must be bathed and fumigated first;
>
> . . .
>
> . . . you must be fasting; only, take
> Three drops of vinegar in at your nose,
> Two at your mouth, and one at either ear;
> Then, bathe your fingers' ends and wash your eyes,
> To sharpen your five senses, and cry "hum"
> Thrice, and then "buz" as often; and then, come.   (1.2.144, 165–70)

In 3.4 and 3.5, we learn that from the vinegar and clean shirt to the humming and buzzing, Dapper has performed the ceremonies that were enjoined him. Later, having been blindfolded, gagged, pinched, and overcome by privy fumes, Dapper may justifiably be imagined to have broken into a sweat.

For unremitting toil, both what we see and what we are to imagine off stage, we must look chiefly, however, to the trio of adventurers. Subtle is not alone, it turns out, in objecting "his pains." Face too wants credit for his hard work and for the expenses he incurs:

> . . . you think I am at no expense
> In searching out these veins [dupes], then following 'em,
> Then trying 'em out. 'Fore God, my intelligence
> Costs me more money than my share oft comes to . . .   (1.3.105–08)

At the beginning of 1.3, Subtle must pacify "[g]ood wives" clamoring at Lovewit's door. At the beginning of 1.4, Dol has to fend off "[y]onder fishwife" and "your giantess / The bawd of Lambeth" (1.4. 1–3). With Sir Epicure fast approaching, still more taxing provisions must be made: "Face, go you and shift. / Dol, you must presently make ready too" (1.4.9–10). Midway through the play, Dol, Face, and Subtle have so many plots running concurrently that Face can only hope that Drugger will stay away "[t]ill our new business be o'erpast" (3.3.61). Of course, this is the predictable signal that things are only just beginning to heat up. Ingenious plotting now must be accommodated to time and stage management schemes, since the reappearance of Dapper coincides perilously with the arrival of Drugger and Kastril ("'Slight, here are more!" – 3.3.81):[89]

FACE   Queen of Faery,
> On with your tire [*Exit Dol*] and, Doctor, with
>   your robes.
> Let's dispatch him, for God's sake.
SUBTLE   'Twill be long.
FACE   I warrant you, take but the cues I give you,
> It shall be brief enough. (3.3.77–81)

Next, the inopportune arrival of Mammon ("Please you to walk / Three or four turns . . . and I am for you. [*Aside.*] Quickly, Dol!" – 3.5.59–61) necessitates disposing of Dapper in "Fortune's privy lodgings" (3.5.79). Face, who, meanwhile, has scrambled into his costume as Lungs, cannot help but elicit a laugh from the audience when he greets Sir Epicure with, "O, sir, y'are come i' the only finest time" (4.1.1).[90]

The trick for Jonson is to get everyone on or back stage at once; and for the venturers tripartite, to keep all their balls in the air at once. This is the spirit in which Face hits upon the idea of substituting Dame Pliant for Dol when Surly grows impatient. Subtle and Face adapt themselves after a brief negotiation to their loss of the "chance to have her" (4.3.67). Since all their "venter / Now lies upon't" (4.3.65–67), they defer to "the common cause" (4.3.76). Such dexterity and postures of courtesy, evidence of hard work no less than mocking intent, answer to Jonson's artifice and the tricksters' chicanery (just as sadness and bating sanction the merchant of Venice's efforts). When Surly catches out Face and Subtle in 4.6, we arrive at a moment comparable to the first trial in *Volpone*: both playwright and tricksters face a hurdle we know they must and will clear. We take pleasure in the ingenuity of their escape. On stage, at least, we are struck also by the level of exertion. To this end, it is not enough that Kastril should neutralize Surly; in addition, Drugger and Ananias must be brought into the fray as well.

Lovewit's appearance at the start of the fifth act marks out a sharp division in *The Alchemist*. Like the prince with the gravediggers ("the hand of little employment hath the daintier sense"), the gentle landlord amidst the lesser orders would refine labor into, or perhaps with, wit.[91] "I love a teeming wit as I love my nourishment" (5.1.16) Lovewit proclaims, arrogantly and mistakenly conjoining *essen* and *moral*, which Brecht insisted observe a strict sequence. If, insofar as "mouldy . . . thin threaden" (1.1.35–36) Subtle and Dol are concerned, they are merely laboring in their vocation, it is Lovewit who will consolidate their gains. Thus it falls to Hal to make Hotspur his factor, to merchants like Watts to sublimate privateering into commercial shipping, and to Jonson to distill cast lines into art. Jonson's work becomes *The Workes of Ben Jonson*. Alchemy, more like industrial than nascent capitalism, stands for transmuting labor into profit. There is even room for a canny worker like Face to cash in. Knowing that Lovewit is "wont to affect mirth and wit" (5.3.80), he asks leave to make the best of his fortune (5.3.82), in effect, to venture in his master's future. In no time, an admiring Subtle is commending his erstwhile confederate as "the precious king / Of present wits" (5.4.13–14). And Face is exercising his "servant's wit" (5.5.150) to arrange an alliance between Dame Pliant and Lovewit.

One might advance numerous explanations for the discrepancy between Lovewit's success and Volpone's failure, pointing to Jonson's changing temperament, to the absence of a widow in the earlier play, to Volpone's refusal to "glue" himself "into a family" (5.12.87–88) or his boast that he neither has nor wants "wife . . . parent, child, ally" (1.1.73), or to Lovewit's proto-bourgeois status compared with Volpone's as magnifico. To these might be added the difference that whereas the alliance between Volpone and Mosca breaks up, in *The Alchemist*, "indenture tripartite" (5.4.131) gives way to Lovewit's self-serving partnership with Face. The servant has become the landlord's factor, now called to strict account and ready to engross a rich widow for his master. Hard-working, clever Face can lead Lovewit to the kind of marriage Drugger (or Mosca) finds himself barred from. Of course Face must also give up his dream of marriage to Dame Pliant; but it is his capacity for self-discipline that Subtle has failed to imagine when he complains that "the slave will run a-wiving, Dol, / Against the instrument that was drawn between us" (5.4.80–81). Jonathan Haynes has written that, "Face's real strength is his ability to participate in a comic settlement that reins in but does not reject the practices of a new social economy, accommodating it to the strength and durability of the status quo."[92] Small fry like Dapper and Drugger stand no chance matched against a combine with resources like those available to Face and Lovewit, not to mention the audience which Face and Jonson solicit with their "pelf" in the closing lines of the play.[93]

IV

"The Argument" to *The Alchemist* refers to a pair of "[c]oz'ners at large" who acquire a "House to set up" from a servant with whom they "contract / Each for a share, and all begin to act" (ll. 6–8). The play's precise reference to "the friers" suggests that it almost certainly was intended for the Blackfriars, the indoor playhouse which reverted to the King's Men in 1608. Venturing in the Blackfriars and its acting companies seems to have entailed its own measure of pain and travail as various investors contended, "each for a share."[94] Without question some of the principals toiled in the courts at great length and I imagine considerable cost. Ten years before the first performance of *The Alchemist*, in 1600, Richard Burbage entered into a bond with a Welsh scrivener named Henry Evans (and with his son-in-law, Alexander Hawkins), leasing the Blackfriars playing space for twenty-one years, at £40 a year.[95] Two years later, Evans and Hawkins entered into partnership with Edward Kirkham, the Yeoman of the Revels, William Rastall, a merchant, and Thomas Kendall, a haberdasher. Kirkham *et al.* were to pay Evans 8 shillings per week during playing times, and they also seem to have paid him £300–400 to buy their way into the apparently lucrative partnership. In return, they were entitled to half of the profits. Evans kept control of the property lease, but having been caught up in the nasty business of the abduction of a young boy into the Children of the Revels, he was under Star Chamber prohibition from managing either the theatre or the children's company. In early 1604 Samuel Daniel (about whom more, shortly) secured a new license for the company from the new king and queen. They might now call themselves Children of the Revels to the Queen, or Children of the Queen's Revels. The *Isle of Gulls* débâcle in 1606 resulted in Kirkham's being thrown off the management team and in the loss of the Queen's patronage. The company would have to settle for calling itself the Children of the Revels or of Blackfriars.

Enter Robert Keysar, a London goldsmith, who bought a share in the assets and revenues of the company and assumed an active role in its day-to-day operations. This arrangement, alas, was not to last for long. In 1608, outraged at the French scenes in Chapman's Byron plays and at still another, earlier play thought to be demeaning to him, King James ordered players thrown into prison, the troupe disbanded, and the playhouse closed. With no profits in sight and thinking he had Kirkham's consent, Evans began to negotiate the surrender of his lease to Richard Burbage. In 1608 Burbage gave Evans the original £400 bond for cancellation and took over occupancy of the playing space on behalf of the King's Men (Evans managed to keep a hand in the enterprise). Meanwhile, Keysar seems to have kept the company of boys together, to have gotten them Court performances as the Children of Blackfriars during the Christmas season (1608–09), and to have moved them in 1609 into the Whitefriars as Children of the Whitefriars. Philip Rosseter, Keysar's new partner, a composer and one of King James's lutenists, received a new patent for the company (in early 1610), as Children of the Queen's Revels once again.[96]

The lawsuits which enable us to piece together much of what we know about the Blackfriars partnerships center on Evans, and to a lesser extent Burbage. At issue was Evans's surrender of the lease, an act which both Keysar and Kirkham deemed fraudulent. In 1610, the year *The Alchemist* premiered, Keysar lodged a bill of complaint against Burbage and the Blackfriars housekeepers (presumably Shakespeare among them). Keysar wanted the one-sixth share that he said he purchased from John Marston for £100 – an interest Marston had reputedly purchased from Evans. Keysar's claim to have been defrauded of his share of the playhouse goods, lease, and profits depended upon his belief that Burbage and company had assured him that they would make no overture toward Evans without first satisfying Keysar. He complained that Burbage coerced Evans into surrendering the lease and so cut Evans out. As a result, Keysar asserted, he suffered the loss of not just his share in the Blackfriars profits since 1608, but the £100 he paid Marston, and the £500(!) he insisted he had spent maintaining the boys in hopes of reinstalling them in the Blackfriars. With an "inveterate and increasinge mallice towardes him," Burbage planned to "[s]upplante" him from "anye Commerce or deallinge in any mattrs of playes or enterludes."[97]

Burbage replied that Keysar's complaint was merely "for molestacion and vexacion sake" (345) and that Keysar's replication was "very incerteine, scandalous, untrue and insufficiente in lawe to be rejoyned unto for many apparant faltes and imperfections slaunders and absurdeties therein conteined. And that the same is so made and contrived of meere malice and spleene" (352). He knew nothing of Keysar's share, he never met with Keysar nor offered to pay him off, and he did not think Keysar had even purchased an interest, since Evans was not entitled to assign any part of the premises to Marston. Burbage also denied that he and his fellows had profited to the tune of £1,500 since the time they had resumed their lease. Keysar simply could not "bridle his envy toward these deftes But ceaseth not most unchristianlike to charge them wth falsehood Cosenage treachery perfidiousness mallice fraude practize . . . & many other lewde & slaunderous supposalls" (356).[98] This is certainly within the realm of Subtle and Dol plotting to supplant "this o'erweening rascal, / This peremptory Face" (5.4.78–79). Even the charges of righteous indignation couched in legal formulas cross over easily into playhouse name-calling: the Face who has tripped up his partners is called a "rogue" and "precious fiend" (5.4.142 and 138).

In 1611 Kirkham, the sole survivor of his "venture tripartite" with Rastall and Kendall, commenced his own series of suits against Evans. Kirkham had a number of complaints, but his foremost grievance was based upon his conviction that as a result of his ownership of one-half of the Blackfriars lease, he was entitled to a moiety of all present and future Blackfriars profits.[99] Like Keysar, Kirkham set out to prove that Evans defrauded him of his rightful profits when he surrendered the lease to Burbage. Burbage and Evans were said to have "practized amongest themselves how to dispossesse this said replyant."[100] Evans insisted that he had Kirkham's implied consent and encouragement to give up the lease, and that in any case there never was any agreement about the *lease* that involved Kirkham.[101] Kirkham was entitled to operating profits – to anything that concerned provisioning and profiting from the acting company and its plays. In dismissing Kirkham's suit, the Court of Chancery held that the parties' articles of agreement, not the lease itself, was at issue, and that even if it were, any agreement to convey part of it to Kirkham had never been "perfected and sealled" (250). This last bit of fudging may not be sufficient to vindicate Kirkham (Irwin Smith, at least, doubts the validity of Kirkham's claim), but, in the present context, Evans and Burbage neatly pushing Kirkham out of the picture calls to mind Face and Lovewit dispossessing everyone from Subtle and Dol to Mammon and the Brethren. Like Lovewit, Burbage was something of an absentee landlord who conveniently returned to the scene at just the moment the Blackfriars company was in shambles.[102] If Lovewit can manipulate the city officers in 5.5 to his own advantage, we have no reason to think Burbage any less capable at law.

At moments when the energy and effort men like Kirkham and Keysar invested in running the Blackfriars companies were balked, they rechanneled it into law. Hence the regular laments about vexatious and malicious lawsuits. In the case of the Blackfriars, John Marston was not the only poet and playwright who seems to have had a stake in the company. Samuel Daniel was also drawn into the financial and legal contention. It is in fact Daniel who invokes the affective trope that we first heard from Robarts, then Sanderson, and then Ralegh. The patent that Daniel secured for the company from King James and Queen Anne specified that no "Playes or Shewes shallbee presented before the said Queene our wief by the said Children or by them any where publiquelie acted but by the approbacion and allowaunce of Samuell Danyell."[103] Daniel was not, however, merely the company's new licenser and censor. Chambers notes that when the boys performed at Court in January 1605, Daniel was one of the payees. Furthermore, although no money is mentioned in the royal patent, "a deposition filed by Kirkham and Anne Kendall in 1609 reveals that the Blackfriars managers were obligated to pay Daniel £10 per year, and that they gave him their bond in the amount of £100 as security for the due performance of their obligation."[104] As Daniel answered in Chancery, it was in "consideracion of his greate paynes & travell" (his "paynes formerly taken") that he had won for himself a sinecure at the Blackfriars.[105] In this case, pain and travail stand for the technique demanded of those who would successfully negotiate advantage for themselves or others in the new king's court. That Daniel was himself wheeling and dealing not much less than Face or Subtle is suggested by his assignment of the £100 bond to one John Gerrard as early as April 1605, and still more clearly by Kirkham's allegations in Chancery. Daniel, he averred, "having occasion to use monye woulde still importune and Request the said Kyrkham and Kendall to pay to him his money before the day did come that the same was due and somtymes to pay the same to others to whom the said Danyell did stande indebted" (335–36). As far as Kirkham was concerned, and in language dear to the courts and the stage, Daniel had "a greedy and Covetous minde" (336).

Painful endeavor and great travail were sometimes literal, more often figurative ways of characterizing the affect attendant upon mental and physical stress in the course of collaborative financial ventures. When a dispute broke out in 1634–35 over shares in the Globe and the Blackfriars, three players who were trying to become shareholders petitioned the Lord Chamberlain that they would "reape some better fruit of their labours then hitherto they have done." It was not fair, they argued, that "some of the sayd Housekeepers who have the greatest shares, are neither Actors nor his Mate servantes . . . & yet reape most or the chiefest benefitt of the sweat of their [the players'] browes, and live upon the bread of their Labours, without takeing any paynes themselves."[106] Once again, pain, sweat, and labor are the mainstays of hazarding and the right to capital investment. Although John Shanks, one of the players' chief targets, alleged that they were "well recompenced for their labour & paines" (370), the Lord Chamberlain sided with the actors, granting them a right to buy shares. Irwin Smith notes that Shanks died still possessed of his shares, but that in this case, at least, a Burbage (Cuthbert, along with his former sister-in-law, now Mrs. Robinson) "[p]resumably" obeyed the Lord Chamberlain's order and sold one of his shares in the Globe.[107] Whether or not such a sale took place, Cuthbert's protest that first his father, and then he and his brother, fitted out the Blackfriars "with great charge & trouble" (371) fell on deaf ears. Although Burbage argued that the players had not yet put in enough sweat equity to be awarded the right to purchase shares ("men soe soone shott up . . . they should come to it by farre more antiquity and desert" – 370), the "[c]oz'n[ing]" actors in the "[h]ouse . . . [the Burbages] set up" were permitted to "contract / Each for a share" (*The Alchemist*, "The Argument," 6–8).

Afterword

It has recently been argued that affect largely governed two very important decisions made by the King's Men. In *The Shakespearian Playing Companies*, Andrew Gurr twice narrates and tries to make sense of the King's sharers' decision, first, to continue to use the Globe after the Burbage brothers had reacquired the Blackfriars lease in 1608 (they could have abandoned the Globe or they could have let out the Blackfriars playhouse – instead, each playhouse was left dark for one half of the year), and second, to rebuild the Globe, at very great expense, after it burned down in 1613.[1] What the sharers were giving up after 1608, according to Gurr, "was the doubled rents they would have obtained if either playhouse had been let to another company" (118). Had they not rebuilt the Globe, "their income would have remained much the same from playing at the Blackfriars all the year round . . . In fact, by 1613 they must have known that the Blackfriars *could* bring in consistently higher returns than the Globe" (118).[2] Gurr concludes that although the Burbages and their fellow sharers must have thought that they were making "sound investment[s]" (297), their decisions were "eccentric" (116) and in the "short term, financially . . . quixotic" (115). To explain such seemingly "uneconomical" choices (297), Gurr again and again recurs to nostalgia, to "substantial," "quixotic," and "costly" nostalgia (117 and 297). Theirs was "much more an investment in nostalgia than an investment for profit" (118). "They could afford the self-indulgent and extravagant luxury of buying themselves a new system based largely on nostalgia for the old time" (296). Theirs was a nostalgia for the days when companies played during the summer at amphitheatres and in city inns during the winter. It was a nostalgia for diverse audiences that included artisans as well as gentry.[3] And it was a nostalgia for "collective landlordism" (117) of the sort that was inaugurated at the Globe in 1599.

Since few of us are prone to think of economies governed solely by laws, or of actors within these economies rationally pursuing their goals, it is reasonable even if only hypothetically to identify a space for affective economies. The early modern English economy, considerably less theorized than our own, must certainly have operated according to a blend of cognition and affect. Gurr's explanation for the sharers' conduct is premised upon such an amalgam, upon what we nowadays call "feeling nostalgic." Hence "the player's sense of traditional values" won out over "commercial wisdom" (118). This strikes me as plausible, but, as I have been suggesting, particular economic decisions may be bound up with a wide variety of affect. Consequently, a number of other emotional factors might be at least as helpful in explaining the sharers' choices. Gurr himself mentions self-indulgence and extravagance. He also mentions pride. We the King's Men, and no one else, can afford to do this, no matter the cost. Like Gresham dissolving a pearl in wine and drinking it off, the King's Men might want simply to jet their plumes or to enjoy their power in the marketplace.

Because we know very little beyond what a few surviving wills and a smattering of commendatory epistles and verses tell us, we are hard-pressed to characterize the affective bonds among the King's Men. Does the offer of shares in the Blackfriars property to Globe shareholders imply a fraternity among men who had been working together for years? Was this initial stock offering a sign of amity? Was it an early modern version of insider trading?[4] Or were Cuthbert and Richard Burbage prudently limiting their exposure by sharing their risk? Conjectures such as these might lead one to believe that tenderness or prudence or even anxiety, not nostalgia, held sway. After all, the Lord Mayor had recently assumed control over what had been the liberty of the Blackfriars. Gurr imagines that the "company was confident that it could mount plays there daily where previously there had only been weekly performances" (296); but it is equally possible that the Burbages were worried that what had befallen their father, when he proved unable to establish an indoor playing space for his company in the Blackfriars, might repeat itself. The King's Men might have been well established in 1608–09, but they still had to contend with a distant, probably unreliable patron. Moreover, to insist that "the reconstruction of the Globe was [financially] unneces-sary" (297) is to overlook the possibility that some shareholders were not sanguine about their prospects for playing within the walls of the city.

Perhaps there were company members whose adrenaline flowed only when they were performing amidst the commotion that we presume was typical at a playing space like the Globe. Exhilaration, as opposed to nostalgia, might explain the desire to maintain an amphitheatre presence. We are familiar with the playwrights', not to mention Hamlet's com-plaints about audiences at the open-air theatres. But what was the actors' point of view? Does the *The Knight of the Burning Pestle* tell us anything about the frustration (boy) actors may have felt with a Blackfriars audience? Rock-and-roll bands that make considerable fortunes from compact disks and music videos continue to mount lavish live-performance tours held at huge outdoor venues. Might there have been players who were, as we now say, committed to playing for popular audiences? Then too, one wonders what sort of thrill (quite apart from profit) derived from playing at the Globe. Were there effects that could be achieved outdoors but not indoors? With good reason we assume that playing indoors in the winter was more comfortable than playing in the cold without a roof overhead. Is it possible that playing outdoors in the summer was more pleasant than playing indoors? Outdoor summer music and theatre festivals are common throughout Europe and North America. Profit, community, festivity, not to mention nostalgia, may all be motives for open-air performance.

Gurr suggests that the King's Men could have rented the Globe to another company: "more companies had patents to play in London than there were theatres for them to play in" (296). Given that the Globe had become the primary venue for the city's preeminent playing company, what cachet would the sharers have been granting a rival company by allowing them to perform in the house the Burbages had built? Once again pride, but also emulation and condescension seem pertinent. An inferior company in residence at the Globe might as easily tarnish as burnish the reputation of the King's Men. The boy actors who had been playing at Burbage's Blackfriars theatre seem to have done much to jeopardize their license. Did the boys put not only themselves but their rented playhouse at risk? There were certainly men and women living in the Blackfriars who still would have been happy to shut down the theatre in their precinct. Fear or caution might well have tempered the sharers' thoughts about profit. Affective economies must have come into play.

Affect bears upon the economy in ways that may be judged ethical or unethical, enabling or disabling. Feelings of nostalgia may secure moral approbation, but perhaps not if one has evidently contributed to the demise of that for which one feels nostalgia. Certainly, we are familiar with widespread commercial exploitation of nostalgia. The affective postures that I have inventoried are nuanced. Embarrassment, which might well be a sign of moral health, can be put to shrewd use in the marketplace. There is a potential righteousness to tenacity, but it is easy enough to imagine it crossing over toward abrasiveness, even offensiveness. Pain that attends toil can be genuinely exculpatory, or it may remind us of the blood that flows when Bardolph tickles his nose with speargrass. The early modern English economy at times prompted, at other times coerced, notably varied affective responses. No master trope, even an implicitly affective trope premised upon a transition from passions to interests, is adequate to the multiplicity of men's and women's affective engagements with a changing economy. The amplitude of aphorism is more arresting but less revealing than the fine grain of particularism.

Notes

1 Three important exceptions are Lorraine Daston, "Curiosity in Early Modern Science," *Word & Image*, 11 (1995), 391–404; Michael MacDonald, *"The Fearefull Estate of Francis Spira*: Narrative, Identity, and Emotion in Early Modern England," *Journal of British Studies*, 31 (1992), 32–61; and Steven Mullaney, "Mourning and Misogyny: *Hamlet, The Revenger's Tragedy*, and the Final Progress of Elizabeth I, 1600–1607," *Shakespeare Quarterly*, 45 (1994), 139–62. Mullaney observes that "[u]nlike the pulpit . . . the stage was an affective rather than a didactic forum . . . As a forum for the representation, solicitation, shaping, and enacting of affect in various forms, for both the reflection and, I would argue, the reformation of emotions and their economies, the popular stage of early modern England was a unique contemporaneous force . . . it certainly served as a prominent affective arena in which significant cultural traumas and highly ambivalent events . . . could be directly or indirectly addressed, symbolically enacted, and brought to partial and imaginary resolution" (144).

   Cf. Jonathan Bates's review, "Love Locked Out: The Downgrading of the Affections in New Shakespearean Criticism," *The Times Literary Supplement*, 24 December 1993, 3–4.

   There is, of course, a vast literature on the humors and, implicitly or explicitly, their relation to joy, grief, fear, etc. that explains the arousal of affect in terms (body and soul) different from my own. Key early modern English texts include Timothy Bright, *A Treatise of Melancholie* (1586), Thomas Wright, *The Passions of the Minde* (1601), Thomas Walkington, *The Optick Glasse of Humors* (1607), and Robert Burton, *The Anatomy of Melancholy* (1621); important modern treatments begin with John W. Draper, *The Humors and Shakespeare's Characters* (1945), Laurence Babb, *The Elizabethan Malady* (1951), and Bridget Gellert Lyons, *Voices of Melancholy* (1971), and now include Gail Kern Paster's seminal *The Body Embarrassed: Drama and the Disciplines of Shame in Early Modern England* (Ithaca: Cornell University Press, 1993).

2 Versions of this transition have been discussed by historians (economic, political, and social) far too numerous to cite. Among those who have interpreted cultural practices informed by this transition are Jean-Christophe Agnew, *Worlds Apart: The Market and the Theater in Anglo-American Thought, 1550–1750* (Cambridge: Cambridge University Press, 1986); Walter

Cohen, *Drama of a Nation: Public Theater in Renaissance England and Spain* (Ithaca: Cornell University Press, 1985); William Flesch, *Generosity and the Limits of Authority: Herbert, Shakespeare, Milton* (Ithaca: Cornell University Press, 1992); Patricia Fumerton, *Cultural Aesthetics: Renaissance Literature and the Practice of Social Ornamentation* (Chicago: University of Chicago Press, 1991); and Frank Whigham, *Ambition and Privilege: The Social Tropes of Elizabethan Courtesy Theory* (Berkeley: University of California Press, 1984). Medievalists have begun to argue that this putatively early modern transition was already under way in the thirteenth century. David Aers, for example, pointedly suggests that "literary scholars take note of the pre-capitalist market economy [in late-thirteenth-century England] and explore what consequences it may have for their version of both the medieval period and the early-modern." See "A Whisper in the Ear of Early Modernists; or, Reflections on Literary Critics Writing the 'History of the Subject'," in *Culture and History 1350–1600*, David Aers, ed. (Detroit: Wayne State University Press, 1992), 180 (and 193); also Lee Patterson, "On the Margin: Postmodernism, Ironic History and Medieval Studies," *Speculum*, 65 (1990), 87–108.

When this transition has been figured by, for instance, Marcel Mauss, in terms of gifts and commodities, it has been argued that it traces the emergence of an economic sphere increasingly divorced from the social sphere (in which affect has been prominent). "People come to see economic transactions as impersonal and rational; they come to see social transactions as personal and affective." See James G. Carrier, *Gifts and Commodities: Exchange and Western Capitalism Since 1700* (London: Routledge, 1995), 10 and *passim*. For a healthy dose of skepticism about hard-and-fast differences between gift and commodity exchange, and between impersonal, rational market societies and those founded upon feelings and interpersonal bonds, see Jonathan Parry and Maurice Bloch, "Introduction: Money and the Morality of Exchange," in Parry and Bloch, *Money and the Morality of Exchange* (Cambridge: Cambridge University Press, 1989), 2–19 and 28–30.

3 Raymond Williams, *Marxism and Literature* (Oxford: Oxford University Press, 1977), 131–32.

4 See Antony Easthope, "History and Psychoanalysis," *Textual Practice*, 9 (1995), 349.

5 *A Thousand Plateaus: Capitalism and Schizophrenia*, Brian Massumi, trans. (Minneapolis: University of Minnesota Press, 1987), 400.

6 Cf. Laura C. Stevenson, *Praise and Paradox: Merchants and Craftsmen in Elizabethan Popular Literature* (Cambridge: Cambridge University Press, 1984): "the Elizabethan economic atmosphere combined stagnation and development, poverty and prosperity, personal opportunity and corporate conservatism in a puzzling mixture, and . . . Elizabethans reacted to this atmosphere (according to their temperaments, ranks, and opportunities) with aggression, complacency, indifference, confusion, dissatisfaction, anxiety, anger, or despair" (23).

7 Cited in J. Coulter, "Affect and Social Context: Emotion Definition as a Social Task," in *The Social Construction of the Emotions*, Rom Harré, ed. (Oxford: Basil Blackwell, 1986), 122.

8 J. Coulter, "Affect and Social Context," 120 and 126. Cf. Michelle A. Rosaldo, "Toward an Anthropology of Self and Feeling," in *Culture Theory: Essays on Mind, Self, and Emotion*, Richard A. Shweder and Robert A. LaVine, eds. (Cambridge: Cambridge University Press, 1984), 141 and 143: "[a]ffects . . . are no less cultural and no more private than beliefs. They are instead, cognitions – or more aptly, perhaps, interpretations – always culturally informed . . ." "Feelings are not substances to be discovered in our blood but social practices organized by stories that we both enact and tell. They are structured by our forms of understanding."

In "The Anthropology of Emotions," *Annual Review of Anthropology*, 15 (1986), 405–36, Catherine Lutz and Geoffrey M. White provide an overview of more than a decade of widely varying anthropological research into the emotions, citing those who define emotion as a "socially validated judgment" (408) and others for whom "emotions are a primary idiom for defining and negotiating social relations of the self in a moral order" (417). They point to a considerable body of scholarship in which "emotional meaning systems" both reflect and help to structure social relations (419). Peggy A. Thoits provides a comparable, discipline-specific overview in "The Sociology of Emotions," *Annual Review of Sociology*, 15 (1989), 317–42. While Thoits emphasizes the "important degree" to which what she calls "emotional beliefs" are "socially acquired and socially structured" (319), she expresses reservations about the "structural-functional approach to emotion culture," in particular, the assumption that "emotion norms are produced by and function to sustain dominant institutional arrangements" (336).

9 Peter N. Stearns and Carol Z. Stearns, "Emotionality: Clarifying the History of Emotions and Emotional Standards," *American History Review*, 90 (1985), 813–36; also Carol Z. Stearns, "'Lord Help Me Walk Humbly': Anger and Sadness in England and America, 1570–1750," in *Emotions and Social Change: Toward a New Psychohistory*, Carol Z. Stearns and Peter N. Stearns, eds. (New York: Holmes and Meier, 1988), 39–68.

10 E. Virginia Demos, ed., *Exploring Affect: The Selected Writings of Silvan S. Tomkins* (Cambridge: Cambridge University Press, 1995), 56.

11 Eve Kosofsky Sedgwick and Adam Frank, eds., *Shame and Its Sisters: A Silvan Tomkins Reader* (Durham: Duke University Press, 1995), 37.

A recent neurobiological account suggests that "reason may not be as pure as most of us think it is or wish it were, that emotions and feelings may not be intruders in the bastion of reason at all: they may be enmeshed in its networks." See Antonio R. Damasio, *Descartes' Error: Emotion, Reason, and the Human Brain* (New York: G. P. Putnam's Sons, 1994), xii. Damasio hypothesizes that an encounter with any event or entity gives rise to a mental evaluative process in which neural representations are formed (compare Coulter's "appraisals and judgements"). The neural and chemical signals that are then unleashed trigger emotions, or what Damasio describes as collections of changing body states in juxtaposition with the initial perceptual images. Feelings are what Damasio takes to be our experience or monitoring of bodily changes (emotions), also already juxtaposed to the mental images which initiate the cycle (see chapter 7). Despite the fact that this neurobiological description pertains to how we "mind the body" (159), there remains room for an important concession: "While there appears to be a large biological component to what I have called primary emotions [happiness, sadness, anger, fear, disgust], the way we conceptualize secondary emotions [remorse, embarrassment, vindication, etc.] is relative to particular cultures" (285n16). The likes of melancholy, euphoria, and shyness are, as Damasio nicely puts it, "tuned by experience" (149).

12 I owe the phrase "knowledge deficit" to Elizabeth Hanson.

13 E. Virginia Demos, ed., *Exploring Affect*, 57. Cf. William Ian Miller, *The Anatomy of Disgust* (Cambridge: Harvard University Press, 1997): "Emotions are feelings connected to ideas, perceptions, and cognitions and to the social and cultural contexts in which it makes sense to have those feelings and ideas. Emotions also have functions and often are motives for action" (8).

14 Cf. Antonio Damasio: "In many circumstances of our life as social beings . . . we know that our emotions are triggered only after an evaluative, voluntary, nonautomatic mental process. Because of the nature of our experience, a broad range of stimuli and situations has become associated with those stimuli which are innately set to cause emotions. The reaction to that broad range of stimuli and situations can be filtered by an interposed mindful evaluation. And because of the thoughtful, evaluative filtering process, there is room for variation in the extent and intensity of preset emotional patterns . . ." (*Descartes' Error*, 130).

Analyzing what might be called the relationality of emotions, Lorraine Daston argues that "the felt substance of an emotion depends to a significant degree on the company it keeps . . . What we might call the structure of emotion changes with its neighbors" ("Curiosity in Early Modern Science," 392).

15 Eve Kosofsky Sedgwick and Adam Frank, eds., *Shame and Its Sisters*, 49 and 62.

16 The relationship between drives and affects is for Tomkins one of "co-assembly," linking the digital (on/off) potential of the former with the analogue (amplificatory) potential of the latter. Affects are drives' *necessary* amplifiers. See Eve Kosofsky Sedgwick and Adam Frank, "Shame in the Cybernetic Fold: Reading Silvan Tomkins," *Critical Inquiry*, 21 (1995), 504.

17 I am again "indebted" to Elizabeth Hanson for helping me to this formulation and to much of what I have arrived at thus far in my introduction.

My attempt to work at a much lower level of generality than is entailed by master affects (or anti-affects, like asceticism) and by widespread trends toward affect moderation (or drive control) in early modern England explains the absence of Max Weber and Norbert Elias from most of my discussion. Nonetheless, one is ill-advised to proceed in these matters without having consulted *The Protestant Ethic and the Spirit of Capitalism* (1904–05) and *The Civilizing Process* (1939). Elias, for example, writes that "the strength, kind and structure of the fears and anxieties that smoulder or flare in the individual never depend solely on his own 'nature' . . . They are always determined, finally, by the history and the actual structure of his relations to other people, by the structure of society, and they change with it." See *The Civilizing Process*, vol. I, *State Formation and Civilization*, Edmund Jephcott, trans. (Oxford: Basil Blackwell, 1982), 327.

18 I am thinking not only of Agnew's stimulating *Worlds Apart*, cited in note 2, but back to L. C. Knights, *Drama and Society in the Age of Jonson* (London: Chatto & Windus, 1937), on to Don Wayne, "Drama and Society in the Age of Jonson: *An Alternative View*," *Renaissance Drama*, 13 (1982), 103–29, and up to the recent work of Douglas Bruster, *Drama and the Market in the Age of Shakespeare* (Cambridge: Cambridge University Press, 1992), Lars Engle, *Shakespearean Pragmatism: Market of His Time* (Chicago: University of Chicago Press, 1993), and Paul Yachnin, *Stage-wrights: Shakespeare, Jonson, Middleton, and the Making of Theatrical Value* (Philadelphia: University of Pennsylvania Press, 1997). Many more titles could be adduced to fill in this chronology.

19 Note, for example, Lars Engle's interest in "the historic and economic *idea* of the market" and his demonstration of how "Shakespeare takes up the market economy both as a *social concept* useful in describing the complex erotic and economic circuits which bind the parties in a single short-term transaction, and as a *historical metaphor* useful in keeping track of the wider set of transactions involved in a long-term process of dynastic change and legitimation" (*Shakespearean Pragmatism*, 21 and 23; my emphasis).

20 For a related argument that points in a different direction, see Christopher Pye, "The Theater, the Market, and the Subject of History," *ELH*, 61 (1994), 501–22. Responding to Stephen Greenblatt's historicism, Pye notes "the ease with which economic description seems to lend itself to a generalized metaphorics of speculation and exchange, to a thrilling measure of discursive liquidity . . . Freed from the particularities of the market, the discourse of 'negotiation,' 'liquidity' and 'exchange' comes to articulate an account of the entire social field, all under the rubric of 'the circulation of social energies'" (502).

21 See Thomas Wilson, *A Discourse Upon Usury* (1572), R. H. Tawney, ed. (London: G. Bell, 1925); R. H. Tawney, *Religion and the Rise of Capitalism* (London: John Murray, 1936); and Norman Jones, *God and the Money-lenders: Usury and the Law in Early Modern England* (Oxford: Basil Blackwell, 1989).

22 See Barry Supple, *Commercial Crisis and Change in England, 1600–1642* (Cambridge: Cambridge University Press, 1959): "England . . . was perpetually threatened with a harmful reduction in its supplies of coins and bullion of one metal – and sometimes of both [gold and silver]. Where, as was the case for most of the period, silver was being lost, considerable inconvenience was felt, which partly goes to explain the vehemence of contemporary complaints concerning a 'scarcity of money'" (14).

Margaret Spufford looked at surviving inventories from Chippenham in Cambridgeshire, 1576–1700, and discovered that "a third of the people who were well enough off to be appraised at death were involved in money-lending." These were "retired yeomen and husbandmen, prosperous crafts-men, and widows and spinsters." What Spufford calls the "money-lending system in rural society . . . permitted a man to stave off the immediate effect of a bad harvest, and to prevent a foreclosure on his holding when he was unable to pay the rent." See *Contrasting Communities: English Villagers in the Sixteenth and Seventeenth Centuries* (Cambridge: Cambridge University Press,

1974), 212 and 78–80; cf. J. A. Chartres, *Internal Trade in England 1500–1700* (London: Macmillan, 1977), 52–54.

23 For the "chain linking credit to trust and trust to a pervasive commitment [in Restoration writings] to the performance of obligations," see Joyce Oldham Appleby, *Economic Thought and Ideology in Seventeenth-Century England* (Princeton: Princeton University Press, 1978), 189. For the "long chain of dependence that involved the poor in small debts, the roving chapman in medium debts, the merchant in the local market in the largest debt of all," see Joan Thirsk, *Economic Policy and Projects: The Development of a Consumer Society in Early Modern England* (Oxford: Clarendon Press, 1978), 170.

24 Cf. Bruce G. Carruthers, *City of Capital: Politics and Markets in the English Financial Revolution* (Princeton: Princeton University Press, 1996): "[t]he same obligation that binds the debtor to the creditor also, in a curious way, binds the creditor to the debtor. This creates the potential for a complex balance of power between debtors and creditors, and modifies the usual picture of a debtor beholden to his or her creditors" (9). Carruthers also comments on the way relationships based on credit "would seem to provide a perfect opportunity to witness *homo economicus* unbound . . . When discussed by contemporaries [in the second half of the seventeenth century], however, credit relations were interpreted through an ethos of neighborliness, and framed by a language of moral obligation" (192).

25 For more detail about the points that follow in this paragraph, see Richard Grassby, *The Business Community of Seventeenth-Century England* (Cambridge: Cambridge University Press, 1995), 215–18.

26 Richard Grassby, *The Business Community of Seventeenth-Century England*, 215 (my emphasis); see also Charles Spinosa, "The Transformation of Intentionality: Debt and Contract in *The Merchant of Venice*," *English Literary Renaissance*, 24 (1994), 370–409.

27 For a premature dating of across the board "liquidity of the commodity form" see Jean-Christophe Agnew, *Worlds Apart*, 11–12 and *passim*. Cf. P. G. M. Dickson, *The Financial Revolution in England: A Study in the Development of Public Credit, 1688–1756* (London: Macmillan, 1967), 39–41 and *passim*.

28 R. D. Richards, *The Early History of Banking in England* (1929; rpt. London: Frank Cass, 1958), 43–50.

29 Richard Grassby, *The Business Community of Seventeenth-Century England*, 217.

30 For recent monographs on the culture of credit in the late seventeenth and early eighteenth centuries, often indebted to the seminal writings of J. G. A. Pocock, see Colin Nicholson, *Writing and the Rise of Finance: Capital Satires of the Early Eighteenth Century* (Cambridge: Cambridge University Press, 1994), Sandra Sherman, *Finance and Fictionality in the Early Eighteenth Century: Accounting for Defoe* (Cambridge: Cambridge University Press, 1996), and James Thompson, *Models of Value: Eighteenth-Century Political Economy and the Novel* (Durham: Duke University Press, 1996).

31 Refreshingly straightforward and telling remarks about the emotions of humility and embarrassment (as well as humiliation and shame) may be found

in William Ian Miller, *Humiliation and Other Essays on Honor, Social Discomfort, and Violence* (Ithaca: Cornell University Press, 1993), 131–74.

32 The distinction between embarrassment and *incipient* humiliation is significant. William Ian Miller notes that "[h]umiliation is dark, embarrassment light. Humiliation is rough justice, embarrassment a gentle slap on the wrist. Embarrassment is a very close relative of amusement, for it takes only a very subtle shift in context, distance, or involvement to turn embarrassing situations into causes for mirth both for observers *and* for the person embarrassed. But one senses that if humiliation has anything to do with amusement, that amusement would be dark indeed" (*Humiliation*, 148–49, also 150–65).

33 This is to take issue with Lawrence and Jeanne C. Fawtier Stone's conviction that there was a "close and easy co-operation" between the early modern English "elite" and "a powerful upper bourgeoisie of overseas merchants and bankers." See *An Open Elite? England 1540–1880* (Oxford: Clarendon Press, 1984), 423.

34 Cf. William Ian Miller, "Contempt is the emotional complex that articulates and maintains hierarchy, status, rank, and respectability. And differentiated status and rank are the eliciting conditions of contempt." Miller nicely distinguishes between contempt and disgust: "Contempt marks social distinctions that are graded ever so finely, whereas disgust marks boundaries in the large cultural and moral categories that separate pure and impure, good and evil, good taste and bad taste." See *The Anatomy of Disgust*, 217 and 220.

35 "My little beagle": so begin a number of James's letters to Cecil; see, for example, HMC Salisbury MSS, 20.269 and 287.

I   CREDIT CRUNCH

1   R. H. Tawney, "Introduction" to Thomas Wilson's *A Discourse upon Usury* (1925; rpt. New York: A. M. Kelley, 1963), 88; cf. Eric Kerridge, *Trade and Banking in Early Modern England* (Manchester: Manchester University Press, 1988), 68 and 75. See also Margaret Spufford, *Contrasting Communities: English Villagers in the Sixteenth and Seventeenth Centuries* (Cambridge: Cambridge University Press, 1974): "Borrowing and credit appear to have underpinned the whole of rural society" (80). Needless to say, credit relations obtained between various sorts of people in England before the sixteenth century. In the realm of trade, see, for example, Pamela Nightingale, "Monetary Contraction and Mercantile Credit in Later Medieval England," *Economic History Review*, 43 (1990), 560–75; also N. J. Mayhew, "Population, Money Supply, and the Velocity of Circulation in England, 1300–1700," *Economic History Review*, 48 (1995), 238–57 ("what really kept trade going was the practice of sales on credit," 253). The pervasiveness of such relations, their increasing theorization and rationalization, as well as the attendant flood of debt litigation, all indicate something new.

C. W. Brooks, *Pettyfoggers and Vipers of the Commonwealth: The 'Lower Branch' of the Legal Profession in Early Modern England* (Cambridge: Cambridge University Press, 1986), charts the spectacular rise in the absolute and relative frequencies of actions of debt in Common Pleas and King's

Bench from 1560 to 1640 (69). Brooks notes that the litigants were men "below the rank of gentleman" (110) and argues that "[b]orrowing and lending were widespread" among not only gentry and merchants, but yeomen and artisans (95–96).

Economic and legal historians' notions of credit are, of course, not exhaustive. "Credit," which gives us credence and credibility and credentials, as well as incredible and discredit, derives from *credo*, to entrust or commit, to trust, to believe, to think. Benveniste writes that "*Credo* . . . is *literally* 'to place one's **kred*', that is 'magical powers', in a person from whom one expects protection thanks to 'believing' in him." See Emile Benveniste, *Indo-European Language and Society*, Elizabeth Palmer, trans. (London: Faber and Faber, 1973), 99; and Pierre Bourdieu, *Language and Symbolic Power*, Gino Raymond and Matthew Adamson, trans. (Cambridge: Harvard University Press, 1991), 118–19 and 192–93. The role played by gender, and the advent of humanism, in the redefinition of credit in early modern England are the subjects of Lorna Hutson's *The Usurer's Daughter: Male Friendship and Fictions of Women in Sixteenth-Century England* (London: Routledge, 1994).

In France, Jonathan Dewald writes, "'credit' became a central metaphor of seventeenth-century public life. Contemporaries typically described the standing of leading figures in terms of the 'credit' they enjoyed." Dewald goes on to make the larger, and convincing, argument that late-sixteenth- and seventeenth-century France witnessed not "the rise of self-interest or of economic rationality . . . [but] the rise of credit and the need for economic independence." See *Aristocratic Experience and the Origins of Modern Culture: France, 1570–1715* (Berkeley: University of California Press, 1993), 157 and 172. I owe this reference to Nancy Klein Maguire.

2 Robert Tittler, "Money-Lending in the West Midlands: the Activities of Joyce Jefferies, 1638–49," *Historical Research*, 67 (1994), 251. That Antonio's credit relations in *The Merchant of Venice* should include both Bassanio and Shylock suggests that transactions founded in *Gesellschaft* were not only subsequent to, but often coterminous with, those founded in *Gemeinschaft*. Or, as Clifford Geertz has noted in the context of "the Javanese attitude toward credit: its main function is not simply to capitalize trade but to stabilize and regularize ties between traders, to give persistence and form to commercial relationships." See *Peddlers and Princes: Social Change and Economic Modernization in Two Indonesian Towns* (Chicago: University of Chicago Press, 1963), 39.

3 Tittler, "Money-Lending in the West Midlands," notes that even as credit transactions were being rationalized in the seventeenth century, "'[c]redit' still meant trust" (260). He posits a geographically uneven and an evolutionary, as opposed to a revolutionary, transition from what Tawney described as casual and personal credit relations to the transactions typical of Adam Smith's professionals (263). Peter Spufford, who writes that "il est manifestment habituel, dans l'est du Kent au XVIIe siècle, de vivre, au moins en partie, avec l'argent des autres," finds that while many of the century's credit relations extended no further than among family members, "[n]éanmoins, une partie non négligeable de l'investissement intervient entre des parties qui n'ont aucun contact personnel immédiatement réparable par l'historien." See "Les

liens du crédit au village dans l'Angleterre du XVIIe siècle," *Annales: Histoire, Sciences Sociales*, 49 (1994), 1361–62 and 1369–71. An earlier, slightly different version of this essay appears as "Credit in Rural England before the Advent of Country Banks," *Atti della Società Ligure di Storia Patria*, 31 (1991), fasc. II, 893–911.

4 Renato Rosaldo notes that "the term *nostalgia* (from the Greek *nostos*, 'to return home,' and *algia*, 'a painful condition') dates from the late seventeenth century." See "Imperialist Nostalgia," *Representations*, 26 (1989), 108; also Jean Starobinski, "The Idea of Nostalgia," *Diogenes*, 54 (1966), 81–103 ("In psychiatry . . . we no longer underline the desire to return but, on the contrary, the failure of adaptation," 101). The term "nostalgia" was coined by Johannes Hofer. See "Medical Dissertation on Nostalgia by Johannes Hofer, 1688," Carolyn Kiser Anspach, trans., *Bulletin of the History of Medicine*, 2 (1934), 376–91; and see George Rosen, "Nostalgia: A 'Forgotten' Psychological Disorder," *Clio Medica*, 10 (1975), 28–51. I owe these two references to Susan Snyder.

According to Phyllis Rackin, nostalgia "forms a constant feature of Renaissance thought." Writing specifically about *Richard II*, Rackin argues that "[i]nitially identified with a lost medieval world, Richard is now associated with the emergent capitalism that was transforming English society in Shakespeare's own time, with the same threatening mercantile forces that produced the longing for an idealized feudal past which must have drawn many of Shakespeare's original audience to see the play in the first place." See *Stages of History: Shakespeare's English Chronicles* (Ithaca: Cornell University Press, 1990), 117n63 and 123. Jonathan Hall notes "elements of nostalgia in the new national theatre" as well as a new subject, "a nomadic adventurer, whose desires challenge all formerly established boundaries, [even as] s/he is profoundly marked by regressive and narcissistic desires for an absent center or origin." See *Anxious Pleasures: Shakespearean Comedy and the Nation-State* (New Jersey: Fairleigh Dickinson University Press, 1995), 35.

5 Not just Shylock, but Antonio too (my colleague Marshall Grossman suggests), makes manifest a supplement unassimilable to the formation nostalgically evoked. *The Merchant of Venice* is thus itself generically recursive, knowingly and nostalgically if not necessarily neurotically recurring to the Pauline text.

6 Sigmund Freud, *Beyond the Pleasure Principle*, James Strachey, trans. (New York: W. W. Norton, 1961), 43. Jean-Joseph Goux explicates the neurotic subject in history in terms of repression and replacement – at the level of the unconscious – not recursion. "The progress of civilization, leaving beneath and behind it the signifying modes of production which it outmodes and interdicts, produces a neurotic *succession*." "Just as on the level of neurosis the symptom substitutes for a repressed idea, we can say that on the historical scale *neurosis is the symptom of a repressed historical period*. For the idea repressed by neurosis is the ideology of a superseded period, and the neurotic individual becomes the symptom of the era left behind." *Symbolic Economies: After Marx and Freud*, Jennifer Curtiss Gage, trans. (Ithaca: Cornell University Press, 1990), 85.

7 A socio-economic basis for this gap broadens the etiology for it that has been adduced by Edward Snow in his deeply moving account of Faustus, a debtor who makes Lucifer his creditor when he binds his soul by deed of gift. See "Marlowe's *Doctor Faustus* and the Ends of Desire," in *Two Renaissance Mythmakers: Christopher Marlowe and Ben Jonson*, Alvin Kernan, ed. (Baltimore: Johns Hopkins University Press, 1977), 70–110. In the final sections of this chapter, I suggest that both the embarrassed creditor's expenditure of energy on memorialization and the debtor/creditor's self-depletion (Timon's, in my account, but I suspect this applies to Faustus's too) also have as their telos, death.

8 All citations are from the Arden edition, John Russell Brown, ed. (London: Methuen, 1955).

9 *The Philosophy of Money*, Tom Bottomore and David Frisby, trans. (Boston: Routledge & Kegan Paul, 1978), 176.

10 *OED*, sufficient, adj. A4. In his sermon, *The Godly Merchant* (London, 1613), 23, William Pemberton reminded his Paul's Cross auditors that "*Our sufficiency is from God*" who alone need not worry about credit because He alone is "*El-schaddai, the almighty* and *al-sufficient God.*"

11 The business of maritime insurance, and its relation to usury, was very much in the air; a general account of "assurances" may be found in Gerald Malynes, *Consuetudo, Vel Lex Mercatoria* (London, 1622), 146–66. On maritime insurance under Elizabeth, see note 49, below.

12 Cf. Walter Cohen, *Drama of a Nation: Public Theater in Renaissance England and Spain* (Ithaca: Cornell University Press, 1985), 202, where Antonio is described as "the harbinger of modern capitalism."

13 Cf. Lars Engle, "'Thrift in Blessing'. Exchange and Explanation in *The Merchant of Venice*," *Shakespeare Quarterly*, 37 (1986), 27. See also the expanded version of this essay in *Shakespearean Pragmatism: Market of His Time* (Chicago: University of Chicago Press, 1993), 85. Like Engle, I focus on credit and obligation, and on the relations between emotions and finance.

14 For the way Antonio's "social function" fills him with sadness, see Michael Nerlich, *Ideology of Adventure*, vol. I, Ruth Crowley, trans. (Minneapolis: University of Minnesota Press, 1987), 145–46 and 159. For a brilliant analysis of what I would call a recursion from both the marketplace and a gift, or patronage, economy to an artisanal, corporate economy founded on labor and in the workshop, see Jane Tylus's "Resisting the Marketplace: The Language of Labor in Benvenuto Cellini's *Vita*," in *Reconfiguring the Renaissance: Essays in Cultural Materialism*, Jonathan Crewe, ed. (Lewisburg: Bucknell University Press, 1992), 34–50.

15 *Drama of a Nation*, 200 and 203. Cf. Michael Ferber: "Shakespeare wanted Antonio to have noble virtues, however improbable his calling makes them . . . One might take his sadness as a sign of his foundering under the burden of so much heterogeneous ideological cargo." See "The Ideology of *The Merchant of Venice*," *English Literary Renaissance*, 20 (1990), 438.

16 Marc Shell has noted Heinrich Heine's remark that Antonio's Christian "brothers" in Venice do not lend him the ducats he needs. See *Money, Language, and Thought: Literary and Philosophical Economies from the Medieval to the Modern Era* (Berkeley: University of California Press, 1982),

67. In Shakespeare's probable source story, *Il Pecorone*, "many merchants joined together in offering to pay the money." See Geoffrey Bullough, ed., *Narrative and Dramatic Sources of Shakespeare*, vol. I (London: Routledge & Kegan Paul, 1957), 472.

17 Renato Rosaldo writes of nostalgia as "a form of mystification," a process by which "people mourn the passing of what they themselves have transformed"; one attempts "to establish one's innocence and at the same time talk about what one has destroyed"; see "Imperialist Nostalgia," 108–09.

18 Julie Solomon informs me (pers. comm.) that in early seventeenth-century bookkeeping, a "waste book" was a disposable, rough account book in which one would note all and sundry transactions prior to entering them more carefully in a journal or ledger.

19 Cf. Lars Engle's reading of the play's relation to the Elizabethan credit and marriage markets, and his suggestion that Antonio's sadness "is a market-linked phenomenon," in "'Thrift is Blessing,'" 20, 28 and *passim*. David Lowenthal notes that "[s]eventeenth-century nostalgia was a physical rather than a mental complaint, an illness with explicit symptoms and often lethal consequences . . . To leave home for long was to risk death." Cited by Renato Rosaldo, "Imperialist Nostalgia," 109.

20 Here and in what follows, I advance various responses to credit and debt. A note may suffice to indicate a joyful version of Antonio's morbid involvement in both Bassanio's debts and the composition of his own epitaph. Michael Nerlich (*Ideology of Adventure*, I.101–07) instances Panurge's paradoxical encomium to debtors and creditors. In Rabelaisian terms, financial debts are the very basis of "Faith, Hope, and Charity." Panurge (who, Nerlich writes, represents "the merchant, the avant-garde of the bourgeoisie") begs Pantagruel *not* to absolve him of all his "past owings." Since "Nature created man for no other purpose but to lend and borrow," to be unencumbered would be to die: "from now on not a fart will blow off . . . that isn't aimed at my nose. For every farter in the world says as he farts: 'Now we're quits!' My life will soon be over . . . I leave you [Pantagruel] the making of my epitaph. For I shall be pickled in farts." See François Rabelais, *The Histories of Gargantua and Pantagruel*, J. M. Cohen, trans. (New York: Penguin, 1979), 298–303. What I have called joyful, Nerlich deems possibly "naive," then "burlesque irony" (103).

21 See Karen Newman, "Portia's Ring: Unruly Women and Structures of Exchange in *The Merchant of Venice*," *Shakespeare Quarterly*, 38 (1987), 19.

22 Cf. Engle, "'Thrift is Blessing,'" 33 (*Shakespearean Pragmatism*, 93); and Harry Berger, Jr., "Marriage and Mercifixion in *The Merchant of Venice*: The Casket Scene Revisited," *Shakespeare Quarterly* 32 (1981), 161: Portia "uses the additional gift of the ring to convert this first gift [of her property and herself] to a loan, a bond."

23 For a different juxtaposition of Portia with Elizabeth, see Leah Marcus, "Shakespeare's Comic Heroines, Elizabeth I, and the Political Uses of Androgyny," in *Women in the Middle Ages and the Renaissance*, Mary Beth Rose, ed. (Syracuse: Syracuse University Press, 1986), 135–55.

24 Richard Bonney, *The King's Debts: Finance and Politics in France 1589–1661* (Oxford: Clarendon Press, 1981), vii. See also James B. Collins, *Fiscal Limits*

of Absolutism: Direct Taxation in Early Seventeenth-Century France (Berkeley: University of California Press, 1988), 1.

25 A. W. Lovett, "The Vote of the *Millones* (1590)," *Historical Journal*, 30 (1987), 2–3.

26 A. W. Lovett, *Early Habsburg Spain 1517–1598* (Oxford: Oxford University Press, 1986), 228–29; also see A. W. Lovett's "The General Settlement of 1577: An Aspect of Spanish Finance in the Early Modern Period," *Historical Journal*, 25 (1982), 1–22. I. A. A. Thompson notes that the "term 'bankruptcy' can be misleading," especially since Spanish "'bankruptcies' were an integral part of the financial system of the Monarchy": "[t]hese events . . . were a rescheduling of debts, but they did not mean that the Crown was without resources. Determined unilaterally by the Crown, they did not involve any legal process, nor any sequestration of the Crown's assets; neither did they stop the Crown taking on more loans." Thompson adds that "[t]he consolidation of the debt was the key to the long-term ability of the Spanish Monarchy to live beyond its immediate means, for it made possible a continuous renewal of the cycle of borrowing in advance of progressively retreating and hence progressively less attractive incomes." See "Castile: Polity, Fiscality, and Fiscal Crisis," in *Fiscal Crises, Liberty, and Representative Government, 1450–1789*, Philip T. Hoffman and Kathryn Norberg, eds. (Stanford: Stanford University Press, 1994), 160–61.

27 Bonney, *The King's Debts*, 29, 33, and 36. Cf. Philip T. Hoffman, "Early Modern France, 1450–1700," in *Fiscal Crises, Liberty, and Representative Government*: "By the end of the sixteenth century, public credit had largely disappeared, and the monarchy was reduced to the medieval practice of having the king's councilors take out loans in their own name" (233).

28 M. Berger de Xivrey, ed. *Recueil des Lettres Missives de Henri IV*, vol. III (Paris: Imprimerie Royale, 1846), 658–60.

29 Bonney, *The King's Debts*, 54–57; cf. Hoffman, "Early Modern France," 243–44. According to Collins, *Fiscal Limits of Absolutism*, 67, one of Henri's "main concerns between 1596 and 1604 was to decide which debts to pay"; see also, pp. 67–98.

30 R. B. Wernham, "Queen Elizabeth and the Portugal Expedition of 1589," *English Historical Review*, 66 (1951), 4.

31 *State Papers Relating to the Defeat of the Spanish Armada anno 1588*, vol. I, ed. John K. Laughton (London: Spottiswoode & Co., 1894), 285.

32 M. J. Rodríguez-Salgado, "The Anglo-Spanish War: the Final Episode in the 'Wars of Roses'?" in *England, Spain, and the Gran Armada 1585–1604*, M. J. Rodríguez-Salgado and Simon Adams, eds. (Edinburgh: John Donald, 1991), 25.

33 R. B. Wernham, *After the Armada: Elizabethan England and the Struggle for Western Europe 1588–1595* (Oxford: Clarendon Press, 1984), 78.

34 See G. D. Ramsay, *The City of London in International Politics at the Accession of Elizabeth Tudor* (Manchester: Manchester University Press, 1975), 50; for European monarchs, see Immanuel Wallerstein, *The Modern World-System* (New York: Academic Press, 1974), 176.

35 Wernham, "Queen Elizabeth and the Portugal Expedition," 5; for a schematic account of typical royal negotiations with the City of London, see Robert

Ashton, *The Crown and the Money Market, 1603–1640* (Oxford: Clarendon Press, 1960), 27.

36 R. B. Wernham, *After the Armada*, 81.

37 "Queen Elizabeth and the Portugal Expedition," 5.

38 *Annales of Queen Elizabeth* (1635), cited in Lawrence Stone, *An Elizabethan: Sir Horatio Palavicino* (Oxford: Clarendon Press, 1956), 129.

39 Karl Marx, "Excerpts from James Mill's *Elements of Political Economy*," in *Early Writings*, Rodney Livingstone and Gregor Benton, trans. (New York: Penguin, 1975), 263–64. Julie Solomon has called my attention to Elaine Scarry's comments on "Marx's writing when he is acknowledging the body's presence in . . . money, fixed capital, circulating capital" and on capital's presence *as* the body: "Capital. It is colossal. It is magnificent. And it is the capitalist's body": in *The Body in Pain* (Oxford: Oxford University Press, 1985), 249–50 and 264.

40 Cf. Frederick Engels, "The merchant was the revolutionary element in this [medieval] society . . . he is the starting point of its transformation. Not, however, as a conscious revolutionary; on the contrary, as its own flesh and blood." See the "Supplement to Volume 3 of *Capital*," Karl Marx, *Capital*, vol. III, David Fernbach, trans. (London: Penguin, 1981), 1038.

41 Karl Marx, "Excerpts," 264.

42 "Embarrassment" and "embarrass," like "nostalgia," first appear in English later in the century. The *OED* begins with Pepys writing in his diary, in 1664, of his "embarras" (the French word dates back to the mid-sixteenth century). William Ian Miller notes that the "*OED* finds it [embarrass] in the late seventeenth century referring to the state of being perplexed, but it is not until almost exactly to the year that *humiliating* means what it does to us that *embarrassment* does too: perplexed, yes, but with particular reference to awkwardness about the propriety of certain actions." My sense that the emotion we associate with Gresham is embarrassment, not shame, runs counter to Miller's account, according to which, before 1700, shame "clearly seemed to occupy much of the ground we would now call embarrassment and most all the ground we would call humiliation." See *Humiliation and Other Essays on Honor, Social Discomfort, and Violence* (Ithaca: Cornell University Press, 1993), 176, 179, and Miller's discussion of shame, humiliation, and embarrassment in *Sir Gawain and the Green Knight* (183–95).

43 All citations are from Madeleine Doran's edition of *If You Know Not Me You Know Nobody, Part II* for the Malone Society (Oxford: Oxford University Press, 1935).

44 Richard Grassby notes that the "credit and reputation of prosperous merchants was . . . such that they could often manage without cash: their bills were accepted in anticipation of profits, and additional capital could be attracted from relatives and friends at a low rate of interest. Business fortunes were exposed to uncertainty but they had the advantage of flexibility": see "English Merchant Capitalism in the Late Seventeenth Century. The Composition of Business Fortunes," *Past & Present*, 46 (1970), 105.

45 Edward T. Bonahue, Jr., "Social Control, the City, and the Market: Heywood's *2 If You Know Not Me, You Know Nobody*," *Renaissance Papers 1993*, Barbara J. Baines and George Walton Williams, eds. (Southeastern Renais-

sance Conference, 1994), 78; Alexander Leggatt, *Jacobean Public Theatre* (London: Routledge, 1992), 173; Barbara J. Baines, *Thomas Heywood* (Boston: Twayne, 1984), 35.

46 On Antonio, see René Girard's "'To Entrap the Wisest': A Reading of *The Merchant of Venice*," in *Literature and Society*, Edward W. Said, ed. (Baltimore: Johns Hopkins University Press, 1980), 100–19.

47 Craig Muldrew provides evidence for the avoidance of "wranglinge or suit of law" by means of informal or structured arbitration (of the sort to which Ramsey and Gresham submit themselves) in "The Culture of Reconciliation: Community and the Settlement of Economic Disputes in Early Modern England," *Historical Journal*, 39 (1996), 931–37.

48 "By the terms of his [Gresham's] will . . . the Exchange and other properties came jointly into the hands of the City of London and the Mercers' Company for the performance of certain charitable trusts, including the establishment of Gresham College." See W. K. Jordan, *The Charities of London 1480–1660* (London: George Allen & Unwin, 1960), 253. I. R. Adamson suggests that the Corporation of the City of London, which had been led by Gresham to believe that it would inherit the Exchange and "share its unencumbered profits," was none too happy to discover, in 1575, that Gresham's will called for the endowment of a college out of the profits of the Royal Exchange. The Corporation had, after all, paid £3,500 for the land upon which Gresham built the Exchange. See "The Administration of Gresham College and its Fluctuating Fortunes as a Scientific Institution in the Seventeenth Century," *History of Education*, 9 (1980), 14–15.

49 Reginald R. Sharpe, *London and the Kingdom*, vol. I (London: Longmans, Green, 1894), 500. See W. J. Jones, "Elizabethan Marine Insurance: the Judicial Undergrowth," *Business History*, 2 (1960), 53–66, where it is noted that in 1576 a "monopoly for the registering of [maritime insurance] policies was granted . . . to Richard Candler, Gresham's representative in London" (63). See also J. S. Kepler, "The Operating Potential of London Marine Insurance in the 1570s," *Business History*, 17 (1975), 45 and *passim*.

50 Some cause for embarrassment may be found in Edmund Howe's edition of Stow's *The Annales, or Generall Chronicle of England* (London, 1615). Here we read that for two or three years after it was built, the building stood empty, and that "a little before" the Queen was to visit, Gresham "went twice one day round about the upper pawne, and besought those few shopkeepers then present, that they would furnish, and adorne with wares . . . as many shoppes, as they either coulde, or would & they would have, all those shops so furnished rentfree that yeare" (868). Of the Queen's visit itself, we read: "In the yeare 1570, on the 23. of Jannuarie, the Queenes Majestie, attended with her Nobilitie, came from her house at the Strand called Sommerset house, and entered the citie by Temple Barre . . . to sir *Thomas Greshams* in Bishopgate streete, where she dined. After dinner, her Majestie returning through Cornehill, entered the Bursse on the southside, and after that she had viewed every part therof above the ground, especially the Pawne, which was richly furnished with all sorts of the finest wares in the Citie: she caused the same Bursse by an Herauld and a Trumpet, to be proclaimed the *Royal Exchange*." See John Stow, *A Survey of London* (1603), vol. I, Charles L. Kingsford, ed.

(Oxford: Clarendon Press, 1908), 193.

S. T. Bindoff speculates that Elizabeth proclaimed Gresham's burse *her* Royal Exchange "in obedience to her instinct to defend the royal prerogative in all its branches" (in this instance, to control the trade in bills of exchange). But he goes on to note that far from catering to "merchants of all nations and bills on every market," the Exchange soon merely "ousted St Paul's as the customary place for the discharge of debts." See *The Fame of Sir Thomas Gresham* (London: Jonathan Cape, 1973), 19. Later cause for embarrassment is registered in *The Royal Exchange* (Harlem, 1597), when John Payne wishes "both young men and reputed virgins there [in the upper shops] to win credit to the house and to themselves by desert of better fame then is abroad" (15).

51 On progress through Kent in 1573, Elizabeth visited Gresham at his estate. She paid him yet another visit, at Osterley, in 1576.

   On the "embarrassment of riches" and the sanction of "clergy and laity," see Simon Schama, *The Embarrassment of Riches: An Interpretation of Dutch Culture in the Golden Age* (New York: Knopf, 1987):

   A strong sense of the reprehensible nature of money-making persisted, even while the Dutch amassed their individual and collective fortunes. The odd consequence of this disparity between principles and practice was to foster expenditure rather than capital accumulation, as a way to exonerate oneself from the suspicion of avarice. Admittedly, the forms of such expenditure had to be collectively sanctioned and regarded as morally unblemished by clergy and laity alike. But that might extend from obviously virtuous expenditures like philanthropy, to less sacrificial gestures, like lending to public institutions at low rates and on long terms . . . (334).

52 One or another variant of the phrase "her Majesty's honor and credit" fills Gresham's correspondence with Burghley; see John William Burgon, *The Life and Times of Sir Thomas Gresham*, 2 vols., vol. I (London: Effingham Wilson, n.d.), *passim*. As early as 1588, Gresham emphasized reciprocity between sovereign and subject, advising Elizabeth "to kepp [up] your creditt, and specially with your owne marchants, for it is thaye must stand by youe att all eventes in your necessity" (Burgon, I.486).

53 Doran, ed., Heywood, *If You Know Not Me You Know Nobody, Part II*, xvii–xviii.

54 Julia Gasper calls *Part II* a "terrible hotchpotch of a play" in "The Reformation Plays on the Public Stage," *Theatre and Government under the Early Stuarts*, J. R. Mulryne and Margaret Shewring, eds. (Cambridge: Cambridge University Press, 1993), 203.

55 See Richard Johnson's *The Plesant Conceites of Old Hobson, The Merry Londoner* (London, 1607).

56 Bindoff, *The Fame of Sir Thomas Gresham*, 10.

57 Burgon, *Sir Thomas Gresham*, I.89–92.

58 *Ibid.*, I.138 and 133.

59 *Ibid.*, II.12–13.

60 *Ibid.*, II.26–27.

61 The majority of Tudor and early Stuart bankrupts – those who were liable to be proceeded against by creditors – were "craftsmen, shopkeepers, and small middle-men: bakers and butchers, simple drapers and mercers, buttonsellers,

fishmongers, and upholsterers" – see W. J. Jones, *The Foundations of English Bankruptcy: Statutes and Commissions in the Early Modern Period* (Philadelphia: American Philosophical Society, 1979), 5.

62 Paul S. Seaver, *Wallington's World: A Puritan Artisan in Seventeenth-Century London* (Stanford: Stanford University Press, 1985), 123.

63 Anon., *The Death of Usury, or, the Disgrace of Usurers* (Cambridge, 1594), E4v.

64 Cited in Norman Jones, *God and the Moneylenders: Usury and Law in Early Modern England* (Oxford: Basil Blackwell, 1989), 54 and 67.

65 John Wheeler, *A Treatise on Commerce* (London, 1601), B2; Malynes, *Lex Mercatoria*, 221.

66 W. J. Jones, *Foundations of English Bankruptcy*, 8.

67 See A. W. Lovett, *Philip II and Mateo Vázquez de Leca: the Government of Spain (1572–1592)* (Geneva: Librairie Droz, 1977), 66; Lovett cites other examples at 66n35.

68 Cited in José Gentil da Silva, "Réalités économique et prises de conscience: Quelques Témoignages sur le XVIe siècle," *Annales: Economies, Sociétés, Civilisations* 14 (1959), 737; a footnote of Marc Shell's put me onto this citation, although Shell exercises some license, translating "cambios and interesses" as "immaterial money" – see *Money, Language, and Thought*, 5.

69 All citations are from the Arden edition of *Timon of Athens*, H. J. Oliver, ed. (London: Methuen, 1959).

70 Michael Chorost, "Biological Finance in Shakespeare's *Timon of Athens*," *ELR*, 21 (1991), 357; cf. Timon "tries to ignore money itself" (352).

71 Stanley Wells and Gary Taylor, *William Shakespeare: A Textual Companion* (Oxford. Clarendon Press, 1987), 303.

72 For the former, see John Wallace, "*Timon of Athens* and the Three Graces: Shakespeare's Senecan Study," *Modern Philology*, 83 (1986), 360; for the latter, Chorost, "Biological Finance," 350.

73 Kahn, "'Magic of bounty': *Timon of Athens*, Jacobean Patronage, and Maternal Power," *Shakespeare Quarterly*, 38 (1987), 34–57.

74 For Bacon's concern about the precedent set when Parliament "was once in taste with the matter of bargain" and Cecil's justification of bounty, see F. R. Foster, *Proceedings in Parliament 1610*, vol. I (New Haven: Yale University Press, 1966), 105 and 6; cf. Linda Levy Peck, "'For a King not to be bountiful were a fault': Perspectives on Court Patronage in Early Stuart England," *Journal of British Studies*, 25 (1985), 31–61. On James's willingness to "strike a bargain," see Alan G. R. Smith, "Crown, Parliament and Finance: The Great Contract of 1610," in *The English Commonwealth 1547–1640*, Peter Clark, Alan G. R. Smith, and Nicolas Tyacke, eds. (New York: Barnes and Noble, 1979), 111 and *passim*.

75 *Timon of Athens* (London: Harvester Wheatsheaf, 1989), 77. In another context, Nuttall remarks on the way Shakespeare, in *Timon*, moves beyond *The Merchant of Venice* to do "what Shylock was prevented from doing, he rips open the heart of the Giver" (125). This is to presume Antonio's "pure altruism" ("He is the unmercenary merchant") and to make a case for Shakespeare's development (*Timon* "growing out of *Merchant*"): comedy to tragedy, satisfying to disturbing, etc. I have argued that the question Nuttall

assigns to *Timon* – "Does love really ask for nothing, or is another order of reciprocity and obligation involved?" – is a question posed more acutely in *Merchant* (124–25).

76 Timon goes on to ask, "must my house / Be my retentive enemy, my gaol?" – 3.4.79–80. The pervasive assumption was that bankrupts kept to their houses to avoid arrest; cf. Lucius's Servant at 3.4.72–75, also Thomas Dekker, *The Seven Deadly Sinnes of London* (1606), in *The Non-Dramatic Works of Thomas Dekker*, vol. II, Alexander. B. Grosart, ed. (London: Hazell, Watson, and Viney, 1885), 23: "the politick Bankrupt barricadoing his Sconce with double locks, treble dores, invincible bolts, and pieces of timber 4. or 5. storyes hye, victuals himself for a moneth or so."

77 Lawrence Stone, *The Crisis of the Aristocracy 1558–1641* (Oxford: Clarendon Press, 1965), 543–44. In what follows, I concentrate on aristocratic indebtedness; Coppélia Kahn reads Timon's bounty in the context of King James's in "'Magic of bounty,'" 41–48 and 55–57. On late-sixteenth-century Norman *parlementaires'* indebtedness and the credit mechanisms available to them, see Jonathan Dewald, *The Formation of a Provincial Nobility: The Magistrates of the Parlement of Rouen, 1499–1610* (Princeton: Princeton University Press, 1980), 229–45. Dewald documents a marked increase in borrowing on the part of *parlementaires* during the last years of the sixteenth century and the first decade of the seventeenth; "magistrates were drawn into a much more intense round of credit relations after the 1570s" (240).

78 Peck, *Court Patronage and Corruption in Early Stuart London* (Boston: Unwin Hyman, 1990), 158–59; cf. "corrupt practices . . . became a matter of increasing concern in the early seventeenth century. The extent and scale of corruption appears to have increased especially from the 1590s" (5). Important earlier studies of corruption in early modern England include Joel Hurstfield, *Freedom, Corruption and Government in Elizabethan England* (Cambridge: Harvard University Press, 1973) and Gerald Aylmer, *The King's Servants* (London: Routledge & Kegan Paul, 1961) and his *The State's Servants* (London: Routledge & Kegan Paul, 1973). Hurstfield, who is inclined to show a good deal of tolerance, writes that following the death of Robert Cecil, in 1612, patronage was more and more often "corrupted into favouritism" (153).

79 See Peck, *Court Patronage and Corruption*, 11 and 135; also Stone, *Crisis of the Aristocracy*, 421: "James lacked the strength of mind to support the reformers, and immediately began exempting his friends from the ban" on pensions in 1621. James C. Scott has written of "proto-corruption – that is, of practices that are corrupt only by present-day standards" – in early Stuart England. "Practices that are today corrupt were an integral part of the mercantilist and revenue farming arrangements of the seventeenth century." See *Comparative Political Corruption* (New Jersey: Prentice-Hall, 1972), 37 and 52. While it is important to keep in mind that much of what we deem corrupt practices, Jacobean Londoners would have taken for acceptable patron–client or Crown-sponsored relations, even my brief rehearsal of the Suffolk case suggests that early modern English people could find criteria for distinguishing between what we might call acceptable and unacceptable corruption. It should go without saying that personal and political factors

influenced the deployment of these criteria. One person's or one moment's false dealing might be another's patronage.

Cf. Sharon Kettering's remarks about political corruption in early modern France: "By early modern standards, many illegal practices were not considered corrupt. Some modern abuses – embezzlement of state funds, forgery, fraudulent accounting at the expense of the state – were considered corrupt in the seventeenth century. But other practices fell into a gray area . . . The concept of corruption did exist in seventeenth-century France." See *Patrons, Brokers, and Clients in Seventeenth-Century France* (Oxford: Oxford University Press, 1986), 204 and 192. I owe this reference to Nancy Klein Maguire.

80 See Lawrence Stone's chapters on "Office and the Court," "Credit," and "Conspicuous Consumption" in *Crisis of the Aristocracy*, 383–588, and Stone's *Family and Fortune: Studies in Aristocratic Finance in the Sixteenth and Seventeenth Centuries* (Oxford: Clarendon Press, 1973).

81 Cited in Stone, *Family and Fortune*, 282. My discussion of Suffolk (1561–1626) is based upon Stone, 268–86; Peck, *Court Patronage and Corruption*, 181–84; A. P. P. Keep, "Star Chamber Proceedings against the Earl of Suffolk and Others," *English Historical Review*, 13 (1898), 716–29; and Anthony F. Upton, *Sir Arthur Ingram* (Oxford: Oxford University Press, 1961), 52–85; further sources appear in the notes that follow. Further references to Keep and Upton will appear parenthetically in the text.

82 Stone, *Family and Fortune*, 282.

83 These arrangements are also discussed by Robert Ashton, who puts the 1612 figure at £3,500; see *The City and the Court 1603–1643* (Cambridge: Cambridge University Press, 1979), 22–23.

84 *Family and Fortune*, 279. Cf. Cecil, who while negotiating a new grant of the Great Farm in 1611, "permitted" the farmers to assume £20,000 of his debts, including more than £9,000 which were due to the farmers themselves (*Family and Fortune*, 26).

85 As Kent Cartwright has asked me, "what can it mean to talk of Falstaff's subversiveness when a man like Suffolk is operating from the very center of power?"

86 Cf. Peck, *Court Patronage and Corruption*, 182: "The Countess of Suffolk and Bingley required merchants, customs farmers, courtiers, and citizens granted pensions and favors from the king to kickback to them between 5 per cent and 15 per cent of the value of the grant. If 5–10 per cent was the usual douceur, 15 per cent must have seemed avaricious." Menna Prestwich writes that "[b]ribe after bribe was exposed, and Bacon summed up by saying that 'my lady kept the shop, Bingley was the prentice that cried "what do you lack?", but all went into my lord's cash.'" See *Cranfield: Politics and Profits under the Early Stuarts* (Oxford: Clarendon Press, 1966), 221–22.

87 *The Letters of John Chamberlain*, vol. II, Norman E. McClure, ed. (Philadelphia: American Philosophical Society, 1939), 207.

88 Stone, *Family and Fortune*, 285. When brought before the Star Chamber in 1619, Suffolk drew a fine of £30,000. But even this additional burden could be made to disappear: King James remitted all but £7,000 of the fine and, in the end, only £1,397 of the Star Chamber imposition made it into the Exchequer. See *ibid.*, 282; also Frederick C. Dietz, *English Public Finance 1558–1641*

(1932; rpt. London: Frank Cass, 1964), 177–78. In France, at roughly the same moment, "the crown was generous in making cash gifts, particularly to great nobles in financial trouble. The crown gave the duc de Vendôme 150,000 livres to pay his debts in 1622." See Sharon Kettering, *Patrons, Brokers, and Clients*, 156.

89 Stone, *Crisis of the Aristocracy*, 542–43 (cf. 423–34); and Stone, *Family and Fortune*, 25.

90 See Stone, *Crisis of the Aristocracy*: "staggering arrears meant that an official could live vastly beyond his means in his lifetime, leaving the Crown to extract the money as best it could from the heirs" (424). Thus if not in the life of a particular indebted noble, then "[i]n the life of a noble family it [death] was the moment of truth, when for a brief instant they faced up to the realities of their financial position" (529).

91 Also writing about ethics, but in a different key, is A. D. Nuttall (*Timon of Athens*): "freedom may indeed be the most radical idea in the play, linking the original liberality with the ultimate disengagement of the hero" (141).

92 I have drawn some of the language in the first sentences in this section from David Sacks's helpful response to a draft of this chapter in February, 1995. Of course, it would be foolhardy even to suggest that self-interest suddenly appeared on the scene at some definable start of the early modern moment, a moment at which personal bonds and loyalties suddenly disappear.

2   DEBT RESTRUCTURING

1 See Marjorie K. McIntosh, "Money Lending on the Periphery of London, 1300–1600," *Albion*, 20 (1988), 557–71; esp. 570–71. Norman Jones notes that "most types of financing were not usurious, even though money or goods were advanced and payment was received for their use. So long as the lender shared the risk, there was no usury." See *God and the Moneylenders: Usury and Law in Early Modern England* (Oxford: Basil Blackwell, 1989), 4. B. A. Holderness addresses what he refers to as Tawney's investigation of the pathology of usury, arguing that "[m]oney-lending played a part in pre-industrial England that was more positive than the mere entrapment of humble men in the toils of the bloodsucker." Holderness observes that "[a]mong the tens of thousands of disputes brought before officials . . . the cases of usury are numbered in the dozens, and in many records feature not at all." See "The Clergy as Money-Lenders in England, 1550–1700," in *Princes and Paupers in the English Church 1500–1800* (Leicester: Leicester University Press, 1981), 195 and 197.

2 McIntosh documents credit and debt at "lower levels of society" and in surprising circumstances. Thus one William Ellis, of Havering in Essex, had "meager possessions and £2 in ready money at the time of his death in 1616 but had loaned out cash totalling £33." At his death in 1567, the Romford butcher John Ellis was found to have "loaned £6 to other people but himself owed a total of £165 to twenty-two people, debts ranging in size from 5s. to £40" ("Money Lending on the Periphery of London," 568). Cf. C. W. Brooks, *Pettyfoggers and Vipers of the Commonwealth: The "Lower Branch" of the Legal Profession in Early Modern England* (Cambridge: Cambridge

University Press, 1986), 95–96. Holderness, "The Clergy as Money-Lenders," cites William Harrison's *A Description of England* to the effect that "[u]sury [is] now perfectly practised almost by every Christian and so commonly that he is accounted but for a fool that doth lend his money for nothing" (206).

3 Craig Muldrew, "Interpreting the Market: the Ethics of Credit and Community Relations in Early Modern England," *Social History*, 18 (1993), 173.

4 It is significant that in *The Debt Book* (London, 1625), Henry Wilkinson's subject is primarily debt (and the "borrower [who] is not alwaies so innocent as is supposed" – 72), not usury. Wilkinson is, to my knowledge, the first clergyman to take up the inevitability of indebtedness "while humane contracts stand," without focusing on "grievous exactions" (3; "Dedicatorie").

In *Praise and Paradox: Merchants and Craftsmen in Elizabethan Popular Literature* (Cambridge: Cambridge University Press, 1984), Laura C. Stevenson argues that in the 1590s the formerly moralized greedy usurer is replaced on the Elizabethan stage by a moneylender who is primarily an unjust father. Condemnation gives way to comic exposure at a time when both the legality of taking interest and the necessity of borrowing are widely acknowledged (see especially, 98–104). Whereas Stevenson goes on to suggest that the Jacobean usurer is reconceived as "social climber" (105; see also my note 5, below), I want to continue to stress the economic, as well as the social, function of the usurer *qua* creditor.

See also Karl Marx, *Capital*, vol. III: "The credit system develops as a reaction against usury. But this should not be misconstrued, nor by any means taken in the sense of the ancient writers, the Fathers of the Church, Luther or the early socialists. It means neither more nor less than the subordination of interest-bearing capital to the conditions and requirements of the capitalist mode of production." Cited in Michael Nerlich, *Ideology of Adventure*, vol. I, Ruth Crowley, trans. (Minneapolis: University of Minnesota Press, 1987), 231n68.

5 Kenneth Burke, *A Grammar of Motives* (1945; Berkeley: University of California Press, 1969), 114. Here, as so often, Burke anticipates the conclusions of scholars whose range is, understandably, narrower than his. I have in mind Norman Jones's observation that in "Jacobean drama the usurer's sin is no longer greed, it is social ambition" (*God and the Moneylenders*, 173; Jones's footnotes may not *fully* indicate just how precisely this formulation is indebted to Stevenson's *Praise and Paradox*, 104–05: "the sin . . . objected to was not greed, but social ambition"). Jones begins with the assumption that in "the Elizabethan economy it was more and more difficult to believe that only the needy borrowed and that the borrower was always oppressed by the lender" (200). When Jones argues that the "theocentric, communal, and theologically defined approach to moneylending [that underwrites the Act Against Usury of 1571] had been replaced [by 1624] by one that was secular, individualistic, and defined by economic thought" (199), he rehearses the familiar-sounding trajectory that Craig Muldrew, "Interpreting the Market," rejects. When Jones writes that what was understood in terms of God's law was progressively reinterpreted in terms of individual conscience, in terms, that is, of "Protestant theology and an increasingly

complex economy" (205), he more closely approximates the revisionist account (see below).

6 Craig Muldrew, "Interpreting the Market," 177; see also Muldrew's "The Culture of Reconciliation: Community and the Settlement of Economic Disputes in Early Modern England," *Historical Journal*, 39 (1996), 915–42. Cf. Richard Grassby, *The Business Community of Seventeenth-Century England* (Cambridge: Cambridge University Press, 1995): "Because every businessman was at the same time a debtor and creditor, indebtedness, far from creating a subordinate relationship reinforced connections and confidence." While there was much sharp practice, it was nonetheless the case that the "whole structure of credit depended on 'mutual trust among private men'" (177 and 298).

   J. G. A. Pocock finds in the late-seventeenth-century writings of Charles Davenant the "beginnings . . . of a civic morality of investment and exchange, and indeed of an equation of the commercial ethic with the Christian. It is when men realize that their well-being depends upon mutual support that credit is converted into confidence, into a mutual trust and a belief in one another . . ." Pocock describes Defoe's and Addison's attempts to translate credit "into virtue, in the entirely moral and societal sense of that word." Whereas I am arguing that at the turn of the seventeenth century, the usurer and prodigal are reinterpellated as creditor and debtor, Pocock argues that at the turn of the eighteenth century, "[t]he ideological thrust was constantly toward the absorption of stockjobber into merchant: the rentier, who frightened the social theorists, into the entrepreneur, who did not." See *The Machiavellian Moment: Florentine Political Thought and the Atlantic Republican Tradition* (Princeton: Princeton University Press, 1975), 440 and 456.

7 Cf. *An Appeale to Heaven, and Heavens Ministers: . . . From all the Prisoners, imprisoned for Debt, in the severall Gaols within the Kingdome of England . . .* (1644), Thomason Tracts E.8[23]: debtors' "miserable bodies are daily sacrificed by the merciless Common Law, unto the tyranny of Jaylors." "[I]nsnared in holes, and hid, yea, buried in prison-houses . . . wee are set apart for a prey to oppression, and . . . a spoyle to Lawyers and Jaylors" (2 and 6). James Horn writes that both "Virginia and Maryland provided a distant refuge for immigrants fleeing from creditors." But Horn also notes that as many as "40 per cent of new arrivals may have died within their first few years in the Tidewater, commonly of a variety of ailments associated with malaria and intestinal diseases." See James Horn, "'To Parts Beyond the Seas': Free Emigration to the Chesapeake in the Seventeenth Century," in *"To Make America": European Emigration in the Early Modern Period*, Ida Altman and James Horn, eds. (Berkeley: University of California Press, 1991), 104; and J. P. P. Horn, "Moving on in the New World: Migration and Out-Migration in the Seventeenth-Century Chesapeake," in *Migration and Society in Early Modern England*, Peter Clark and David Souten, eds. (London: Hutchinson, 1987), 176.

8 For this distinction in relation to truth and credibility, see Steve Shapin, *A Social History of Truth: Civility and Science in Seventeenth-Century England* (Chicago: University of Chicago Press, 1994), 63–64 and 81.

9 Commenting on Defoe's rhetoric in 1706, Pocock writes that Defoe describes

credit "in precisely the idiom employed by Machiavelli to describe *fortuna* . . . [c]redit typifies the instability of secular things, brought about by the interactions of particular human wills, appetites and passions . . ." Pocock characterizes credit as an "innovative conquering force which, in the most dynamic moments of Machiavelli's vision, created the disorder . . . which it then set out to dominate" (*The Machiavellian Moment*, 452–54).

10 Morris Palmer Tilley, *A Dictionary of the Proverbs in England in the Sixteenth and Seventeenth Centuries* (Ann Arbor: University of Michigan Press, 1950).

11 William Fennor, *The Counter's Commonwealth* (1617) cited A. V. Judges, *The Elizabethan Underworld* (London: Routledge, 1930), 483.

12 *A Petition to the Kings most excellent Majestie . . . Wherein is declared the mischiefe and inconveniences, arising to the King and Common-wealth, by the Imprisoning of mens bodies for Debt* (London, 1622), D1.

13 All citations are from George Chapman, Ben Jonson, and John Marston, *Eastward Ho*, R. W. Van Fossen, ed. (Manchester: Manchester University Press, 1979).

14 On fear of derogation, see Golding's lines in 3.2: "I am born a gentleman, and by the trade I have learned of my master (which I trust taints not my blood) . . ." On the prevalence of gentle apprentices, see, for example, Steve Rappaport, *Worlds Within Worlds: Structures of Life in Sixteenth-Century London* (Cambridge: Cambridge University Press, 1989), 304–11, and R. Grassby, *The Business Community of Seventeenth-Century England* (Cambridge: Cambridge University Press, 1995), 166–70. Grassby cites a Star Chamber ruling, in 1634, in favor of a gentleman, that it was "no disparagement nor stain to him to have been a woollen draper as long as he carried himself honestly and with integrity" (42).

15 Edmund Bolton, *The Cities Advocate* (1629), A1 and A2v. Bolton poses the hypothetical case of a gentleman wanting "to breed up" a son not merely "out of a stocke of wit, or learning, but out of a stocke of money, and credit" (C2). "Defender of the credit of the City" though he may be, Bolton cautiously devotes all of the last part of his "Apologie" to assuring his readers that he does not mean to "confound degrees": in the end, "Citizens, as Citizens, are not Gentlemen, but Citizens"; they remain forever "of a degree beneath the meere Gentlemen" (G4). Cf. J. P. Cooper, "Ideas of Gentility in Early-Modern England," in *Land, Men and Beliefs: Studies in Early-Modern History* (London: Hambledon, 1983), 71–73 and *passim*. Both Cooper and Gertrude E. Noyes note that *The Cities Advocate* was probably written some ten to twelve years before it was published. See Cooper, *Men and Beliefs*, 71n162 and Noyes, *Bibliography of Courtesy and Conduct Books in Seventeenth Century England* (New Haven: Tuttle, Morehouse & Taylor, 1937), 30.

Steven R. Smith suggests that "[p]lacing young gentlemen as apprentices led to role confusion"; see "The London Apprentices as Seventeenth-Century Adolescents," *Past & Present*, 61 (1973), 160. R. Grassby (*The Business Community of Seventeenth-Century England*, 45) argues that as to whether or not apprenticeship extinguished gentility, the "underlying problem was that budding merchants were lumped together with handicraftsmen and paupers

. . . What determined the status of an apprentice was the standing of his master and the precise conditions of his binding."

16 C. G. Petter, ed., *Eastward Ho* (London: Ernest Benn, 1973), 9n. Editors of the play from Schelling (1903), Julia Hamlet Harris (1926), and Herford and the Simpsons (1950) to Petter and Van Fossen, all have credited J. E. Hodgkin's description of this panel in *Notes and Queries*, 4 (1887), 323–32.

17 Van Fossen cites J. T. Henke's *Renaissance Dramatic Bawdy (Exclusive of Shakespeare): An Annotated Glossary and Critical Essay* (Salzburg Studies in English Literature, 1974) for the suggestion that "horn" means "penis" (73n).

18 Cf. Gertrude's comment about her father's tightfistedness: "we shall as soon get a fart from a dead man as a farthing of court'sy here [from my father]" (4.2.161–62). And cf. Quicksilver's prescription for Golding when the latter asks how he should comport himself: "be like a gentleman . . . Wipe thy bum with testons, and make ducks and drakes with shillings" (1.1.138–40). Van Fossen cites Henke's suggestion that this alludes to "the proverbial evacuating abilities of ducks" (76n).

19 Touchstone imagines Golding's "thrifty course" ("not a week married, chosen commoner and alderman's deputy in a day!") being "remembered the same day with the Lady Ramsey and grave Gresham." He recognizes in the apprentice-makes-good story a performance equal to that staged in Heywood's *If You Know Not Me*: "thy deed [shall be] played i' thy lifetime, by the best companies of actors, and be called their get-penny" (4.2.60–89). Credit consists of actions that a man might play.

20 Editors since Dodsley (1774) have assigned the play's "EPILOGVS" to Quicksilver.

21 R. A. Foakes and R. T. Rickert, *Henslowe's Diary* (Cambridge: Cambridge University Press, 1961), 86.

22 S. P. Cerasano, "Edward Alleyn: 1566–1626," in *Edward Alleyn: Elizabethan Actor, Jacobean Gentleman*, Aileen Reid and Robert Maniura, eds. (Dulwich Picture Gallery, 1994), 23.

23 *Memoirs of Edward Alleyn*, John Payne Collier, ed. (London: Shakespeare Society, 1841), 131. In the 1616 edition (Q4) of *English Villainies*, Dekker writes: "[i]n thy wants of money let thy pen neither dig the mine too often nor in too many places. Letters are but bladders to fill which a prisoner keeps a-puffing and blowing; but they to whom they are sent let all out in the very opening." See *Thomas Dekker*, E. D. Pendry, ed. (Cambridge: Harvard University Press, 1968), 269.

24 *Memoirs of Edward Alleyn*, John Payne Collier, ed., 186. Less nuanced appeals to Alleyn for financial help were common. See, for example, Thomas Bolton's letter of 14 April 1619. Bolton, "has 'bin prisoner in the Marshalsey 28 weekes att the suite of one Low, a scrivener, upon a bond of x li,' and entreats him to send something towards his release and payment of his fees." *Catalogue of the Manuscripts and Muniments of Alleyn's College of God's Gift at Dulwich*, G. F. Warner, ed. (London: Longmans, Green, 1881), 109. Another solicitation, almost identical to Dekker's, was sent to Alleyn by Thomas Chard, printer and prisoner in Ludgate; see Warner, 102–04.

25 For "good credit," see Cerasano, "Edward Alleyn," 26; for players' debt, see *Memoirs of Edward Alleyn*, 126–30.

26 Thomas Dekker, *English Villainies* (Q6), in *Thomas Dekker*, E. D. Pendry, ed., 275–76.
27 *Ibid.*, 273–74.
28 *The Statutes of the Realm* (1819), vol. IV, part II, 1029–34. Cf. 21 Jac. I, c.19. Cf. Ian P. H. Duffy, "English Bankrupts, 1571–1861," *American Journal of Legal History*, 24 (1980), 284–85.
29 *A Collection of Seventy-nine Black-letter Ballads and Broadsides*, J. O. Halliwell-Phillipps, ed. (London: Joseph Lilly, 1867), 16–17.
30 *The humble petition of the poore distressed prisoners in the hole of the poultry compter* (London, 1644), Thomason Tracts E.21[32].
31 "Introduction," *Thomas Dekker*, 6; emphasis added.
32 "Introduction," *Eastward Ho*, R. W. Van Fossen, ed., 4. Van Fossen includes the prison letters in his Appendix 2. All further citations are drawn from this edition. Although less confident than Van Fossen that Chapman and Jonson's prison letters "almost certainly" pertain to *Eastward Ho*, Richard Dutton writes: "[w]ith some hesitation . . . I conclude that all these documents related to the same business and that . . . it stemmed from *Eastward Ho*." See *Mastering the Revels: The Regulation and Censorship of English Renaissance Drama* (Iowa City: University of Iowa Press, 1991), 172–73.
33 I assume that the two clauses to which Chapman refers are precisely that, the two sentences that are censured. If "two clauses" can refer to two passages, then Chapman may have in mind the lines in 4.1 about "knighthood" as well as the Virginia passage. Herford and Simpson take the latter tack in *Ben Jonson*, vol. I (Oxford: Clarendon Press, 1925), 191. Cf. Richard Dutton, *Mastering the Revels*, 175–76.
34 We will never know who was responsible for the offending lines. In his letter to the King, Chapman seems to point the finger at Marston, but he could be blaming the players.
35 Mention of a "first Error" in his letter to Cecil probably refers to Jonson's share in *The Isle of Dogs* and his subsequent imprisonment; however, there was also *Sejanus*, which was of still more recent memory.
36 Dutton (*Mastering the Revels*, 179) speculates that Suffolk released Chapman and Jonson from prison, and was repaid when Jonson wrote *Hymenaei* for the wedding of Lady Frances Howard and the Earl of Essex. David Riggs suggests that Jonson's release followed upon Lord D'Aubigny's intervention. He adds that "Jonson felt a profound sense of gratitude toward his benefactor." In his epigram "To Esmé, Lord Aubigny" he calls "*Posteritie* / Into the debt" he owes the King's Scottish cousin. See Riggs, *Ben Jonson* (Cambridge: Harvard University Press, 1989), 125–26. Cf. Janet Clare, *"Art made tongue-tied by authority": Elizabethan and Jacobean Censorship* (Manchester: Manchester University Press, 1990), 120–21.
37 Van Fossen, ed., "Introduction," *Eastward Ho*, 5, notes that "the letters written to the Earl of Salisbury and the Earl of Montgomery could not have been written before 5 May 1605, when the two earldoms were created . . . Since we know that on 9 October of that year Jonson was one of the guests at a party given by Robert Catesby . . . the imprisonment cannot have lasted more than twenty weeks."
   What I have called bravado, or self-assertiveness, David Riggs describes as

Jonson's "chronic rebelliousness" and "audacity." Riggs seems to ascribe the anti-Scottish humour in *Eastward Ho* to Jonson, explaining that "most of Jonson's prospective benefactors bore a grudge against the Scots." See *Ben Jonson*, 123–4 and 141.

Citing Chapman's escape from arrest (three years after *Eastward Ho*) for staging the Queen of France quarreling with her husband's mistress, Millar MacLure desribes a "temerarious . . . [i]ntransigent, querulous" Chapman. See *George Chapman: A Critical Study* (Toronto: University of Toronto Press, 1966), 20–21.

38 Play-writing as a prodigal expenditure of wit may call to mind Richard Helgerson's argument in *The Elizabethan Prodigals* (Berkeley: University of California Press, 1976). However, Helgerson understands prodigality to mean waste (of time, education, and ability) and rebellion, not indebtedness on its way to default. Helgerson's writers repent and then try to give up what came before; in the texts I consider, repentance leads to repetition or some form of reintegration through renewed indebtednes. As I argue in my discussion of *Greene's Tu Quoque* at the end of this chapter, prodigality understood in terms of waste readily lends itself to moral judgment; when it is conceived of as indebtedness, it lies primarily within the sphere of the socio-economic.

39 Fennor, *The Counter's Commonwealth* (1617), cited in A. V. Judges, *Elizabethan Underworld*, 443–44; see all of Chapter 4: "Containing: I. The subtlety of many unconscionable citizens that entangle young gentlemen and lap them into bonds."

40 Petter, ed., notes that Mercury's "'nimble-spirited' antics (especially subduing gold) exasperate the alchemist, but the promise of gold or, still better, *lumen novum*, philosophers' gold, helps him to persist." *Eastward Ho*, 4.

41 In this and other comedies Middleton is perfectly willing to stigmatize a character onomastically. Andrew Lethe, born Andrew Gruel, and Sir Petronel Flash are obvious examples in *Michaelmas Term*. Although late in the play, a defeated Quomodo calls Easy "Master Prodigal Had-land" (5.1.119), Middleton opted for a name that does not quite so clearly peg the man. All citations are from my edition of *Michaelmas Term* in *The Collected Works of Thomas Middleton* (forthcoming, Oxford: Oxford University Press).

42 At 2.3.384–85 Easy is told, "you rest too much upon your R's [arse]." For a discussion of sodomitical reference in this play, see my "Redeeming Beggary/Buggery in *Michaelmas Term*," *ELH*, 61 (1994), 53–70.

43 In 3.4 Easy is brought before Quomodo by Shortyard and Falselight, disguised as sergeant and yeoman ("we told him . . . that it lay in your worship's courtesy to arrest" him – 55–56). Quomodo pretends he would rather they had brought "Master Blastfield, the more sufficient man" (29). Of course, he has been angling for Easy all along, and now archly insists that the only courteous thing to do is to demand repayment of Easy: "I have no reason to refuse you; I should show little manners in that" (39–40).

44 For Norman Jones's argument that the usurer's sin changes from greed to ambition, see note 5, above.

45 Quomodo is no less interested in his reputation after death than Antonio, Gresham, or Timon. Unable to guarantee his posthumous credit, Quomodo

masochistically orchestrates a staging of his death that confirms his own worst suspicions.

46 The account which follows depends upon Charles William Wallace's pioneering work, *The First London Theatre: Materials for a History* (Lincoln: University of Nebraska, 1913). This was published as volume 13, nos. 1–3 of the series University Studies. Some new ground is broken and much recovered in William Ingram's *The Business of Playing: The Beginnings of the Adult Professional Theater in Elizabethan London* (Ithaca: Cornell University Press, 1992), 182–218. See also Herbert Berry, "A Handlist of Documents about the Theatre in Shoreditch," first published in *The First Public Playhouse*, H. Berry, ed. (Montreal: McGill-Queen's University Press, 1979), 97–133, and reprinted in Berry's *Shakespeare's Playhouses* (New York: AMS Press, 1987), 19–44. Page references for citations from Wallace appear parenthetically in the text.

47 Edward Collins's deposition supports Myles's account of Brayne's collapse. Collins says that Brayne was soon in so far over his head as a result of construction costs that he was forced to sell to Collins's father the "lease of the howse wherin he dwelled/ for one C li" and to Collins himself

all suche wares as he had left/ and all that longed therunto Remayning in the same for the some of one Cxlvii li . . . And after wardes the said Brayne tooke the matter of the said building so upon him/ as he was dryven to borow money to supplye the same/ . . . and that he found not towardes it above the value of ffiftie poundes/ some parte in money/ and the rest in stuff. (137)

48 Bett also notes that he "did write certaine peticions, for the same Braine and Myles, to crave favore at ther Creditors handes, to whom thei did owe about viii or ix C li, the wch was not (as he takethe it) for any matter conceruinge the Theatre, but for matters concerninge the Inn called the george" (87).

49 Wallace describes the deed of gift of property to save it from creditors as "a favorite method of Brayne (and others) when heavily indebted" (8). Among those others was Burbage himself, or so at least claimed Giles Allen in Star Chamber proceedings, 1601–02:

James Burbage had in his lyefe tyme made A deede of guift of all his goodes to the sayd Cuthbert Burbage and Richard Burbage his sonnes, whoe after the death of the sayd James Burbage procured Ellen Burbage his widdowe being a verye poore woman to take the Administracion uppon her wch was done to defraude your Subject and other Creditors of the sayd James Burbage. (278)

50 Uneasy about relying on a unique statement referring to a mortgaged lease, Ingram will say no more than that the case "for the lease's having been pawned in 1577 is problematic." See *The Business of Playing*, 198.

51 Myles deposed that he had heard Burbage tell Brayne that the cost of the playhouse would not exceed £200, that Brayne soon charged that he had spent £500, and that Burbage responded that he should "be contented/ it wold shortlie quyte the cost unto them bothe" (140).

52 Ingram, *The Business of Playing*, 202–03, writes that when a London haberdasher got a sergeant to arrest Burbage for settlement of a £5 debt in June 1579, Burbage was quickly able to discharge the obligation (and therefore, *pace* Ingram, "secure his release from prison"). While Ingram concludes that "the incident suggests that Burbage was not without financial

resources in the summer of 1579" (shortly before mortgaging the lease to Hyde), it should be noted that covering a £5 debt corresponds to a magnitude of financial encumbrance altogether different from the costs associated with building and operating the Theatre.

53 Ingram, *The Business of Playing*, 213, reminds us that even as Burbage was under arrest, Brayne was "eluding arrest": in 1582, for a suit brought against him in the matter of £100 debt; in 1583, for a debt of £80. In both instances, the bailiff was forced to return *non est inventus*.

54 From 1585 until his death in 1597 Burbage tried to get Allen to sign a new lease. Allen refused. He not only objected to the playhouse but claimed that Burbage overestimated the cost of his improvements. Burbage twice hired appraisers to substantiate his claims, and each time Allen refuted the evidence.

   Also in 1582, Allen's own title to the Shoreditch property was challenged by the Peckham family. One tactic the Peckhams employed in the prosecution of their suit against Allen was to harass Burbage as he tried to operate the Theatre. As a result, Burbage took to paying men wages for the sole purpose of fending off the Peckhams. As Oliver Tilt, a former tenant of Burbage, deposed, Burbage employed men like Tilt "soe longe as the contrav*e*rsie was betw*e*ene mr Allen and mr Peckham and mr James Burbadge was muche disturbed and trobled in his possession of the Theater and Could not Quietlye and peaceablie enjoye the same./ And therefore the players for sooke the said Theater to his great losse" (242). The painter Randolph May deposed that Burbage was "once in danger of his owne lyffe by keepinge possession thereof from Peckham and his servan*t*es." Furthermore, Burbage "loste much money by that controve*e*rsie and troble for yt drove manye of the players thence" (240).

55 Ingram, in *The Business of Playing*, 227–36, speculates about the Brayne–Burbage–Laneman arrangement and Burbage's possible purchase of the Curtain.

56 See Wallace, *The First London Theatre*, 23; also, from the *Sharers Papers* of 1635: "[n]ow for the Blackfriers that is our inheritance, our father [James Burbage] purchased it at extreame rates, & made it into a play house wth great charge & trouble." See E. K. Chambers, "Dramatic Records: The Lord Chamberlain's Office," *Malone Society Collections*, vol. II (Oxford: Oxford University Press, 1931), pt. 3, 371.

57 See note 49, above.

58 It may be worth noting that the 1576 lease did permit James Burbage and his heirs "to take downe & Carrye awaye to his & their owne pro*p*er use for ever all such buildinges & other thinges as are alredye builded erected or set upp & wch herafter shalbe builded erected or sett up . . . eyther for a Theater or playinge place or for any other lawfull use" (177). This is not to suggest that Allen had no grounds for later suits; the same lease stipulated, for instance, that the right to take down buildings extended for only twenty-one years. For an extremely succinct summary of *Burbages* v. *Allen*, see Herbert Berry, *Shakespeare's Playhouses*, 39–40.

59 "Wee," said Cuthbert and William Burbage in 1635, "at like expence built the Globe, wth more summes of money taken up at interest, which lay heavy on

us many yeeres." See E. K. Chambers, "Dramatic Records: The Lord Chamberlain's Office," 371.

60 Ingram, *The Business of Playing*, 115–18. "Let-the-facts . . ." is not Ingram's formulation; but this is: "I hope to . . . content myself . . . with looking at the raw materials of all the stories, with an eye to laying out the ingredients from which a larger narrative, or alternative larger narratives, might be put together" (118). We may imagine historians less cautious than Ingram mixing these ingredients and confabulating their own narratives. I note that Mary Edmond has recently questioned the veracity of the broomstick episode, and of Nicholas Bishop's deposition, in particular. See her "Yeomen, Citizens, Gentlemen, and Players: The Burbages and Their Connections," in *Elizabethan Theater: Essays in Honor of S. Schoenbaum*, R. B. Parker and S. P. Zitner, eds. (Newark: University of Delaware Press, 1996), 34–35.

61 Ingram, *The Business of Playing*, 196–97.

62 *Ibid.*, 228. Arguing that "Brayne and the players could not have failed to notice" if Burbage was stealing from the box for *two* years, Mary Edmond concludes that Myles's claim is "barely credible." See "Yeomen, Citizens, Gentlemen, and Players," 35.

63 Tenacity as firmness of purpose, or persistence, and as miserliness or parsimony, were equally available meanings in Burbage's day (see *OED*, tenacity, 1 and 3). The character Tenacity, in *The Contention Between Liberalitie and Prodigalitie* (London, 1602), suggests something of both senses. He is "old, sparing, covetous niggard, Tenacity" and he claims that "*I truely labour day and night, / To get my living by my toile*" (ll. 350 and 453–54).

64 William Ingram, *A London Life in the Brazen Age: Francis Langley 1548 1602* (Cambridge: Harvard University Press, 1978), 71–72. Further citations from Ingram's wonderful biography appear parenthetically in the text.

65 Herbert Berry, *The Boar's Head Playhouse* (New Jersey: Associated University Presses, 1986), 26. My account radically condenses Berry's monograph.

66 See E. K. Chambers, *The Elizabethan Stage*, vols. III and IV (Oxford: Clarendon Press, 1923), III.269 and IV.178; and Alan Berman's "Introduction" to his edition of *Greene's Tu Quoque or, The Cittie Gallant*, by J. Cooke (New York: Garland, 1984). All citations are from Berman's critical edition.

67 For Cooke's "experimenting with different attitudes to the prodigal story without fusing these attitudes into a coherent whole," see Alexander Leggatt, *Citizen Comedy in the Age of Shakespeare* (Toronto: University of Toronto Press, 1973), 42. As Marshall Grossman has pointed out to me (pers. comm.), a psychologically coherent narrative might well require generic incoherence.

68 Christoper Marlowe, *Edward II* (2.1.42–43) in *Doctor Faustus and Other Plays*, David Bevington and Eric Rasmussen, eds. (Oxford: Clarendon Press, 1995), 346.

69 In *A Meditation upon the Lord's Prayer* (London, 1619), King James writes that "[o]ur sinnes are called debts in Saint Mathew . . . and in Saint Luke they are called sinnes" (55–56). Both Tyndale and the Book of Common Prayer have recourse not to debts but to trespasses. Sir Richard Baker explains that Christ used a "Syriacke" word ("Choba") which "signifies both Debts and

Trespasses." See *Meditations and Disquisitions upon the Lords Prayer* (London, 1636), 149.

70 Cf. Michael Walzer: "Through the covenant men became the 'bondsmen' of God – not the children – and the image implied the voluntary recognition of an existing debt, a legal or commercial obligation. God was the creditor of all men, but some were enabled by his grace to acknowledge the debt and, through obedience, in part to repay it." *The Revolution of the Saints: A Study in the Origins of Radical Politics* (Cambridge: Harvard University Press, 1965), 168.

71 Lancelot Andrewes, *Institutiones piae*, 3rd edn. (London, 1640), 165.

72 Lancelot Andrewes, *Scala Coeli* (London, 1611), 181. Cf. William Gouge, *A Guide to Goe to God* (London, 1636): "[a]s the greatnesse of the debt wherein men standeth obliged to God, so also mans impotency, and impossibilitie to discharge it, aggravateth that wretched state whereinto man by sinne is implunged, and giveth him much more occasion and matter of humiliation" (150–51).

73 William Perkins, *An Exposition of the Lords Prayer* (London, 1595), 44–45.

74 Cf. John Smith, *A Paterne of True Prayer* (London, 1624), 351 and 361–62. Christ as surety and creditor derives from what Benjamin Nelson and Joshua Starr call "the classic ransom theory of atonement." See "The Legend of the Divine Surety and the Jewish Moneylender," *Annuaire de L'Institut de Philologie et d'Histoire Orientales et Slaves*, 7 (1939–44), 333. St. Ambrose, for example, writes to his sister, "let no one be startled at the word 'creditor'. . . He [Christ] gave to me a new kind of acquittance, changing my creditor because I had nothing wherewith to pay my debt," *A Select Library of Nicene and Post-Nicene Fathers of the Christian Church*, vol. X, *St. Ambrose* (Oxford: James Parker, 1896), 446. Luther, of course, very carefully circumscribes the right to stand surety. What was within God's purview was both "unseemly" and "presumptuous" for a man. See Benjamin Nelson, *The Idea of Usury: From Tribal Brotherhood to Universal Otherhood* (Princeton: Princeton University Press, 1949), 152.

75 *A Petition to the Kings most excellent Majestie*, F2. Further citations appear parenthetically in the text.

76 Phillip Shaw, "The Position of Thomas Dekker in Jacobean Prison Literature," *PMLA* 62 (1947), 366–91: see 389n10.

77 Henry Wilkinson writes that "in many cases it is a servile thing to be indebted . . . By Debt a mans state and person is in a manner mancipated to the lender." See *The Debt Book* (London, 1625), 5.

78 The 1622 petition finesses the issue of a debtor's complicity: "the Debtor is not *volens*, for it is against every Debtors will to pay Usury or Forfaiture; but hee is pressed thereunto by his owne necessity on the one side, and by the Creditors uncharitable will on the other, who will not lend but for Usury and Forfaiture" (D1).

79 See John P. Dawson, "The Privy Council and Private Law in the Tudor and Stuart Period: I," *Michigan Law Review*, 48 (1950), 410–16.

80 In 1589, the Council took note of the fact that creditors were threatening Commissions with lawsuits: "some contemptuous persones" have set out to "molest them for their procedinges . . . by suites and other vexacions by

lawe." The Council was unable to do much more than refer this "difficulty" to the "advice and counsell of the two Lordes Chief Justices, being of the same Commission" (*Acts of the Privy Council*, 15 September 1589). Dawson speculates that the "doubtful legality of the commissioners' powers" explains their demise under King James ("The Privy Council and Private Law," 416).

81 *Acts of the Privy Council*, 2 April 1592. In 1598 the Council came to the defense of the "decaied and empoverished" Southampton merchant, John Mercer. Seeking mediation with two "rigorous" creditors on Mercer's behalf, the Council can do little more than threaten unspecified "farther order for his releefe and for redreese of their [the creditors'] extreeme and unconscionable dealing." *APC*, 7 October 1598.

82 *Ibid.*, 13 March 1616–17. When Edward Barnes, a mercer £16,000 in debt but "well knowne to have ben a cittizen of good worth and creditt" sought relief from the Council, it was because of creditors who "doe so presse for present paymentes and use such violent courses to force him . . . to his utter ruyne." Some of his creditors "being more unmercifull then the rest would neither forbeare their money, take debtes nor wares under valued, nor yet landes at an under rate, but doe secke onely their owne endes, tending to his utter ruine who is whollie bent for their satisfaction." The Barnes case first comes to the attention of the Council in 1622. A third entry devoted to Barnes informs us that by 1624, the mercer had paid all but £500 of his original debt. The Council attributes this success to the "good use he had made of the former time in discharging so great a proportion of his debtes." See *APC*, 15 July 1622, 25 June 1623, and 16 June 1624.

83 See Jay Cohen, "The History of Imprisonment for Debt and Its Relation to the Development of Discharge in Bankruptcy," *The Journal of Legal History*, 3 (1982), 153–71. Cohen notes that "imprisonment for debt stands out as a typical form of coercive imprisonment." If debtors took affront, it may well be because, as Cohen writes, it "was meant to *compel* payment of the debt, not as punishment for the previous failure to pay" (155; emphasis added).

84 Geffray Mynshul, *Essayes and Characters of a Prison and Prisoners* (1618; Edinburgh: James Ballantyne, 1821), 61–62. For "insulting jaylor," see p. 75. Further citations will appear in the text. E. D. Pendry writes that prisoners in the Fleet "were easily moved to complain because many of them were highborn and well-connected, and loath to submit to the ordinary conditions of captivity." Pendry quotes from Court of Requests records which include complaints against a Fleet officer, John Hore ("a person of small worth and most odious conditions") "who lately coming to the Fleet a poor boy of no value, and servant to one of the servants of this house, is by his cunning and rare dealings, and exactions against your said good subjects . . . grown to be of excessive pride and insolency, boasting also to be of great wealth." See *Elizabethan Prisons and Prison Scenes*, vol. II (Salzburg: Universität Salzburg, 1974), 207–08 and 203.

85 William Shakespeare, *The First Part of King Henry IV*, A. R. Humphreys, ed., The Arden Shakespeare (London: Methuen, 1960), 1.3.107–08.

86 William Bagwell, *The Distressed Merchant* (London, 1645), K2 and F3.

87 Alexander Harris, *The Oeconomy of the Fleete: or An Apologeticall Answeare*

of Alexander Harris (Late Warden There) Unto XIX Articles Sett Forth Against Him by the Prisoners (1621?), Augustus Jessopp, ed. (London: J. B. Nichols, 1879), 134–35 (further citations appear in the text). Harris answers each of Lee's nine complaints and then appends thirty of his own complaints against Lee. For example, Harris charges that Lee "Was the first that used incouragement to kill the Warden"; "Conferred with others to Cutt the throats of all that gave intelligence to the Warden"; "Never paid the Warden anything" (137).

88 Prisoners lodge specious complaints against Harris, "thinking that if the Warden fayle in his place and credit, then there will be none to call them to accompt for what they owe him" (63).

89 *Journals of the House of Commons*, vol. I, 596 (28 April 1621).

90 Fennor, *The Counter's Commonwealth*, 485. Further citations will appear in the text. Fennor's account of the governance of the Hole is not confirmed, so far as I know, by any other source. There are a number of indications that it is at least partly facetious, which is to say that it is no more or less indicative of affective responses to indebtedness than other texts discussed in this chapter. For what it is worth, a play by Thomas Jordan, *The Walks of Islington and Hogsdon, with the Humours of Woodstreet-Compter* (London, 1657), includes a Hole steward, constable, and chamberlain (F2).

91 Sir Thomas Gresham left £50 per annum to the prisoners and poor persons in Newgate, Ludgate, King's Bench, Marshalsea, and Woodstreet Prison. See William Burgon, *The Life and Times of Sir Thomas Gresham*, vol. II (London: Effingham Wilson, n.d.), 492. Such legacies, if often less generous, were not uncommon. Thus Robert Dowe, Merchant Taylor, whose total benefactions amounted to £3,448 in 1612, left £20 per annum to be distributed to "relieve poor prisoners – redeeming them that are in pryson for small debts or for their fees . . ." W. Craven, former Lord Mayor of London, died in 1617, leaving "to the poor Prisoners of Newgate, Ludgate, and the two Compters, the Sum of 40*l*." See Charles M. Clode, *The Early History of the Guild of Merchant Taylors*, 2 vols. (London: Harrison and Sons, 1888–89), I.161–62 and II.323. John Stow writes of one John Fuller who bequeathed land in trust, the profits from which were to be used to relieve prisoners in the Hole. See *A Survey of London*, vol. I, Charles Kingsford, ed. (Oxford: Clarendon Press, 1908), 115.

3 MORTGAGE PAYMENTS

1 See Richard Grassby, *The Business Community of Seventeenth-Century England* (Cambridge: Cambridge University Press, 1995), 392: "Although not ranked on an equal footing, the codes of behaviour characteristic of business and landed society were able to co-exist and were both complementary and mutually dependent."

   Robert Brenner makes a different, but related claim, one that lies at the very heart of his famous essays in *Past & Present*. "English economic development," he writes, "thus depended upon a nearly unique symbiotic relationship between agriculture and industry. It was indeed, in the last analysis, an agricultural revolution, based on the emergence of capitalist class relations in the countryside, which made it possible for England to become the first nation to experience industrialization." Under what Brenner calls a classic commercial landlord/capitalist tenant/wage-laborer system, "[c]api-talist profits were . . . a condition for landlord rents." See the reprints of Brenner's 1976 and 1982 articles in *The Brenner Debate: Agrarian Class Structure and Economic Development in Pre-Industrial Europe*, T. H. Ashton and C. H. E. Philpin, eds. (Cambridge: Cambridge: University Press, 1985), 54 and 315. John Merrington cautions, however, that the period's "fusion of merchant capital and landed property" was not yet by any means evidence of capitalist agriculture. This was still what Merrington calls "rentier feudalism." See "Town and Country in the Transition to Capitalism," in *The Transition from Feudalism to Capitalism*, Paul Sweezy, *et al.*, eds. (London: New Left Books, 1976), 184.

2 Lawrence Stone, *The Crisis of the Aristocracy 1558–1641* (Oxford: Clarendon Press, 1965), 525.

3 Mary E. Finch, *The Wealth of Five Northamptonshire Families 1540–1640* (Oxford: Oxford University Press, 1956), writes of the landowner's "fear of forfeiture" and "ruinous" indebtedness (168). Stone, *Crisis of the Aristocracy*, writes that "[d]ebtors were afraid of mortgages and avoided them when they could . . . foreclosure was regarded as an ever-present threat, a sword of Damocles suspended above the heads of many Elizabethan noblemen" (525). And C. G. A. Clay, *Economic Expansion and Social Change: England 1500–1700*, vol. I (Cambridge: Cambridge University Press, 1984), writes of the widespread "fear of foreclosure" (125).

4 My discussion of the equity of redemption derives from Finch (33 and 167–69), Stone (518–27), and Clay (I.125 and 151–59), all cited in the previous note, as well as from R. W. Turner, *The Equity of Redemption: Its Nature, History and Connection with Equitable Estates Generally* (1931; rpt. Florida: Wm. W. Gaunt, 1986).

5 Mary E. Finch, *The Wealth of Five Northamptonshire Families*, 169. Cf. Robert Ashton, *The Crown and the Money Market 1603–1640* (Oxford: Clarendon Press, 1960), 8–9. David Sugarman and Ronnie Warrington argue that the rationales for the "highly interventionist jurisdiction" entailed by equity of redemption were twofold. First, there was a strong predisposition to protect young heirs. The landowners who pledged their property "out of necessity" required protection from "money-hungry" creditors. Second, the court sought "to ensure that ultimately land was returned to its 'rightful' (often meaning historical or traditional) owner . . . It was as if it were inconceivable that an English gentleman would give up his land, save in wholly exceptional circumstances." See "Land Law, Citizenship, and the Invention of 'Englishness': The Strange World of the Equity of Redemption," in *Early Modern Conceptions of Property*, John Brewer and Susan Staves, eds. (London: Routledge, 1995), 119–20. Sugarman and Warrington understand-ably emphasize the advantages that accrued to landowners; they underplay the extent to which equity of redemption, as they themselves acknowledge in passing, facilitated "the extension of credit and business" (112), that is, it served creditors' interests too (cf. 125 and 134).

6 The loss of their right to take possession of property immediately upon

default probably explains why creditors seem to have backed away from mortgages following the development of equity of redemption. Although Chancery proceedings created a structure within which a mortgagee could collect interest after the assigned date of a mortgage, this may not have been viewed as sufficient compensation for the loss of the property itself. The wariness of creditors may also explain why records do not show large numbers of landowners turning to mortgages to raise money on their land until decades after the acquisition of their new equitable right.

7 R. W. Turner, *The Equity of Redemption*, 21 (my discussion of equity of redemption in this paragraph depends upon pp. 21–41).

8 *Ibid.*, 27. Turner argues that in extending relief to mortgagors, the Chancellor (probably Bacon) was taking his cue from the relief from bonds which Chancery had already begun to offer. By the early seventeenth century Chancery was applying the criteria of conscience to cases of unpaid bonds. First the ability of an English version of Shylock to win strict enforcement of a bond was undermined in Chancery, then followed a curtailment of the ability of versions of Overreach to foreclose upon default. In *A New Way to Pay Old Debts*, both of these credit instruments, as well as statutes and trusts, are in play.

9 R. W. Turner, *The Equity of Redemption*, 36–41.

10 Philip Massinger, *A New Way to Pay Old Debts*, in *The Poems and Plays of Philip Massinger*, vol. II, Philip Edwards and Colin Gibson, eds. (Oxford: Clarendon Press, 1976). All citations are drawn from this edition. "[C]hemical reaction" and "less satisfactory" are Alexander Leggatt's words in *Citizen Comedy in the Age of Shakespeare* (Toronto: University of Toronto Press, 1973), 68.

11 Michael Neill, "Massinger's Patriarchy: The Social Vision of *A New Way to Pay Old Debts*," *Renaissance Drama*, 10 (1979), 194, 203, and 192; Margot Heinemann, "Drama and Opinion in the 1620s: Middleton and Massinger," in *Theatre and Government under the Early Stuarts*, J. R. Mulryne and Margaret Shewring, eds. (Cambridge: Cambridge University Press, 1993), 258 and 260. Keith Lindley reads the play as a conflict between "established landed elites" and a "social parvenu." Neither a nightmare nor a fantasy, Overreach "is very much the voice of the real world in which the ruthless and unprincipled prosper and inherited status and traditional codes of behaviour provide no protection in themselves against social and economic catastrophe." See "Noble Scarlet vs London Blue," in *The Theatrical City: Culture, Theatre and Politics in London, 1576–1649*, David L. Smith, Richard Strier, and David Bevington, eds. (Cambridge: Cambridge University Press, 1995), 183 and 188. Both Lindley and Gail Paster note Overreach's deep craving for admission into the very aristocratic community he is at odds with and from which he finds himself forever excluded. See Lindley, *ibid.*, 189, and Paster's "Quomodo, Sir Giles, and Triangular Desire: Social Aspiration in Middleton and Massinger," in *Comedy from Shakespeare to Sheridan: Change and Continuity in the English and European Dramatic Tradition*, A. R. Braunmiller and J. C. Bulman, eds. (Newark: University of Delaware Press, 1986), 171–77.

12 Martin Butler, "*A New Way to Pay Old Debts*: Massinger's Grim Comedy," in *English Comedy*, Michael Cordner, Peter Holland, and John Kerrigan, eds. (Cambridge: Cambridge University Press, 1994), 122, and "The Outsider as Insider," in *The Theatrical City*, 196. The material that I cite at length appears in the more recent essay, pp. 205–06.

13 Martin Butler, "The Outsider as Insider," 204. Cf. Leggatt's discomfort with putatively high-minded and sober Welborne's recourse to roguish tactics, after the fashion of *A Trick to Catch the Old One*'s Witgood (*Citizen Comedy in the Age of Shakespeare*, 68); and Nancy S. Leonard's characterization of Welborne's tactics as "joyless and morally troublesome," evidence of "aggression, contempt, and cruelty." See "Overreach at Bay: Massinger's *A New Way to Pay Old Debts*," in *Philip Massinger: A Critical Reassessment*, Douglas Howard, ed. (Cambridge: Cambridge University Press, 1985), 181 and 184.

14 Martin Butler, "Outsider as Insider," 206–07.

15 Clay notes that by "the 1620s and 1630s the age of estate building on a grand scale by city men had dawned." See *Economic Expansion and Social Change*, I.153. Finch offers graphic evidence of Sir John Isham of Lamport's profits from mortgages he held, 1622–40, in the table that appears on page 33 of *The Wealth of Five Northamptonshire Families*. She notes that not only did Sir John (grandson of a London mercer and son of a country gentleman) gain a reputation as a lender, but that he invested "[s]pare capital" in land that he then sold at a profit (34).

16 William Ian Miller discusses relevant varieties of contempt: not only familiar downward contempt but also what he calls mutual contempt and upward contempt. The latter, the contempt of the low for the high, is "a kind of remedy for the contempt that is rained down on one, never constitutive, always reactive." Miller argues provocatively that a fairly equal distribution of contempt among a polity's diverse groups may assist democracy. See *The Anatomy of Disgust* (Cambridge: Harvard University Press, 1997), 221, 251, and chapter 9, *passim*.

17 Philip Edwards and Colin Gibson write that the phrase "this, th'undoubted heire" (*The Poems and Plays of Philip Massinger*, V.179) refers to Margaret, who is either her father's heir in expectation, or is soon to administer her father's property, given his madness. However, they also note that Alworth "acquires at least the benefits of ownership."

18 Cf. Martin Butler, "The Outsider as Insider": Massinger's "play's perspective is sufficiently demystified for it to disclose the . . . gap between what is said of the gentry and what disenchantedly they are seen to be, and these are troubling contradictions which have to be left to oscillate within the play and cannot be fully discharged at the end" (207).

19 Philip Edwards and Colin Gibson, *The Poems and Plays of Philip Massinger*, I.xxi–xxii.

20 Menna Prestwich, *Cranfield: Politics and Profits under the Early Stuarts* (Oxford: Clarendon Press, 1966), 358 (hereafter *C*). Ingram and Cranfield were both knighted in 1613.

21 Philip Edwards and Colin Gibson (*The Poems and Plays of Philip Massinger*, V.278) note that Patricia Thomson compares Overreach with Cranfield in her

essay "The Old Way and the New Way in Dekker and Massinger," *MLR*, 51 (1956), 170.

22 Anthony F. Upton, *Sir Arthur Ingram* (Oxford: Oxford University Press, 1961), 211. Future citations from this volume (hereafter *AI*) will appear in the text.

23 A sketch of Cranfield's and Ingram's careers should be sufficient, given my focus. Cranfield was born in 1575, the second son of a mercer. He married his master's daughter, was made free of the Mercers' Company in 1597, and became a Merchant Adventurer in 1601. Through the first decade of the seventeenth century Cranfield was engaged in overseas trade, lending and foreclosing, buying and selling Crown lands, and leasing customs farms from nobles. He entered the Court as a client of the Earl of Northampton and in 1613 was made Surveyor-General of the Customs. Northampton put Cranfield forward after the failure of the Great Contract because he appeared to be the sort of "technocrat" (*C*, 105) who could bring order to the Crown's finances. By the time of Northampton's death in 1614, Cranfield was deriving his profits from office not merchandise. In 1616 he was made Master of Requests and began to attach himself to the Villiers. In 1618–19, the scope of Cranfield's reform efforts broadened as he became, first, Master of the Wardrobe, then Master of the Wards. Following the death of his first wife in 1617, Cranfield was rewarded by King James for agreeing to marry Anne Brett, the dowryless daughter of Buckingham's mother's sister. Cranfield reached his apogee as a courtier when he became Lord Treasurer in 1621. By this same date he owned not only Chelsea House but great houses and large estates at Pishobury, Copt Hall, Wiston, Milcote, and Ebury. Buckingham turned on Cranfield for thwarting his war plans, and with Prince Charles closely supervised the Lord Treasurer's impeachment for extortion and accepting bribes. In the years that followed his fall and preceded his death in 1645 Cranfield, though till the end a fabulously wealthy man, wrestled with debts and oversaw the sale of well over half the land he had acquired prior to 1624.

Born in 1565, Arthur Ingram was the son of a Yorkshireman who prospered in sixteenth-century London, lending money and profiting from Anglo-Dutch trade. First a client of Cecil, then of the Howards, and always in some relation of partnership or clientage with Cranfield, Ingram began his career brokering leases, licenses, and farms, arranging syndicates, and retailing Crown lands. While generally working as a middleman, Ingram also invested heavily in the alum business and in land too. Although he soon owned land all over England, with the exception of the vast Yorkshire properties where he built his family estate, he was mostly speculating. Ingram first entered government service as a controller of customs of the port of London. At various times between 1609 and the late 1620s he served in Parliament. In 1613, Ingram was made Secretary and Keeper of the Signet to the Council of the North. The following year he became a member of the Council and in 1615, he momentarily achieved his highest Court office as Cofferer of the Royal Household. Upton estimates that at his death in 1642 Ingram was worth at least £10,000 a year (*AI*, 210).

24 Historical Manuscripts Commission, *Report on Manuscripts in Various Col-*

lections, Vol. VIII. The Manuscripts of the Hon. Frederick Lindley Wood; M. L. S. Clements, Esq.; S. Philip Unwin, Esq. (London: His Majesty's Stationery Office, 1913), 5.

25 As a basis for comparison, it may be noted that in 1642, only 10.8 percent of Yorkshire gentry families had annual incomes in excess of £1,000. See Keith Wrightson, *English Society 1580–1680* (New Brunswick: Rutgers University Press, 1982), 25.

26 These are John Chamberlain's words in his letter of 23 November 1616 to Dudley Carleton. See *The Letters of John Chamberlain*, vol. II, Norman E. McClure, ed. (Philadephia: American Philosophical Society, 1939), 39.

27 *Ibid.*, II.150 and I.585. When Chamberlain mistakenly reported that Cranfield was about to be made Lieutenant of Dover Castle, he wrote that he could "hardly beleve yt" that "a marchant of this towne of Ingrams profession" might achieve such office (I.463). In the course of Cranfield's impeachment proceedings, Bishop Williams spoke of "a man *plebeius*, creeping into so many offices, where there are so many worthy and learned noblemen" (*C*, 451).

28 Prestwich takes this from Gardiner, who describes it as a story told "long afterwards" by John Williams, Lord Keeper, later Bishop of Lincoln. See S. R. Gardiner, *History of England*, vol. V (London: Longmans, Green, and Co., 1883), 229.

29 The gypsy who reads the Lord Treasurer's palm in Ben Jonson's *The Gypsies Metamorphosed* predicts that he will set his "office upright, and the *Kinge* out of debt; / To putt all that have pensions soone out of theire paine, / By bringing th'Exchequer in Creditt againe." See *Ben Jonson*, vol. VII, C. H. Herford and Percy and Evelyn Simpson, eds. (Oxford: Clarendon Press, 1941), 584. Herford and the Simpsons identify this Lord Treasurer as Sir Henry Montagu (*Ben Jonson*, X.624). David Riggs, perhaps influenced by the ironic foreshadowing to be found in the gypsy's assertion that this is a Lord Treasurer whose "palme is not foule" and aware that Cranfield became Lord Treasurer in 1621, assumes that this is Cranfield (see David Riggs, *Ben Jonson* [Cambridge: Harvard University Press, 1989], 273). Given that the Windsor performance of the masque, the only one in which lords' fortunes are told, probably took place in early September 1621 (see John Nichols, *The Progresses, Processions, and Magnificent Festivities, of King James the First*, vol. IV [London: J. B. Nichols, 1828], 716); and given that on 30 September Montagu surrendered his office to Cranfield; the H&S identification is almost certainly correct. As Prestwich notes, Cranfield wasted no time proposing a stop to all pension payments – payments which cost the Crown nearly one-sixth of its revenue (*C*, 341) – thereby giving a new meaning to the gypsy's prediction that pensioners soon would be put out of their pain.

30 Cf. Menna Prestwich, *Cranfield*, 455. To his credit, James saw the danger inherent in relying upon judicial procedure in Parliament to bring Cranfield down. As he informed Buckingham, "By God, Steenie, you are a fool, and will shortly repent this folly, and will find, that, in this fit of popularity, you are making a rod with which you will be scourged yourself." Cited in Robert E. Ruigh, *The Parliament of 1624: Politics and Foreign Policy* (Cambridge: Harvard University Press, 1971), 356.

31 R. H. Tawney, *Business and Politics under James I: Lionel Cranfield as*

Merchant and Minister (Cambridge: Cambridge University Press, 1958), 84, 80, and 97. Tawney nicely imagines "[m]inisters whose solicitude for the revenue [due the Crown] is not expected to preclude a dignified curiosity as to perquisites for themselves, surrounded by concession-hunters versed in that aristocratic weakness and quick to play upon it" (98).

32 *Calendar of the Manuscripts of Major-General Lord Sackville*, vol. I, *Cranfield Papers, 1551–1612*, A. P. Newton, ed. (London: His Majesty's Stationery Office, 1940), 328–29 (hereafter *CP*).

33 *The Letters of John Chamberlain*, I.319; also cited in *AI*, 37.

34 Martin Butler, "Outsider as Insider," 197. In "Massinger's Grim Comedy," Butler writes that "Overreach's threats here [3.2.140–54] are directed at his daughter, but they establish his ability to compete within the aristocratic arena on aristocratic terms . . . his boldness for his 'honour' is a quality which means they have to take him seriously" (125).

35 Cf. Gail Paster, "Quomodo, Sir Giles, and Triangular Desire": "Lovell personifies everything that Sir Giles would be and cannot" (175).

36 *AI*, 69–78, provides a detailed account of Ingram's unique attempt to get himself installed at Court. I quote directly from Chamberlain's letters when Upton's citations contain significant ellipses.

37 *The Letters of John Chamberlain*, I.585; cited in part in *AI*, 73.

38 Cf. Menna Prestwich, *Cranfield*, 76: "Frobisher emerges from Cranfield's papers as that stock figure of the Jacobean stage, the country squire gulled by the smart City man."

39 Prestwich compares Ingram with Meercraft and with Mosca (*C*, 61, 64 and 98). She also associates Jonson, at the Mermaid, with Cranfield, who diverted himself at the Mitre ("it is very difficult to believe that Jonson did not know the members of the 'Mitre' club, and that, even if he never ran across Ingram and Cranfield, he did not hear of them from Brooke and Hoskyns, and especially from Martin, who as their lawyer had a good knowledge of their ways" – *C*, 98). Christopher Brooke, John Hoskyns, Richard Martin, John Donne, and Inigo Jones could be found at both taverns.

40 The debt to Cranfield stood at £1,280 as early as 1608. Cranfield responded by taking a mortgage, via a trusteeship, on rents from parsonages Greville had purchased from the Crown's commissioners. Their agreement stipulated that if Greville or his assigns repaid the debt in 1609, the rents would be reconveyed. It is doubtful that Cranfield expected any such thing.

41 Prestwich notes that while the value of the Greville land was estimated to be £3,000 a year at the time of the exchange, Cranfield was getting £3,400 in 1630. Clearly, he could claim no losses from this portion of his swap with Ingram. See *C*, 409.

42 This was, after all, the same man who, in 1601–02, enclosed the Stratford town commons, offered "minaces to the Baileefe Aldermen & Burgesses of Stratforde," and countenanced an assault on Shakespeare's friend, Richard Quiney. See Mark Eccles, *Shakespeare in Warwickshire* (Madison: University of Wisconsin Press, 1961), 97–99.

43 Citations from the sonnets are drawn from the modernized text in *Shakespeare's Sonnets*, Stephen Booth, ed. (New Haven: Yale University Press, 1977), 115–16.

44 In Sonnet 142, she has "sealed false bonds" and "Robbed others' beds' revenues of their rents" (ll. 7–8).
45 Cf. 125.12: "But mutual render, only me for thee" and cf. Thomas M. Greene, who suggests that "the affirmation of the 'mutuall render' between the two men acquires in the context of the whole collection a peculiar resonance." See "Pitiful Thrivers: Failed Husbandry in the Sonnets," in *Shakespeare and the Question of Theory*, Patricia Parker and Geoffrey Hartman, eds. (New York: Methuen, 1985), 230 and *passim*.

4 VENTURE CAPITAL

1 On Robarts, see Louis B. Wright, "Henry Robarts: Patriotic Propagandist and Novelist," *Studies in Philology*, 29 (1932), 176–99 and Wright's *Middle-Class Culture in Elizabethan England* (Chapel Hill: University of North Carolina Press, 1935), 515–24. Documents relating to the expedition may be found in Kenneth R. Andrews, ed., *The Last Voyage of Drake & Hawkins* (Cambridge: Cambridge University Press, 1972).
2 Robarts seems to have known only one note. Ten years earlier, he was already coupling toil with soil in *A most friendly farewell, Given by a welwiller to the right worshipful Sir Frauncis Drake* (London, 1585): "When true report had blased abroad ye iii. yeares takē toile, / Of that rare knight Syr Francis *Drake* through many a forraine soile . . ." (Bv). Here too, the "gallant Gentes" (B3) who "adventured both life, goodes, and all" (A3) are distinguished from "dastardes [who] use at home to stay, and there will sit & talke" (B2v).
3 Kenneth R. Andrews cites Robarts's newsletter celebrating Grafton, *OUR LADYS RETORNE to England* (London, 1592), in *Elizabethan Privateering: English Privateering During the Spanish War 1585–1603* (Cambridge: Cambridge University Press, 1964), 151.
4 Henry Robarts, *A most friendly farewell*, A3 and Bv.
5 Mary C. Fuller writes that the English "colonial relation to America was envisioned and disastrously realized precisely as venture without return, trade without profit, labor without fruit." While of course the privateers' ventures could not be advertised as profitless, their efforts, like the colonialists', were said to depend upon rigor, discipline, and the banishment of idleness. See *Voyages in Print: English Travel to America, 1576–1624* (Cambridge: Cambridge University Press, 1995), 86, 28 and *passim*.
6 I note in passing that after having decided to return to *The Merchant of Venice* in a chapter entitled "Venture Capital," I (re)discovered C. L. Barber's comment that "Antonio's loan is venture capital." See *Shakespeare's Festive Comedy: A Study of Dramatic Form and its Relation to Social Custom* (Princeton: Princeton University Press, 1959), 175.
7 Sir Walter Ralegh, *The Discoverie of the large and bewtiful Empire of Guiana*, V. T. Harlow, ed. (London: Argonaut Press, 1928), 4 and 6. For Cecil's estimation, see *CSP Domestic 1591–1594*, 273; 21 September 1592.
8 Michael Ferber locates in Antonio a basis for what he calls Shakespeare's "imaginary alternative to the Weber Thesis." Where Weber linked "habits of asceticism" to early capitalism, Shakespeare "tied capitalism to . . . uncalcu-

lating acts of sacrifice and risk." See "The Ideology of *The Merchant of Venice*," *English Literary Renaissance*, 20 (1990), 447–48. Of course, Antonio does not imagine himself to be at risk (he has full confidence in his ships' success: "My ships come home a month before the day" – 1.3.177); it is Bassanio who sees himself hazarding all he has, whether with arrows (1.1.140–52) or caskets. Toil (asceticism) and risk consistently appear not as alternatives, but in tandem with one another.

9 Cf. Michael Nerlich: "The man who consciously presented himself as an adventurer, as a bold risk-seeking entrepreneur who defies every risk, is gradually becoming, in the presentation of his apologists, an entrepreneur who is subjected to adventures, is exposed to risks, is concerned about the common weal, is at pains to create order . . ." *Ideology of Adventure*, vol. I, Ruth Crowley, trans. (Minneapolis: University of Minnesota Press, 1987), 111–12.

10 *Ibid.*, 133–34.

11 *Ibid.*, 60–61.

12 William Sanderson, "[b]orne a gentleman, bred a Merchant Adventurer," married Margaret Snedall, Ralegh's niece. He "assumed a leading part in sponsoring and managing the voyages undertaken by the navigator John Davis in search of the Northwest Passage ["the onely Merchant that to his great charges with most constant travaile did labour for the finishing"] . . . contributed . . . funds to construct the first globes made in England by Emery Molyneux; and . . . named his first three sons Raleigh, Cavendish, and Drake." See Ruth A. McIntyre, "William Sanderson: Elizabethan Financier of Discovery," *William and Mary Quarterly*, 13 (1956), 184–201; also John W. Shirley, "Sir Walter Ralegh's Guiana Finances," *Huntington Library Quarterly*, 13 (1949), 55–69; David Beers Quinn, ed., *The Roanoke Voyages 1584–1590*, 2 vols. (Cambridge: Cambridge University Press, 1955), I.65–71 and II.576–97; Albert H. Markham, *The Voyages and Works of John Davis* (London: T. Richards, 1880), xii–xvi, 208, and 232; and Sanderson's son William's reply to Carew Ralegh's attack on Sanderson senior: *An Answer to a Scurrilous Pamphlet* (London, 1656).

13 Cf. Philip Edwards, *Last Voyages: Cavendish, Hudson, Ralegh* (Oxford: Clarendon Press, 1988), 184: "Ralegh had everything to lose on this expedition, James nothing. If Ralegh succeeded, James had his gold; if Ralegh failed, James had his head." See also "An Interpretation," in V. T. Harlow, *Ralegh's Last Voyage* (London: Argonaut Press, 1932), 1–99, esp. 87–99; and, contra Harlow, Joyce Lorimer, "The Location of Ralegh's Guiana Gold Mine," *Terrae Incognitae*, 14 (1982), 77–96, esp. 95. In his "Apology" (1618), Ralegh offers as proof of the existence of the elusive Guianan mine not only his, his wife's, and his son's willingness to hazard all, but his "being old and weakly, thirteen years in prison and not used to the air, to travail, and to watching, it being ten to one that I should ever have returned, and of which by reason of my violent sickness and the long continuance thereof no man had any hope, what madness could have made me undertake this journey but the assurance of the mine" (*Last Voyages*, 244).

14 Kenneth R. Andrews, *Elizabethan Privateering*, 100–23.

15 Kenneth R. Andrews, ed., *English Privateering Voyages to the West Indies*

1588–1595 (Cambridge: Cambridge University Press, 1959), 98n3, 101, and 159.

16 Kenneth R. Andrews, *Elizabethan Privateering*, 145 and 267. John Gillies comments very instructively on the distribution of what he calls the "Jason-function" among Bassanio, Gratiano, and Lorenzo. He notes the Medean anxieties latent in the ethic of merchant-adventuring and their suppression in Rubens's 1635 design for an Antwerp pageant arch (*The Pageant of the Mint*) in which Medea becomes "Lady Felicity" and the golden fleece becomes "the golden Indian wealth that has been won for Spain." See *Shakespeare and the Geography of Difference* (Cambridge: Cambridge University Press, 1994), 135–37.

17 Monson, whom Brown cites, writes that he and Sir Robert Duddeley "endured more foul weather and trouble than in the whole voyage besides, by reason of the unwieldiness of the St. Andrew when she came to work in the narrow channel among the sands." See M. Oppenheim, ed., *The Naval Tracts of Sir William Monson*, vol. I (Navy Record Society, 1902), 357.

18 See Kenneth R. Andrews, *Trade, Plunder and Settlement: Maritime Enterprise and the Genesis of the British Empire, 1480–1630* (Cambridge: Cambridge University Press, 1984), 241–43. In *Elizabethan Privateering*, Andrews gives some measure of the interpenetration of foreign policy and plunder at Cadiz:

[i]n such national enterprises, with all their opportunities for malversation, private and public interests were inextricably mingled. Of some 150 vessels engaged in the Cadiz voyage, only 15 or 18 belonged to the Crown; the rest, apart from 24 Dutch ships, were supplied by port towns and private owners. A high proportion of the privateering captains sailed, and they were led by Charles Howard, Essex and Ralcigh – each in his own way a champion of pillage as a system of politics and a method of waging war. (237)

Cf. David B. Quinn and A. N. Ryan on "the treasure-hunting element [of] the Cadiz expedition":

[w]ar against enemy property as a means of serving one's country and making one's fortune was always likely to win an Elizabethan strategic argument . . . the raid developed into an orgy of pillage with Essex's arguments in favour of permanent occupation being submerged in a general desire among all ranks for personal enrichment and a rapid return home with the loot, most of which found its way into private pockets rather than into the treasury.

See *England's Sea Empire, 1550–1642* (London: George Allen & Unwin, 1983), 119–20.

19 See John Gillies, *Shakespeare and the Geography of Difference*, 66; and cf. M. M. Mahood, "Introduction," *The Merchant of Venice* (Cambridge: Cambridge University Press, 1987), 13. Gillies makes the case that "Antonio, too, is a Jason, his argosies laden with the 'fleece' of eastern 'spices' and Mexican gold" (134).

20 Kenneth R. Andrews, ed., *English Privateering Voyages*, 98–101.

21 Mahood explains that the Venetians had lost their part of the spice trade; both Mahood and Gillies note that the Venetians never participated in the new oceanic trade which was dominated by the Iberians. See Mahood's

"Introduction," 13, and Gillies, *Shakespeare and the Geography of Difference*, 66.

22 For "emotions as conduct – as manoeuvres or 'moves' in largely institutionalized social interactions involving clusters of people," see C. Terry Warner, "Anger and Similar Delusions," in *The Social Construction of Emotions*, Rom Harré, ed. (Oxford: Basil Blackwell, 1986), 155. Rather than conceive of, say, anger as merely an "inner experience," Warner accepts the "Wittgensteinian recognition that anger is essentially *avowal*" (155; my emphasis).

23 On status and privilege, see Frank Whigham, "Ideology and Class Conduct in *The Merchant of Venice*," *Renaissance Drama*, 10 (1979), 93–115.

24 Cf. Whigham, *ibid.*: "Bassanio romanticizes in heroic terms the pragmatic web of technique, *effort*, and self-interest which baser men work with more openly" (96; my emphasis).

25 Michael Nerlich associates Morocco with the "swaggering style of the Spanish knightly romances" (*Ideology of Adventure*, I.165).

26 John Gillies, *Shakespeare and the Geography of Difference*, suggests that in these lines Antonio "is imagined as an ancient Stoic for whom . . . the world is 'a stage' (1.1.78) for the tragi-comedy of human existence" (125).

27 René Girard, "'To Entrap the Wisest': A Reading of *The Merchant of Venice*," in *Literature and Society*, Edward Said, ed. (Baltimore: Johns Hopkins University Press, 1980), 115.

28 Michael Nerlich, *Ideology of Adventure*, I.167 and 172.

29 See chapters 4 and 6 of *Elizabethan Privateering*. In chapter 5, Andrews discusses a third group, the "professionals." Cf. Walter Cohen on the "tripartite unity of Antonio, Bassanio, and Portia" in *Drama of a Nation: Public Theater in Renaissance England and Spain* (Ithaca: Cornell University Press, 1985), 203.

30 Michael Nerlich, *Ideology of Adenture*, 8.

31 Andrews, *Elizabethan Privateering*, 61.

32 *Ibid.*, 71.

33 *Ibid.*, 70–79.

34 See G. C. Williamson, *George, Third Earl of Cumberland (1558–1605) His Life and His Voyages* (Cambridge: Cambridge University Press, 1920), 106–10 and *passim*. On 12 December 1592, Cumberland wrote to Burghley of a "desire to relieve my friends and servants in danger of bonds for me, my credit from dying, and my house from falling . . . and for more (if God send it) I will ever be ready to spend it and my life . . . for the gain of Her Majesty and my country" (112).

35 "By guaranteeing an honorable reputation as well as a secure and absolute title to private property, the exemption of the Italian merchant-financier from the stigma of usury provided a necessary spur to the expansion of the new system" (*Drama of a Nation*, 202). Cohen partly justifies his interest in the play's Venetian context when he argues that "no manipulation will convert a comedy in which there are no merchant-usurers and in which the only usurer is a Jew into a faithful representation of English economic life" (199). On the narrow grounds of "faithful representation" this is true of course.

36 Sir Walter Ralegh, *The Discoverie*, 4.

37 See Robert Brenner, *Merchants and Revolution: Commercial Change, Political*

Conflict, and London's Overseas Traders, 1550–1653 (Princeton: Princeton University Press, 1993), 47–48.

38 Carole Shammas, "English Commercial Development and American Colonization, 1560–1620," in *The Westward Enterprise: English Activities in Ireland, the Atlantic, and America 1480–1650*, K. R. Andrews, N. P. Canny, and P. E. H. Hair, eds. (Liverpool: Liverpool University Press, 1978), 173 and *passim*.

39 Henry Stevens, ed., *The Dawn of British Trade to the East Indies as Recorded in the Court Minutes of the East India Company 1599–1603* (London: H. Stevens, 1886), 118. This 22 January 1601 entry goes on to explain that if a prize-taking opportunity were to present itself, the captain is to use his best judgment and make a "meet" agreement with his mariners for shares (118–19).

40 See G. C. Williamson, *George, Third Earl of Cumberland*, 142 and 210–18. The ship was sold for £3,700; however, Cumberland retained a £1,500 interest in her and Thomas Cordell another £500 interest. Cf. Kenneth R. Andrews, *Elizabethan Privateering*, 218–19:

> [t]he most urgent requirement of the East India company in its early years . . . was capital, and . . . privateering was one of the most important means of the accumulation of capital in the fifteen years before the company's first voyage. Over a quarter of the £30,000 initially subscribed or promised in 1599 came from men known to have invested in privateering . . . the economic and maritime strength required to establish and maintain East Indies trade was to a large extent the direct result of fifteen years of continuous commerce-raiding.

41 Michael Chorost, in "Biological Finance in Shakespeare's *Timon of Athens*," 358–59, quotes from Benjamin Jowett's translation of the *Politics* and refers to *Merchant* in this context. For Shylock, "thrift is a blessing" (1.3.85); at 5.1.16, Lorenzo hails "unthrift love."

42 On the capture of the *Madre de Dios*, see E. W. Bovill, "The *Madre de Dios*," *The Mariner's Mirror*, 54 (1968), 129–52; C. R. Boxer, "The Taking of the *Madre de Deus*, 1592," *The Mariner's Mirror*, 67 (1981), 82–84; William Richard Drake, "Notes upon the Capture of 'The Great Carrack,' in 1592," *Archaeologia*, 33 (1849), 209–40; Edward Edwards, *The Life of Sir Walter Ralegh*, vol. I (London: Macmillan, 1868), 145–58; Richard Hakluyt, *The Principal Navigations*, vol. VII (Glasgow: James MacLehose, 1904); C. Lethbridge Kingsford, ed., "The Taking of the *Madre de Dios* Anno 1592," in J. K. Laughton, ed., *The Naval Miscellany*, vol. II (Naval Records Society, 1912), 85–121; M. Oppenheim, ed., *The Naval Tracts of Sir William Monson*, I.278–96; Samuel Purchas, *Purchas His Pilgrimes*, vol. XVI (Glasgow: James MacLehose, 1906), 16–17; Lawrence Stone, *An Elizabethan Life: Sir Horatio Palavicino* (Oxford: Clarendon Press, 1956), 207–30; G. C. Williamson, *George, Third Earl of Cumberland*, 83–112; also HMC Salisbury MSS, vol. IV, and *CSP Domestic 1591–1594*.

43 Edward Edwards, *The Life of Sir Walter Ralegh*, II.45–46. Cf. a letter from Lord Burghley and the Lord Admiral to Ralegh on 23 May 1592 in which they write that the Queen "would have you to direct the course of her ships and yours under Sir Martin Frobisher" (HMC Salisbury MSS, IV.200).

44 M. Oppenheim, ed., *The Naval Tracts of Sir William Monson*, I.287–88.

45 Kenneth R. Andrews, ed., *English Privateering Voyages*, 205.

46 Hakluyt's account includes a gruesome description of "so many bodies slaine

and dismembred . . . miserable people, whose limnes were so torne with the violence of shot, and paine made grievous with the multitude of woundes. No man could almost steppe but upon a dead carkase or a bloody floore, but specially about the helme, where very many of them fell suddenly from stirring to dying." See *Principal Navigations*, VII.114; also cited by Bovill, "The *Madre de Dios*," 135.

47 "The *Madre de Dios*," 135.

48 Ralegh wrote that "the Earl of Cumberland's ships who had the chiefest pillage arrived at Plymouth, made port sale of diamonds, rubies, musk, ambergris and all other commodities" (cited in Bovill, "The *Madre de Dios*," 141).

49 *CSP Domestic 1591–1594*, 272 (not entirely accurately cited in E. W. Bovill, "The *Madre de Dios*," 140).

50 HMC Salisbury MSS, IV.232–34 and 255.

51 The Queen seems at first to have decided, on the basis of Burgh's having taken over the carrack in her name, that the entire prize was hers. When her chancellor of the exchequer reminded her that this would have been to run roughshod over all of the written and unwritten rules of privateering, and so to jeopardize an enterprise from which the Queen profited, she agreed to claim as her own only the pepper. In fact, its sale represented Elizabeth's best chance of profiting from the carrack. With a monopoly hold on the London pepper market, she could set her own price. In the end, she pocketed £80,000 after an initial investment of £3,000!

Cumberland, who had spent £19,000 on his fleet, was awarded £37,000 by the Queen. Hawkins's group fared poorly with £7–8,000 (though Hawkins's captain, who had taken the *Dainty* around to Harwich where none of the Queen's agents were stationed, managed to dispose of £1,200 in booty without hindrance). The London merchants' £12,000 award represented a profit of £6,000. Despite the original commission which granted Ralegh all plunder from the expedition, he and his partners' £34,000 investment yielded them only £24,000. There is no way to know how much was plundered (Purchas says four-fifths of the cargo was embezzled); but some idea of what transpired may be derived from the fact that when Captain Cross, of the Queen's *Foresight*, was accused of having taken spoils worth £10,000, he admitted to £2,000.

52 E. W. Bovill, "The *Madre de Dios*," 148.

53 Edward Edwards, *The Life of Sir Walter Ralegh*, II.45. Here, and in the citations that follow, I draw upon Edwards's collection of Ralegh's letters in the second volume of his biography, 45–78. In the Hatfield House collection there is another letter to Cecil, undated but probably July 1592, in which Ralegh sounds ever so much like Antonio: "[d]o with me now therefore what you list. I am more weary of life than they are desirous I should perish, which if it had been for her, as it is by her, had been too happily borne." HMC Salisbury MSS, IV.220.

54 Stephen J. Greenblatt, *Sir Walter Ralegh: The Renaissance Man and His Roles* (New Haven: Yale University Press, 1973), 56.

55 Cf. Richard C. McCoy, *The Rites of Knighthood: The Literature and Politics of Elizabethan Chivalry* (Berkeley: University of California Press, 1989), 2–3

and *passim*.

For months after the *Madre de Dios* arrived in Dartmouth, Ralegh decried the spoil and repeatedly called attention to his own clean hands. From Hartlebury, on his way to meet the carrack, Ralegh wrote to Burghley: "[i]f I meet any of them [jewelers dealing booty] coming up, if it be upon the wildest heath in all the way, I mean to strip them as naked as ever they were born. For it is infinite that Her Majesty hath been robbed, and that of the most rare things." See Edward Edwards, *The Life of Sir Walter Ralegh*, II.70–71. Ralegh especially resented the Earl of Cumberland's claim on the prize (and, no doubt, on the Queen's affection too). As far as Ralegh was concerned, Cumberland's men had joined the capture late in the day, were not legally in consortship with the Queen, and were responsible for the worst pillage and plunder. It made sense, of course, for the Queen to use Ralegh's squabbling with Cumberland to her own advantage. She asserted, for example, that what Cumberland received derived not from his right or claim but from her bounty.

56 Cf. Carole Shammas, "English Commercial Development and American Colonization, 1560–1620," 158–60; also Louis Montrose, "The Work of Gender in the Discourse of Discovery," *Representations*, 33 (1991), 8–10.

57 HMC Salisbury MSS, IV.250. When Elizabeth was finally in a position to dispose of the pepper, she flat out auctioned it to the highest bidder. In the end, a syndicate of London merchants purchased the pepper, but they never saw a profit. "The only gainer was the Crown, thanks to the skill of its servants in commercial sharp-practice of a somewhat dubious nature." See Lawrence Stone, *An Elizabethan Life*, 220–23.

58 Norman E. McClure, ed., *The Letters and Epigrams of Sir John Harington* (Philadelphia: University of Pennsylvania Press, 1930), 196. Carolyn J. Bishop compares Harington's epigram with one of Sir John Davies's, "In Paulum," which she believes dates from the period of Ralegh's imprisonment and the capture of the *Madre*, and which begins: "By lawfull mart, and by unlawfull stealth / Paulus . . . / Derives . . . much wealth." See "Raleigh Satirized by Harington and Davies," *Review of English Studies*, 23 (1972), 52–56.

59 In the line that follows Cecil's comment about Ralegh's toiling, Cecil wrote that he could not "help laughing to hear him [Ralegh] rage at the spoils" (*CSP Domestic 1591–1594*, 273).

60 Sir Walter Ralegh, *The Discoverie*, 6 and 10.

61 Cited in V. T. Harlow, *Ralegh's Last Voyage*, 111.

62 K. R. Andrews, "Sir Robert Cecil and Mediterranean Plunder," *English Historical Review*, 87 (1972), 513. This is not the only place Andrews presents evidence of Cecil attempting to conceal his interest in a privateering enterprise (see, e.g., 519). See also Lawrence Stone, "The Fruits of Office: The Case of Robert Cecil, First Earl of Salisbury, 1596–1612," in *Essays in the Economic and Social History of Tudor and Stuart England*, F. J. Fisher, ed. (Cambridge: Cambridge University Press, 1961), 92–94.

Cecil's behind-the-scenes calculation encourages us to part company with Antonio in order to consort with Lovewit.

63 HMC Salisbury MSS, IV.232 and 238.

64 E. W. Bovill, "The *Madre de Dios*," 151. I have not been able to locate the

original source for Bovill's citation. He may be borrowing from Sir William Foster, *England's Quest of Eastern Trade* (London: A & C Black, 1933), 137. Foster writes that "An excellent treatise of the kingdome of China" is Hakluyt's translation of the *Madre* volume, first printed in Macao, in 1590. See Hakluyt, *The Principal Navigations*, VI.348–77.

65 Richard Hakluyt, *The Principal Navigations*, VII.116; cited, with incidental differences, in E. W. Bovill, "The *Madre de Dios*," 151. C. R. Boxer argues that the "most important manuscripts seized on board the *Madre de Deus* were the official reports relating to the trade and administration of Portuguese Asia, which were subsequently utilized by Hakluyt and Purchase [*sic*]" ("The Taking of the *Madre de Deus*," 84).

66 Kenneth R. Andrews, *Elizabethan Privateering*, 237.

67 *Ibid.*, 105. For Watt's career I draw on this volume of Andrews (104–09) and on his *English Privateering Voyages*, 97–106.

68 Watts had a fleet of five ships in the West Indies in 1591 and Ralegh was a shareholder in the enterprise. The division of the spoils occasioned a typical letter from Ralegh to Burghley in which the former bemoans the smallness of his profit (although Watts was to value the prizes his ships took at nearly £32,000). See Edward Edwards, *The Life of Sir Walter Ralegh*, II.43–44 and Kenneth R. Andrews, ed., *English Privateering Voyages*, 95–172 (Andrews makes light of Ralegh's complaint, noting that the profit was probably over 200 percent!).

The next year, Watts's *Margaret and John* and his *Alcedo* wound up with Frobisher while the *Madre* was being sacked; nonetheless, as consorts, they entitled Watts to claim a share of the prize. Both ships were also employed in the transshipment of the carrack's cargo from Dartmouth to London, for which Watts received £200. See C. M. Griffiths, "An Account Book of Raleigh's Voyage, 1592," *The National Library of Wales Journal*, 7 (1952), 349 and 351.

69 Andrews, *Elizabethan Privateering*, 108, cites from the company court minutes.

70 *Ibid.*, 230.

71 Kenneth R. Andrews, ed., *English Privateering Voyages*, 40.

72 K. N. Chaudhuri, *The English East India Company: The Study of an Early Joint-Stock Company 1600–1640* (London: Frank Cass, 1965), 26.

73 *Ibid.*, 25.

74 The East India Company was of course not starting entirely from scratch. Nearly half a century earlier the Russia Company had been granted a charter as a joint stock company, and the founding East India company directors had considerable experience in previous, if generally regulated, company partnerships in the intervening years. At the outset, the East India Company was dominated by Levant Company merchants, even first meeting in the Levant Company offices. See Robert Brenner, *Merchants and Revolution*, 21. Brenner argues that in contradistinction to the Merchant Adventurers, those trading in the East "did have to innovate" and "created novel commercial operations" (61).

75 *Ibid.*, 96.

76 Robert Brenner, "The Social Basis of English Commercial Expansion, 1550–1650," *Journal of Economic History*, 32 (1977), 376.
77 William R. Scott, *The Constitution and Finance of English, Scottish and Irish Joint-Stock Companies to 1720*, vol. II (Cambridge: Cambridge University Press, 1912), 93.
78 Philip Lawson, *The East India Company: A History* (London: Longman, 1993), 21–22.
79 Henry Stevens, ed., *The Dawn of British Trade*, 5. Thus, for example, on 31 January 1600, it was decided to "devyse and sett downe certen ordenaunces for the avoiding of private . . . trade" in the first voyage (124). Early on in the company's history, a certain degree of schooling to the habits of joint stock operations was seemingly necessary (cf. the General Court minutes for 10 February 1601, with its second warning against "private traffique barter exchaunge or merchaundizinge" – 130).
80 *Ibid.*, 28.
81 *Ibid.*, 70 (my emphasis).
82 K. N. Chaudhuri, *The English East India Company*, 22.
83 Ben Jonson, *The Alchemist*, Alvin B. Kernan, ed. (New Haven: Yale University Press, 1974), 1.1.135. All further citations are drawn from this edition.
84 C. H. Herford, Percy and Evelyn Simpson, eds. *Ben Jonson* vol. VIII (Oxford: Clarendon, 1947), 392 ("To the memory of my beloved, The AUTHOR Mr. William Shakespeare," line 59).
85 Ben Jonson, *Volpone*, Alvin B. Kernan, ed. (New Haven: Yale University Press, 1962). Further citations are drawn from this edition.
86 Jonathan Haynes, *The Social Relations of Jonson's Theater* (Cambridge: Cambridge University Press, 1992), 114. Cf. Peter Womack: "In another pregnant equivoque, the name for this spiritualization of wealth is 'projection', which in the economic sphere means the speculative investment of capital, but in alchemy means the exposure of inferior substances to the transmuting influence of the Stone. Projection springs money from its fixation on land . . ." "Springs," like Haynes's "neat," intimates an offhandedness that the sweat of the poet and of the projectors qualifies. See Womack's *Ben Jonson* (Oxford: Basil Blackwell, 1986), 164.
87 For the substitution of words for laboratory, see Anne Barton, *Ben Jonson, Dramatist* (Cambridge: Cambridge University Press, 1984), 152.
88 The dizzying, fatiguing, every-which-way directives of farce punctuate *The Alchemist*. Cf., for example, the cozeners' response to Ananias's arrival: "What, more gudgeons! / Dol, scout, scout! Stay, Face, you must go to the door" (2.4.18–19); then

> Let him in.
> Stay, help me off, first, with my gown. Away,
> Madam, to your withdrawing chamber. Now,
> In a new tune, new gesture . . .   (2.4.24–27)

The fever of imperatives is even more pronounced in this instance: "scout, scout . . . Stay . . . must go . . . Let . . . Away . . . to . . . Now . . ."
89 Cf. Alvin B. Kernan's note on commodity schemes: "Face and Subtle are masters at *working* [my emphasis] swindles on three or four levels at once. For

example, having bilked Mammon of all his household goods, they then proceed to sell them to the Anabaptists, and are looking about for a third party to sell them to again." *The Alchemist*, 220.

90 Cf. the beginning of the next scene: Subtle: "Are they gone?"; Face: "All's clear" (4.2.1). Also in 4.3, when Surly asks to see the *señora*:

FACE   'Slid, Subtle, how shall we do?
SUBTLE For what?
FACE   Why, Dol's employed, you know.
SUBTLE   That's true.
        'Fore heav'n I know not. He must stay, that's all.   (4.3.50–52)

91 William Shakespeare, *Hamlet*, Harold Jenkins, ed. (London: Methuen, 1982), 5.1.68–69. Note, too, Lovewit's condescending treatment of his neighbor, the smith (5.1.39–45 and 5.2.40). Hamlet says that the gravedigger has "no feeling of his *business*" (5.1.65, my emphasis) and he complains about "[h]ow absolute the knave is" (5.1.133). Lacking appropriate style, he crudely jowls skulls to the ground. The Shakespearean irony, one that Jonson adopts but moderates in the relation between Face and Lovewit, is that the gravedigger can more than hold his own in a battle of wits with Hamlet.

   Robert N. Watson, *Ben Jonson's Parodic Strategy: Literary Imperialism in the Comedies* (Cambridge: Harvard University Press, 1987), notes that "Lovewit provides Jonson's own sort of conclusion, forgiving the witty for the sake of their wit" (134).

92 Jonathan Haynes, *The Social Relations of Jonson's Theater*, 117. For Face, in this sentence, we can substitute Bassanio.

93 William Empson calls Lovewit a "business-man" who is fully confident "that he is the new ruling class." See *"The Alchemist* and the Critics" (1970) reprinted in *Jonson: Every Man and His Humour and The Alchemist, A Casebook*, R. V. Holdsworth, ed. (London: Macmillan, 1978), 197.

94 S. P. Cerasano notes that

the very language of shareholding, which styled a man "adventurer, storer and sharer," suggests . . . the diverse associations intrinsic to the special relationship between the sharer and his investment. It emphasizes the importance of protection, cooperation, and even trust (financial and otherwise) in the agreements, along with the spirit of nurtured risk inherent in the whole tenuous business. The sense of tidy security conveyed by Chambers's explanation of the sharers' arrangements disregards the fact that theatre entrepreneurship was perilous.

See "The 'Business' of Shareholding, the Fortune Playhouses, and Francis Grace's Will," *Medieval & Renaissance Drama in England*, 2 (1985), 233.

95 I draw upon Irwin Smith's account in *Shakespeare's Blackfriars Playhouse: Its History and Its Design* (New York: New York University Press, 1964).

96 See William Ingram, "The Playhouse as an Investment, 1607–1614; Thomas Woodford and Whitefriars," *Medieval & Renaissance Drama in England*, 2 (1985), 213.

97 Charles William Wallace, "Shakespeare and His London Associates as Revealed in Recently Discovered Documents," *University Studies of the University of Nebraska* 10 (1910), 349. Further citations will appear in the text.

98 We do not know the outcome of *Keysar* v. *Burbage et al.* The case may have been settled out of court. There is no record of testimony from the material witnesses Cuthbert Burbage said that he was prepared to produce.

99 This complaint was formally *Kirkham* v. *Paunton* (or Painton) and it named Henry Evans, Richard Burbage, and John Heminges as co-defendants. Edward Paunton was Alexander Hawkins's (Evans's son-in-law) widow's husband. Paunton claimed that Evans had assigned the lease to Hawkins and that it became his (Paunton's) when he married his wife. Kirkham claimed that when Evans transferred the lease to Hawkins, it was upon trust that he would reassure half of it to Kirkham *et al.* upon request. Burbage and Heminges denied the trust and claimed that any profits due Kirkham derived from playing in the playhouse, not from the lease (a moiety or otherwise). In fact, Burbage and Heminges denied that even Paunton had either a half or a whole share in the Blackfriars.

100 See the proceedings as printed in Frederick G. Fleay, *A Chronicle History of the London Stage, 1559–1642* (London: Reaves and Turner, 1890), 249. Further citations will appear in the text. An abridged version of *Kirkham* v. *Paunton* appears in Irwin Smith, *Shakespeare's Blackfriars Playhouse*, 534–46.

101 In *Evans* v. *Kirkham*, Evans charged that Kirkham had begun to feel the burden of paying rent on the closed playhouse. He alleged that Kirkham had the "Apparells, properties & goods . . . praised and devided" between his partnership and Evans. Furthermore, Kirkham was said to have forwsworn further interest in the whole enterprise, "'for,' qd he, 'yt is a base thing' . . . whereupon [Kirkham] . . . delivered up their Commission, wch he had under the greate seale aucthorising them to plaie, and discharged divers of the partners & Poetts." See Fleay, *A Chronicle History of the London Stage*, 221–22.

102 Given that Lovewit has decamped from London because of the "sickness hot . . . in town" ("The Argument," 1–2), I note in passing that Burbage's rejoinder to Keysar on 19 June 1610 includes the assertion that Keysar's boys were forced to disperse "either through sicknes or for some other cause" (357).

103 E. K. Chambers, *The Elizabethan Stage*, vol. II (Oxford: Clarendon Press, 1923), 49.

104 Irwin Smith, *Shakespeare's Blackfriars Playhouse*, 190.

105 *Kirkham* v. *Daniel* is reprinted in Harold N. Hillebrand, *The Child Actors* (Illinois: University of Illinois Press, 1926), 334–38. Further citations will appear in the text. An abridged version appears in Smith, *Shakespeare's Blackfriars Playhouse*, 514–15.

106 See E. K. Chambers, "Dramatic Records: The Lord Chamberlain's Office," *Malone Society Collections*, vol. II (Oxford: Oxford University Press, 1931), pt 3, 363–64. Further citations will appear in the text. Smith reprints an abridged version of the so-called Sharers' Papers in *Shakespeare's Blackfriars Playhouse*, 553–59.

It appears that at least one of the player-petitioners was already the owner of a third of a share in the Blackfriars, although this is revealed only in Shanks's statement and repeated by Cuthbert Burbage. Certainly this, and the claim that each of the players had earned £180 during the previous year, mitigates their portrayal of themselves as sweating laborers.

107 Irwin Smith, *Shakespeare's Blackfriars Playhouse*, 279.

AFTERWORD

1 Andrew Gurr, *The Shakespearian Playing Companies* (Oxford: Clarendon Press, 1996), 114–19 and 294–98. Subsequent citations appear in the text. For an earlier formulation of the material covered in these pages, see Gurr's "Money or Audiences: The Impact of Shakespeare's Globe," *Theatre Notebook*, 42 (1988), 3–14.

2 I emphasize "could" because Gurr cannot know for certain that the Blackfriars actually did make more money than the Globe. We would need precise attendance figures – as opposed to capacity estimates – to make such a determination.

3 Gurr admits that an element of calculation may have been at work here. He notes "Christopher Beeston's troubles with a mob of apprentices when he took the Red Bull's company to his new Cockpit hall playhouse in 1616" (297–98).

4 The new syndicate included the Burbages, Thomas Evans (a financier), Shakespeare, Heminges, Condell, and Sly. In "Money or Audiences," Gurr writes that the "choice of playing at each playhouse alternately was evidently not a financier's but a company sharers' decision" (9).

Index

Cambridge Studies in Renaissance Literature and Culture

General editor
STEPHEN ORGEL
Jackson Eli Reynolds Professor of Humanities, Stanford University